YOUNG SHAKESPEARE

Young Shakespeare

Russell Fraser

COLUMBIA UNIVERSITY PRESS   *New York*

Columbia University Press
New York   Guildford, Surrey
Copyright © 1988 Columbia University Press

Library of Congress Cataloging-in-Publication Data

Fraser, Russell A.
Young Shakespeare / Russell Fraser.
p.   cm.
Bibliography: p.
Includes index.
ISBN 0-231-06764-X
ISBN 0-231-06765-8 (pbk.)
1. Shakespeare, William, 1564–1616—Biography—Youth.
2. Shakespeare, William, 1564–1616—Contemporary England.
3. England—Social life and customs—16th century.   4. Dramatists,
English—Early modern, 1500–1700—Biography—Youth.   I. Title.
PR2903.F7   1988
822.3'3—dc19

[B]
88-4959
CIP

The author and publisher wish to thank the Rackham School
and the Literary College of the University of Michigan
for contributing to the cost of the jacket and endpapers.

The endpaper maps were planned by Hazelton Spencer and
drawn by Kathleen Voute.

FRONTISPIECE:
Portrait of Shakespeare believed to have been painted by
Gerard Soest in the seventeenth century.
*Photo courtesy of Shakespeare Birthplace Trust and
Jarrold Colour Publications, Norwich, England.*

Design by Jaya Dayal

Printed in the United States of America

c 10 9 8 7 6 5 4 3
p 10 9 8 7 6 5 4 3 2

Hardback editions of Columbia University Press books
are Smyth-sewn and printed on permanent and durable
acid-free paper

Contents

Preface

IN 1594, when my story ends, Shakespeare turned thirty and more than half his life lay behind him. Already a successful playwright and narrative poet, he had eclipsed all his rivals. Predicted by the early years, his best work waited on the future. So Shakespeare's past is prologue, also an absorbing story in its own right, crowded with incident and work of great price.

The work comes first but the life is its seedbed. "Nothing will come of nothing," as true for Shakespeare as anybody else. As a teacher, I have tended to concentrate on Shakespeare's text, downplaying other things, the life, the background, and so on. But practical criticism differs from biography, where the job is to realize the man. Not writing about his own experience, Shakespeare surely wrote from it, and his work (if all were known) is predicable of just this man, no other. On his artistic side even more than in the life, he shows himself to an eye alert for styles and psychologies. A playwright, it seems worth noting, is first of all a "wright" or maker, and resembles a boatwright or cartwright. Where they make boats or carts, he makes plays, leaving his maker's mark on the work. Detecting this is a biographer's business.

Older biographies of Shakespeare indulge the author's fancy, often extravagant. Approved modern biographies, taking disrespectful note, are reserved to the point of taciturnity, and many in their reserve throw out the baby with the bathwater. One account, by an eminent American Shakespearean, begins: "Every writer who wishes to write about the man William Shakespeare longs, but longs in vain, to see him 'in his habit as he lived.' " Caveats are useful, and Shakespeare being of magnitude, no one is going to see him "plain." But there is a kind of unholy glee in asserting that he can't be apprehended at all. Shakespeare's biography is hardly barren of facts, and a multitude of them crowd its margins. Inert in themselves, the facts are only background, a newspaper obit. Sometimes they quicken, though, intimating the man in his habit (or various habits) as he lived.

The man who was Shakespeare isn't just like the rest of us, and Jonson's famous tribute, fair enough, is misleading. "He was not of an age, but for all time!" Shakespeare, who transcends his age, also takes its pressure, revealing this in his life and work. Remote in the dark backward of time, Elizabethan Shakespeare bristles with difference. This has its compensation, and his singularity helps set him before us, "the strangest fellow," as they say of Falstaff, but visibly there. His age, like our own, was more or less myopic, and its vision of things— "purblind" or "sandblind," words he uses—was what he had to work with. Cultural historians, alert to this, emphasize the timeserver or child of his age, truckling to the establishment or the groundlings in the pit or accepting bad ideas uncritically, they being of the atmosphere. This grainy air sustained him, though, even buoyed him up. All art is privation, part of its charm, its efficiency too. Estimating their confinement, a necessary imposition, artists make a virtue of necessity. How Shakespeare did this is part of his story.

The story has been told often, with most authority by E. K. Chambers in his two-volume *Study of Facts and Problems* (1930). As the title suggests, this is specialist work and not intended for the general reader, however literate. The best biography of Shakespeare is S. Schoenbaum's *A Documentary Life* (1975), the second best is G. E. Bentley's *Biographical Handbook* (1961). Neither engages Shakespeare's art, except as matter of fact. Among popular biographies, not always a term of reproach, the most professional is that by Anthony Burgess (1970). Some biographies separate the life, synoptically treated, from the making of the plays. The best of these is Peter Alexander's (1939). No biography exists that is simultaneously a comprehensive and scrupulous account of the life, and a consideration, worth having, of the art. This is the book I have sought to write.

In my account I mean to lay out the facts, circumstantially and with the care they merit, then comment on them, saying what they add up to. I am not writing a biographical romance, and have steered clear of the staple phrases of biography at its wits' end: "Doubtless he" or "It may well have been," etc. I am not writing a textbook either, and don't pretend or wish to be endlessly exhaustive. For example, nine vicars served Stratford in Shakespeare's lifetime. I don't name them all, only those who bear. Much factual material concerning Shakespeare's life is by now in the public domain and doesn't need documentation. Where matter of fact calls for its source, however, I give this in the Notes. A short Reading List precedes the Notes, citing the principal books from which I draw the facts of Shakespeare's early life. Thinking him the best gloss on his work, I try to put one line (or play or poem) against another, intervening as little as possible. This means that quotations from the work, being central to my story and the way I tell it, appear on most pages. Often I leave these quotations unidentified. But they aren't meant for adornment, rather to make a point or buttress an argument, and when their source isn't obvious I locate it in the Notes.

Shakespeare's first editors, addressing "the great variety of readers" in his time, lay down the law for the rest of us. "Read him, therefore; and again, and again." If a life of Shakespeare is to count for much, this injunction ought to be heeded. I have written for the literate reader in and out of academia, supposing that he/she still exists. Knowing Shakespeare some, this reader will want to know him better. Knowing Shakespeare a little before getting started seems important, though.

Anyone who engages to write a book like this one needs all the help he can get. I have had a lot of help and acknowledge it gratefully. (For once it seems indicated to recite the old formula and say that such mistakes as crop up in what follows are mine.) John F. Andrews, John Russell Brown, Susan Cerasano, Lincoln Faller, and Robert Weisbuch commented on parts of my manuscript, and Nicholas Delbanco read it all. William Ingram followed me chapter by chapter, sending up distress signals when called for. He is the definition of a generous scholar.

This book, though biography, is ultimately personal. It comes from teaching Shakespeare and thinking about him, a longtime occupation. My students, making me think twice, have been my collaborators, and I dedicate what I have written to them.

YOUNG SHAKESPEARE

1

The Country

FOUR HUNDRED YEARS AGO, Robert Greene said what Shakespeare was like. A hack writer of genius, Greene was Shakespeare's first critic. Ailing, out of pocket, once the darling of the theater crowd but lately passé, he warned them to beware the up and coming man, night-boding Shakespeare. "Johannes Factotum," Greene called him derisively, a handyman or botcher who tinkered other men's plays. Beneath the player's hide, Greene saw the "tiger's heart."

Later, mutual acquaintance tried to palliate this, saying how Shakespeare, no tiger, was civil, upright in his dealings, polished in his art. "Good sentences and well pronounced," they might do for many men and some women in Shakespeare's time. Vituperative Greene, going for the heart, had the right instinct. He wrote from hatred, aggravated by self-hatred, so made a doubtful reporter. The "divers of worship" who corrected him, knowing this, meant to set the facts straight. Shakespeare's first scholars, they deserve respectful attention. His story begins with mustering facts. But it ends, if worth its salt, with a sally at the question: What was Shakespeare like?

He was William Shakespeare, born in Stratford-upon-Avon, a market town in the Midlands or middle counties of England, on or about April 23, 1564. John Shakespeare, his father, came in from the country to the town. A leather worker and dealer in fleece, he cut an important figure in Stratford, making a good marriage to Mary Arden, a farmer's daughter, well left. Rising through the ranks in the village corporation, he was chosen Stratford's bailiff or mayor. But at the height his fortunes fell. Tradition says that young Shakespeare attended school in Stratford but didn't finish, a casualty of this. He was still in his teens when Anne Hathaway, eight years older, initiated him. Pregnant when they married, she bore him three children. Then for some years, Shakespeare drops from sight. When he turns up again, he is living in London, a professional entertainer. For the next twenty years he labored his craft, making an impersonal testament. He left thirty-eight plays, one hundred and fifty-four sonnets, a moralizing "complaint" saying what happens when woman stoops to folly, two longish narrative poems on erotic subjects, and a mysterious threnody lamenting the death of a pair of chaste lovers. This labor finished, he went back to Stratford and died.

These are the bare bones and fleshing them out has been a problem to many. Henry James, confronting it, threw up his hands. More than once he coped with Shakespeare, a different version of the artist, humble like a catalytic agent. Refined out of existence, James' Shakespeare becomes at last the figment of other men's imaginations, "no such Person." This verdict is entered in the story called "The Birthplace." Speaking for the author, the skeptical hero, a curator, almost talks himself out of a job. The job is promoting The Biggest Show on Earth, Stratford and its Sancta Sanctorum. "He was born *here!*" they want him to say, jamming their umbrellas into the floor. But "the details are naught," the curator says, the links gone, the evidence nil, and anyway "it was so awfully long ago."

Long ago it was, but much matter of fact survives, missed by time's tooth. Over three hundred men wrote for the theater in the English Renaissance. More is known about Shakespeare than any of them, possibly excepting Ben Jonson. He had his proper start in life, "born anew of water and the Holy Ghost." The record identifies the priest who baptized him, and the church has the bowl in which he was dipped—three times, as prescribed by the Book of Common Prayer. Retrieved from a Stratford garden where it functioned as a water cistern, it stands on a pedestal near Shakespeare's grave, much beaten about but there for all to see.

The record of Shakespeare's baptism survives too, entered in the parish register of Holy Trinity, an ancient church beside the Avon on the southern edge of Stratford. The register gives the christening date, April 26, 1564, a Wednesday. Latin still being the canonical tongue, the entry reads "Gulielmus, filius Johannes Shakspere," William, son of John. Parents weren't to defer christening beyond the first Sunday or Holy Day after birth. That is what the Prayer Book told them, and presumably John and Mary, Shakespeare's parents, hearkened to this. The day before the christening honored St. Mark, but spooks walked on this Holy Day. "Black Crosses," they called it, not auspicious for baptizing your child. A contemporary of Shakespeare's remembered how an alewife's house went up in flames when she brewed on St. Mark's Day, "a gentle warning to them that violate and profane forbidden days!" Shakespeare's parents, warned, skipped St. Mark's, going to church a day later. They needed an interval, in any case, after the lying in. St. George's Day fell three days earlier, Sunday the 23rd. Tradition, honoring England's patron saint and best poet together, says that Shakespeare was born on this day.

Then there are the plays, approximately half of them published in Shakespeare's lifetime. Seven years after his death, most were collected in an impressive folio by two friends and fellow actors. Taken together, they offer a likeness of this "sweet swan of Avon," Jonson's phrase in his poem prefaced to the First Folio of 1623. Shakespeare's plays not being true confessions, the likeness is skewed, as with those cunning pictures—"perspectives," he calls them—which when looked at straight on "show nothing but confusion." To sort out the confusion, you have to squint or look awry. Knowing himself for an arrant knave like Hamlet, or rather knowing that "we are arrant knaves all," Shakespeare shies from the first-person pronoun. Writing about others reprieved him from the man he was. But he has his distinctive bias, and though it doesn't "run all one way"—Jonson's description of a "humor" character or cartoon—the bias shows in the plays, open to description.

Shakespeare's people first appear in history in the reign of Henry VIII (1509–47). One chronicler traces them back a lot further, all the way to Adam, surnamed Shakespeare, who died in 1414. This name has its decorum but the provenance seems unlikely. On the paternal side, the Shakespeares lived in Snitterfield, a tiny village four miles northeast of Stratford in rolling hills and meadows, colored yellow with gorse. Richard Shakespeare, the poet's grandfather, adroit or opportunistic, kept his footing in a world slick with change. He knew about history, nobles fighting kings.

Except to those who died, much of the fighting meant little. At the end of *Henry IV*, Part One, Shakespeare's best history play, the soldiers troop off together, resolved to go at it another day. In Warwickshire and environs, this day was always dawning. Southwest of Snitterfield lay the bloody ground of Evesham (1265) where Simon de Montfort, greatest of the barons, died fighting King Henry III. At Bosworth Field, north and east, Henry VII, another maker and shaker, ended the Wars of the Roses in 1485. Shakespeares fought in this battle, or the Heralds' College thought so, a reason for the bristling crest it awarded them later, a falcon shaking a spear.

Coventry, fourth largest city in the kingdom, dominating the Midlands, made a bone of contention in the Wars of the Roses. Mastiffs, York and Lancaster, worried the bone, and burghers in Coventry, keeping history at arm's length, built their fortified walls three feet thick. Falstaff marched his poor perdus through the streets of this city, en route to another famous battle. Six miles from Snitterfield, Warwick was the seat of John Dudley, Duke of Northumberland. Lord Protector of the boy king Edward VI, he wanted the throne for himself. The Duke had a stand-in, Lady Jane Grey, his daughter-in-law. Eight years before Richard Shakespeare died, the two of them died on the scaffold. Not meddling in princes' matters, Shakespeare's grandfather watched the up and down, saying inoffensive things, e.g. "Death is certain" and "What will be, must be." Then he went about his business, prosaic. He looks forward to Shakespeare, resourceful but different, being cumbered with genius and needing to express this.

Richard Shakespeare's house stood on the High Street beside the pike that ran to Warwick. A rising man in Snitterfield, he had an eye to reward and knew how to achieve it. When he died in the winter of 1561, he left goods worth almost £39, more than the neighborhood vicar. Warham, Henry VIII's Archbishop of Canterbury, died with only £30 in hand. He said it was enough for his funeral. Before 1529, the year Richard Shakespeare first appears in the records, he was pasturing cattle on Snitterfield common. The society he lived in, communistic but spelled with a lower-case "c," disappeared beneath the waters that rose in Shakespeare's lifetime. A hundred filaments, vexing and cherishing, bound him to his neighbors. In villages like Snitterfield, "champion" or common-field farmers shared the arable land. It showed like a crazy quilt, sliced by grassy pathways, hedgerows, and balks of turf. No better than they should be, farmers in Snitterfield poached on their neighbor's land or reaped their neighbor's crops. If you didn't mend your hedges, a turn of the plough put you over the line that separated meum and tuum. Richard Shakespeare didn't mend his hedges and in 1538 they told him to do this.

Lady-smocks and crow-flowers bloomed in Snitterfield meadows, also marigolds, "marybud," a common weed. Herbalists like John Gerard said where they grew and didn't, herbs denoting for them any green thing from grasses to trees. Green things made part of a fraternity for Shakespeare, gathered from the life and his reading of Scripture. A boy in Stratford church, he read the First Epistle of Peter: "For all flesh is as grass, and all the glory of man as the flower of grass. The grass withereth, and the flower thereof falleth away."

Stratford's life was the land, not inert but vital, like a man's body. Or the body was like the land. Merging the worker in his vineyard and the other way round, Shakespeare discovered his most potent image, on the tip of his tongue when he groped to say what people were like. Men and women in the plays, not themselves alone, grow and wither like plants and trees. Vaunting "in their youthful sap," they flourish for a while, then decay, "slaves of nature." *King Lear* has a text, intimating connections.

> She that herself will sliver and disbranch
> From her material sap perforce must wither
> And come to deadly use.

"Perforce" is the word, no help for it.

Bearing witness to natural process, Shakespeare suggests a moral order to moral readers. But his laconic appeal goes to sanctions more insistent than the Decalogue. Where the preacher, wanting you to take his word, thunders out an ipse dixit ("thus he said"), Shakespeare and his countrymen looked for verification. Attentive to preachers, they had their homespun text, organic not prescriptive. It speaks in their imagery, matter of everyday. Honoring the Queen, they entertained her with pageants, emblematic tableaux. For her Coronation Day, November 17, they brought on Time and his daughter Truth, also a gigantic rose tree, growing evidently from Henry Tudor, Lancastrian, and his consort Elizabeth of York. Truth in the pageant, not produced from a hat, emerges in the ripened time—"when golden time convents" or summons, is the way Shakespeare puts it—and the Queen, as the tree exfoliates, is nature's bud or scion, sprung from the union of Lancaster and York.

This way of reading the world—not moral, exactly, older than morality and remote from poetic justice—came to Shakespeare in the air he breathed. His people were people of a book, the Bible, if not his favorite text the one he knew best. He heard the Bishops' Bible, standard in most churches, and read the Geneva version, leaning toward Calvin. The Book of Samuel introduced him to Jesse, King David's father. From this remote ancestor came Joseph the carpenter, husband of Mary, mother of God. Matthew in his first chapter gives the begats. Rising branch by branch from the loins of the prophet, the "Jesse Tree" prefigured the rose tree. It showed the lineage of Jesus, more tangible than Salic Law, moldy parchment. Before the Bible, however, Shakespeare consulted the natural world, his *Biblia pauperum*. Showing, not telling, this "poor man's Bible" didn't need words. Empirical Shakespeare made it his study, ratifying connections between men and women and the dungy earth they go back to. This is another version of the bucolic poet, warbling his native woodnotes wild.

The undulating farmland, broken with coppices, hasn't changed much four hundred years later. Sheep and cattle crop the meadows. The sheep have black muzzles and the spotted cattle are black and white. Henry James, playful like an elephant, thought Shakespeare's landscape sinned by excess of nutritive suggestion. "It savors of larder and manger; it is too ovine, too bovine, it is almost asinine; and if you were to believe what you see before you this rugged globe would be a sort of boneless ball covered with some such plush-like integument as might be figured by the down on the cheek of a peach." (In the life, like the art, there were grace notes.) Stands of pine, darkly majestic, dot the countryside but look out of place in this undramatic country. Ivy, a parasite, climbs on the trunks of the deciduous trees. Fencing the meadows, the withies, woven horizontally, are stitched together with stakes. The stakes are the warp, like threads in a carpet, crossed at right angles by the woof. Poplars and chestnut trees grow beside the roads, and some hedges are trees, trimmed to human dimension. "Rank fumiter" still grow in the hedgerows, their flowers waxy red, sometimes yellow.

Coming down from the Middle Ages, big churches serving little flocks of parishioners stood in this open Warwickshire country. Some are still standing, like St. Peter ad Vincula, just around the corner from Snitterfield in the parish of Hampton Lucy. How and why English people supported these churches, bigger than they had to be, is an index of the difference between Shakespeare's time and ours. England before the Reformation, a God-bitten country, made a third place between heaven and hell, "middle earth." Victorians, getting on with it, demolished old St. Peter's, and Sir Gilbert Scott, a Gothic revivalist, helped build the new church. But the church Shakespeare knew survives in parish registers. They tell how in the 1580s his cousins, Lettice and James, children of Henry Shakespeare, were baptized in St. Peter's, the boy dying four years after his birth. Henry was Richard Shakespeare's younger son, a scapegrace. Not much is left of the medieval church. In the south aisle, however, inlaid tiles have little monsters with human faces.

The big church in Snitterfield is St. James the Great, its walls con-

structed of the local stone, lias rubble, a kind of limestone, the slate
roof crowned by a cross within a circle. On the baptismal font, four-
teenth-century work, the professions appear, a mitred bishop, a knight,
a lawyer, perhaps a scholar wearing a close-fitting hood. In the early
years of the seventeenth century, Shakespeare remembered this church.
His heroine Helena in *All's Well That Ends Well,* leaving France for
Florence, goes on pilgrimage to the shrine of St. James the Great in
Compostela, northern Spain. This, as Dr. Johnson remarked long ago,
is rather out of the way. But Shakespeare, having his pieties, made
room for things peculiar to himself.

Remembering, blurred with time's snow or maker's cunning, denotes
him. (This isn't the same as drawing from life or making a roman à
clef.) His drunken tinker in *The Taming of the Shrew,* "old Sly's son
of Burton Heath," comes from Barton, eight miles from Stratford,
or Barton-on-the-Heath, sixteen miles away. Aunt Joan, his mother
Mary's sister, lived in Barton-on-the-Heath, married to Edmund Lambert. Shakespeare's younger sister Joan is named for this aunt Lambert.
The aunt had a neighbor, Sly's drinking companion, "old John Naps
of Greece." He lived in "dingy Greet" across the border in Gloucestershire, home to Clement Perkes of Stinchcombe Hill. A knavish client
of Shallow's makes poor Perkes look foolish. Of little account to
history, these incidental details seemed important to Shakespeare. In
As You Like It, the Forest of Arden to which Rosalind flees is the
Ardennes of France and medieval epic, also his Arden Forest, over the
ridge from Stratford and the valley of the Avon. Shakespeare, faithful
to his origins, declines to sentimentalize them, though. Helena's pilgrimage brings her back to the beginning, and in the Forest of Arden
Rosalind doesn't find a better world.

Youthful memory, flickering in the plays, lights up the private place
the public man resorted to, pleasing or lacerating himself. Another way
to put this is to call the plays a ladder. Wanting to escape his beginnings,
Shakespeare climbed the ladder, never escaping altogether. In *Henry
IV,* Part Two, he thinks back to Snitterfield, where his mother's father
owned land. The family property in Snitterfield being subject to a law
suit, acquisitive Shakespeare, collecting bits of old string, took note of
the commissioners adjudicating this. In 1581 or thereabouts he wrote
their names in his "table book," one Peto among them. This Peto,
dredged from memory, returns as a crony of Falstaff's. Bardolph, a
rogue and toper, is Falstaff's crony too, and Fluellen, a pedantic soldier,
has his part in the play. First, though, these made-up characters were
part of John Shakespeare's story. Delinquents, the three of them didn't
go to church, fearing "process for debt." Stratford churchwardens

reported this in 1592. Seven years later, Shakespeare, escaped from Stratford and absolute despot in his little world of theater, had this Bardolph hanged for stealing a "pax," a paten stamped with the crucifix. Fluellen, however, gets off scot-free, Shakespeare having mercy on whom he will have mercy. *Henry V* tells us what happened. The tip of the iceberg, i.e. a play and impersonal, it rests on the personal life submerged below.

THE LIFE needs its wider context, Tudor England, a world turned upside down. Shakespeare's forcing house, it left him damaged goods but resilient. Cultural shock was his element, one blow succeeding another "like the waves that make toward the pebbled shore." His evasive art is the product of this, also his public face, the mask of Buddha.

The age of the Tudors begins at Bosworth Field in 1485 when the first of them, Henry VII, seized the throne. Shakespeare tells this story in *Richard III*, his first permanent success for the stage. Taking his cue from Tudor propagandists like Holinshed and Hall, he makes the usurper a hero and the deposed king a villain. Contemporary portraits of Henry and Richard tell a different story. Two hang on adjacent walls in the National Portrait Gallery, London. Henry in his likeness is mean, gimlet-eyed, a man up to anything. Richard, anxious and thoughtful, looks like the idea of a king. However, as we learn from *Macbeth*, "There's no art to find the mind's construction in the face," and probably both were villains. Thinking that nothing succeeded like success, Shakespeare gave the victor his due. Others, blurting out the truth, died for opinion's sake or knocked their heads against the universe, like his contemporary Marlowe. Shakespeare, having surrogates and not prone to complaining, kept his opinions to himself.

He had reason. The matrix that nourished him, medieval and Catholic, was broken before he was born. Then it was put back together, then broken again. In the 1530s, his grandfather Richard's young time, Henry VIII, a corrupt adolescent hiding in a man's gross body, made himself head of the Church. Dissolving the monasteries, he evicted the monks, custodians of the old faith of England. He took aim at the Carthusians, a powerful order. Some he had dragged on hurdles or sleds to the three-cornered gallows at Tyburn. This place of public execution in the west of London stood where the Marble Arch stands today.

Hanged on the gallows, the monks were cut down alive. Their arms were torn off, their hearts cut out and rubbed in their faces. In Charterhouse Square where Carthusians had their London quarters, the last prior, Houghton, was cut in fours, one piece being hung on the priory door. Leading his little company of martyrs, the prior said they went to death as cheerfully "as bridegrooms to their marriage." In its secondary sense, death is sexual intercourse, befitting the bridegroom. Very Shakespearean, Houghton is punning even at death's door. Shakespeare's characters do this, one dying bravely "like a smug bridegroom," another hugging darkness in his arms like a bride. Good lines, Shakespeare thought, but he didn't emulate Blessed John Houghton. When Catholic peasants revolted in their Pilgrimage of Grace (1536), the king's generals hanged them on trees in the village gardens, wanting their wives and children to see. Monks they hanged on long pieces of timber "or otherwise," projecting from the church. The hanging went on before Shakespeare's time but he knew all about it, setting down what he knew under color of Jack Cade's rebellion. This angry man of Kent, killed in 1450, gave Shakespeare his first comic scenes. Moderns aren't invariably amused, and to Engels, chronicler of a peasants' rebellion, Cade and company were heroes. Not to Shakespeare, however. As for the rebels, says an officer in his play, let them

> even in their wives' and children's sight,
> Be hanged up for examples at their doors.

In Shakespeare's people, impressionable, this example induced reserve. Taciturn Shakespeare is their scholar.

A decade or so before Shakespeare was born, the wheel turned in England. "Bloody Mary" Tudor, Henry's daughter and a Catholic, came to the throne. Deferring to Rome, this queen harried Protestants. Some went into exile, others got burned at the stake. Her half-sister Elizabeth, steering a tricky course between Rome and Geneva, executed Protestants and Catholics impartially. She was Shakespeare's queen and reigned for forty-five years. A rare bird like Shakespeare, she thought herself endowed "with such qualities that if I were turned out of the realm in my petticoat, I were able to live in any place in Christendom." English being partial to whatever lives long, they praised her to the skies. She was Astraea, goddess of justice, or Cynthia, the Virgin Queen. John Lyly, a fulsome contemporary of Shakespeare's, adorned her with "singular beauty and chastity, excelling in the one, Venus, in the other, Vesta." (Almost all the famous poets swelled this paean of praise but Shakespeare held his peace.)

No doubt "Venus" put it too high. The Queen's nose was hooked, her hair "of an auburn color but false," her teeth black from sucking sugar, a vice of English, Falstaff among them. Vesta she may have been, and many, hymning her virginity, thought so. Coarse Ben Jonson said she had an impenetrable hymen. Likely a scary childhood spent in her father's court, death on women, inclined her to keep her distance from men. She enjoyed teasing them, though, and even at sixty-five, wrinkled with age, appeared in public with her breasts uncovered. "All the English ladies" did this, said a traveler, "till they marry."

A skeptical despot, unlike her bigoted sister but suggesting "Laodicean" Shakespeare, the Queen got on without opinions, not believing in much except herself and England's greatness. In the reign of Elizabeth, if you wanted to save your neck you kept your head down. She said she desired "to open a window on no man's conscience." But this Tudor prince was a child of her age, reveling like others in bloodsports. In her younger time, entertained by bear-baiting at a castle in the Shakespeare Country, she watched the bear "shake his ears twice or thrice with the blood and the slaver." This was "matter of a goodly relief." Mostly, her cruelties were politic. When an incautious pamphleteer came too near her person, she had his hand struck off on a public stage, wanting her people to see what lese majesty got them. Camden the historian, an eyewitness, said they were "mute with fear and commiseration."

Not less than the Pope, the Queen was God's anointed, "next under His Almightiness." Pius V, picking a quarrel with this rival vicar, deprived her of "her pretended right" to the kingdom. The Pope's Bull of Deposition (1570) absolved English "from all duty, fidelity, and obedience" to the royal heretic. This political gesture was consequential for Shakespeare, his family, and friends. Her throne being at risk, Elizabeth turned inquisitor, as savage as any. For the balance of the reign, dissenters went to the stake or the gallows. Catholics, more than 200 of them, headed the procession. None of these malcontents gets a hearing in Shakespeare's plays.

Richard Shakespeare was Catholic but stayed mum on this, or his professing was only lukewarm. When the century was young and he with it, monasteries in England held a fifth of the cultivated land. They held it by old custom, and their tenants and copyholders (men tenured by the manor lord) appealed to custom too. This nice reticulating, where one man's right depended on the rights of others, went out with the monks and the old-time religion. Already dying, the monasteries waited on King Henry to supply the coup de grâce. Monks, like most others, thought that charity began at home. They had their uses, though, sanctifying custom. To Shakespeare, this seemed important. Later, his heroine Imogen, deploring the breach of custom, calls it "breach of all." Her story, a tale of far off things, is set in Roman Britain.

In a dangerous time, Shakespeare's grandfather got on as he could. A "character" writer in the next age, perhaps looking through rose-colored glasses, gave his type. He was a yeoman farmer, that is, one who never uses "cruelty but when he hunts the hare; nor subtlety but when he setteth snares for the snipe or pitfalls for the blackbird; nor oppression but when, in the month of July, he goes to the next river and shears his sheep." Already in the seventeenth century, English had their vision of the good old days. Many think that Shakespeare, back-wardlooking, shared this vision. In *As You Like It,* he brings on stage the "antique world" before the cash nexus and dog eat dog. Faithful Adam in this play embodies the golden world, as it might be Richard Shakespeare's, "where service sweat for duty, not for meed," and Robin Hood, a folk hero, adjusted the balance between rich and poor. But Adam, postlapsarian, prunes a rotten tree, our old stock. If it bears, that isn't thanks to him or his husbandry. Merry England, in Shakespeare's view, predicts "the fashion of these times," having its obligatory serpent. "Country copulatives" in the Forest have to allow for this. None escape "the penalty of Adam." That is point of view and patented Shakespeare, not socioeconomic but respectful of the ills our flesh is heir to.

Shakespeare's villains and naive heroes have their different point of view, saying how "at some time" men are masters of their fate. Splendid locusts on the land, they rose to power by plundering the monks. (Pope Pius called them "obscure men who are heretics.") Most were deaf to commonweal, Hugh Latimer said, like a "hermit closed in a wall." This Reforming clergyman saw how the "too much" amassed by the spoilsmen "causeth such dearth that poor men which live of their labor cannot with the sweat of their face have a living." Latimer's father, like Richard Shakespeare, tilled a small farm. In time of war he put on armor, serving the king. Latimer remembered how "I buckled his harness when he went unto Blackheath Field." An independent yeoman, he sent his son to Cambridge, dowered his daughters and married them off. "He kept hospitality for his poor neighbors, and some alms he gave to the poor. All this he did of the said farm." Times changed, however, and the yeoman went to the wall, no longer able to do "for his prince, for himself, nor for his children, or give a cup of drink to the poor." This came of "private commodity," Latimer said. Commodity means self-interest. Shakespeare in *King John* called it "the bias of the world."

King John is a history play, remembering things past. But the past declares the present. This is Shakespeare's strategy, revealing the feline man, Polonius-like, who finds directions "by indirections" or says one thing in terms of another. Wanting to say his say, he uses history as a stalking-horse. Tudor fowlers, hunting birds, hid behind the stalking-horse, an old nag or a piece of painted canvas. Under cover like a fowler, Shakespeare does this, shooting his arrows. Macbeth, who ruled in Scotland a long time ago, is a stalking-horse. So is King Lear, prehistoric and safe. Reciting their stories, Shakespeare offers his version, always at art's length, of the world turned upside down.

In this anarchic world, the winds, untied, fight against the churches, waves confound navigation, and castles topple on their warders' heads. "Let order die!" cries the anarch, personated by Northumberland in *Henry IV, Part Two.* Shakespeare's bad dream, the annulling of order gets his attention, beginning with his earliest histories. For example, this, from *Henry VI, Part Two:*

> Oh, let the vile world end
> And let the premisèd flames of the last day
> Knit earth and heaven together!

The flames are "premised," sent before their time. Emblem of doomsday, they wait on chaos, an "indigest," rude and shapeless. Very clamant in Shakespeare's tragedies, notably *Timon of Athens, King Lear,* and *Macbeth,* chaos affronts this playwright, no friend of "unaccommodated" man. People often bring him forward as conservative Shakespeare, elaborating the Elizabethan World Picture. Not conservative, liberal either, he wasn't an apologist for the Tudor establishment, like Holinshed and Hall. In a world turned upside down, he stood for survival.

"Cruel are the times," says Ross in *Macbeth,* but the cruelty the Tudors practiced, subtler than the rack or gallows, menaced the spirit. Men turned the wrong side out, inverting the norms and sanctions that make life supportable. Not knowing who they were, they floated on "a wild and violent sea." This is the Shakespearean Tempest. At court and in the country, evacuated men, destitute of principle, crop up on every hand. Stephen Gardiner, a bishop and tool of Henry VIII, is one of these men. Shakespeare gives him a bit part in his late pageant play, dramatizing Henry's reign. Real-life Gardiner went to prison when the king died but lived to be Chancellor under Queen Mary. At the end he said: "I have denied with Peter, and gone out with Peter, but I have not yet wept with Peter." This timeserver died in bed. Oswald in *King Lear,* Shakespeare's version of the timeserver, dies badly, caught in the maelstrom. This is where art, liking the normative case, is wiser than history. The man without principle loses his bearings, pragmatic Shakespeare thinks. His anarch is suicidal, floating on the wild and violent sea.

Shakespeare has an image for Oswald, the halcyon, our kingfisher, often noticed in emblem books, popular collections of moralized pictures. A fabulous bird, the halcyon calmèd the waters. Efficient in other ways, it functioned as a weathervane. If you hung it up by the bill, it turned its bill into the wind. This is like and unlike Shakespeare, faithful to his antecedents and anxious to please. But where the sycophantic man, looking for the wind, hopes to raise his fortunes, Shakespeare is effacing or reserving himself, knowing he had talents to spend. The important question for him is all but put in *Measure for Measure:* What good were your virtues if they didn't go forth of you? Duke Vincentio, a surrogate, raises the question, and Shakespeare gives his answer in the plays. He had a pattern before him in his grandfather Richard, the pattern suggesting what he was and wasn't. Richard Shakespeare, a survivor, born in the Middle Ages, lived into the modern world. His grandson, surviving also, was necessarily circumspect but didn't hide his light under a bushel.

FOR UPWARDS OF thirty years, Richard Shakespeare tilled the Snitterfield farm. Lands in tillage were "leas," disposed in long blocks called "furlongs" and marked off by fences or "meers." Technical language, this gets aired in the plays. Timon in his rantings remembers "plough-torn leas," and Gonzalo, swamped by the tempest, would trade a thousand furlongs of water for an acre of barren ground. Fleeing the fight at Actium, Antony is "the merèd question," marked off from all the rest. An equivocal hero, he made a cynosure with a difference.

In this Saturnian world money was superfluous, or you could say in short supply. Except for paying rent, it didn't often change hands. The average farmer cultivated eighteen acres of land, divided for equity's sake in three parts, good, bad, and indifferent. Besides this, he held two acres of meadow. He grew wheat, red and white, barley, rye, and hops. Rye and wheat were the bread-corn. Shakespeare's lover and his lass, making love in the fields, lie between "the acres of the rye." That is how the song goes but farmers in Snitterfield didn't sow much rye, the soil being too heavy for this. Barley mixed with oats was the drink-corn, the hops went to making beer. Shakespeare's people drank a lot of beer, also cider, claret, muscadine, and charneco, unfortified port. Some, gentrified like Falstaff, preferred sack, Spanish wine or Canary.

"In England," says Iago, who sometimes speaks Scripture, "they are most potent in potting." They drank the Danes dead drunk, overthrew the Germans, and gave Dutchmen a vomit before the next can could be filled. English farmers, not choosy like Falstaff, drank what they grew. Malting and brewing was work for their wives.

The woman on the throne spoke six languages, hunted and hawked, played the virginals, danced "high and disposedly," and made a keen competitor at chess. But her sex was against her. "Had I been born crested, not cloven," she said, raging at her Council, "you would not have dared speak to me thus!" "Cloven" denotes the pudendum, "crested" the cock. Being a prince, the Queen had "two bodies," though, and men took off their caps to this woman. Most women were chattel, valued as they gave use.

Farm women, a valuable commodity, fed the calves, pigs, and poultry. Milking the cows, they skimmed the milk and made butter and cheese. "In time of need," says Fitzherbert, who wrote a book "of husbandry," they helped fill the muck-wain, drive the plough, load the hay, wheat, "and such other." When the frost broke in March, wives planted kitchen gardens. They set out thyme and hyssop, garlic, parsley for stuffing rabbits, saffron to color warden pies. Culling their gardens, they made medicines from herbs, perfumes for the linen chest, and picked salads for the table. Chandlers too, they peeled rushes for the candlewicks. Their thread, homemade, came from nettles, and they spun their own linen and cloth. Spinsters, websters, listers who dyed the cloth, baxters who baked the bread for the family, wives in Shakespeare's England played second fiddle to husbands.

Sometimes Shakespeare dramatizes their humble role, prescribed by Tudor convention, sometimes, departing from convention, he shows his back above the element he lived in. Everybody who reads the plays will feel how they are realistic, rising out of the life that bred them. At their most memorable they overgo real life, however, taking a better way, not ethical or moral, esthetic. In Shakespeare, women rule the roost. Managing less, they manage things better. Unlike men, forthputting, these women defer to Time, a greater power than they can contradict. Ceding authority, they gather it into their hands. This assures the happy ending. That is how it is in the plays, a world turned upside down or right side up. Outside, in the real world, most stuck with St. Paul, an Iron Age psychologist. He said the man was head of the woman.

Country life in Tudor England, not free but constrained, followed the course of the sun. This is life as Shakespeare conceived it, subject to tides beyond wishing and willing. His "good Duke Humphrey," soon to die and not wanting to, knows how bright days turn cloudy, and how,

> after summer, evermore succeeds
> Barren winter with his wrathful nipping cold.

Cares and joys were like this, abounding, then decreasing, "as seasons fleet." The year that mattered, an iron rigol or round, followed the plough. For Shakespeare's people it began in late winter, at Candlemas time (February 2)—Groundhog's Day, Americans call this—or St. Gregory's Day (March 12), when the meadows were put up for hay. Once the harvest was in, cattle, grazing the stubble, had the run of the farm. A common neatherd, shepherd, and swineherd tended the cattle. A keeper with his bow kept an eye out for crows. Maybe he frightened the ladies. He didn't shoot straight, however, so wasn't a match for the crows. "That fellow," says King Lear, "handles his bow like a crowkeeper."

Like jolly folk in a Breughel painting, assimilated to the plough, the villagers had their feast days, a respite from toil. They stuffed themselves on feast days, astonishing travelers from more frugal lands. Italy and France were more frugal, and in culinary matters English put other countries in the shade. Roasting meat was their speciality, afterwards forgotten lore. William Harrison, a Cockney from Bow Lane turned country parson, tells about this in his *Description of England*. "The whole carcasses of many capons, hens, pigeons and suchlike do oft go to wrack, besides beef, mutton, veal, and lamb, all of which at every feast are taken as necessary dishes." This list, meant for exemplary, omits pork, kid, coney or rabbit, venison, fish, fowl, pigs' "pettietoes," and "white meats," dairy products including eggs.

Where villagers ate three meals, gentry ate two, not breaking fast until noon. Sitting down to table, they made up for this. At Kenilworth near Stratford, in Shakespeare's day a splendid castle, now a dull-red ruin, the Earl of Leicester hosted the Queen in 1575. Villagers from Warwickshire turned out en masse, Shakespeare among them, a boy of eleven years and three months. Common folk, not gentry, he stood outside looking in, recording what he saw in the plays. For this festive occasion, two hundred gentlemen served a thousand platters, enough to go round. Gentry and common folk, English lived at full stretch. Any day did for a feast day. Villagers in Snitterfield celebrated Plough Monday on the first Monday after January 6. Lent began with Merry Shrovetide, when the people took their fill of recreation and bought repentance "ere they grow devout." There were Whitsun Pastorals, Church Ales, sheep-shearing feasts, and harvest home at the end of the harvest. In *The Winter's Tale*, Shakespeare's young hero participates in one of these feasts. "Let's be red with mirth," he says, and they were.

Harvest time was Lammas time, celebrated August 1. Richard Shakespeare held Lammas Day in July. Like his grandson, he consulted the Julian Calendar, dating the new year from Lady Day, March 25. English in the eighteenth century changed to the Gregorian Calendar, dropping eleven days from the year. After this, they began the new year January 1. In the calendar he lived by, Shakespeare is Old Style. Some think our modern age, new style, shows a declension. Dryden, a great poet in the age after Shakespeare, thought this. He said that in the old days, antediluvian, there were giants in the earth. Then came the flood, social and political. "It was never merry days in England since gentlemen came up," says a horny-handed philosopher in Shakespeare.

Merry England had another side, "nasty, solitary, brutish, and short." The "gilded puddle" stood on the land, poorly drained and thinly manured. Poor jades got the "bots" or worms. In *Henry IV*, Part One, Shakespeare tells how this happens. The price of oats rose, manipulated, like as not. Idle weeds choked the wheat, and Shakespeare remembers them too, "burdocks, hemlock, nettles, cuckoo-flowers." This disorderly landscape belongs to *King Lear*, etched in dark colors. But *A Midsummer Night's Dream* has its dark colors, Shakespeare's comedy, true to life, needing a moiety of shadow. The oxen stretch their yoke in vain, the ploughman loses his sweat, and the sheep-pen stands empty in the flooded fields. Crows grow fat on the "murrion flock," sick to death.

Rogues and vagabonds—a lot of them in Shakespeare's England—cast eyes on the village farm. The village hayward kept a lookout from seedtime to harvest. Petty thieves he could cope with. But "great oney-ers," men of consequence, preyed on the commonwealth. They were like fern seed, so small you couldn't see it. Finding this seed on St. John's Day made you invisible, Shakespeare's characters thought. Petty villains, they reflect on this in *Henry IV*, Part One. Their masters, playing the same game but on a grander stage, get clear away. "Nobility and tranquillity," they had "the receipt of fern seed."

Common-field farming looked to the past. You could make more profit farming one acre of "several" land than three acres of common, said Tusser, a doggerel poet in Shakespeare's boyhood. "Several" means separate, the way of the future. Shakespeare puns on this difference in *Love's Labor's Lost*. Her lips aren't for kissing, says a woman in the play, "no common, though several they be." Elsewhere Shakespeare looks at the landlord, a voracious feeder. The young dace, small fry, was bait for this old pike. Betting on the future, he swallowed the little farms, "pelting" farms, Shakespeare calls them. This brought a better return on land but pressed hard on the men who got swallowed.

In *Richard II*, Gaunt, a wise old councilor, has his vision of this England, located for safety's sake two hundred years in the past. He sees how the blessed plot, "this earth, this realm," is leased out or bound in with inky blots and parchment. Secure behind his stalking-horse, Shakespeare says what he thinks. In *Timon of Athens*, a fable lifted from Plutarch and tinkered to make a social critique, we hear how the commonwealth has become "a forest of beasts." For Athens read England. "Crack the lawyer's voice," the angry hero urges, "That he may never more false title plead,/Nor sound his quillets shrilly." Quillets are subtleties, dispossessing the poor.

In Hampton Lucy parish, they were moving the poor along before Shakespeare was born. Evicted from their houses, thirty-six people, a crowd in this pelting place, left Hampton in 1517. The houses were pulled down and the tillage reduced by almost two hundred acres. Two of the dispossessors were clergy. Not a friend of the clergy and not hostile either, Shakespeare allowed that some clergy were venal. Others were good, e.g. his Friar Laurence and Abbess Emilia. This impartial reporting, disclosing essential Shakespeare, cancels out point of view. Meanwhile, Catholics like Thomas More and Protestants like Bishop Latimer wrote their angry polemics, attacking the "system." They said how wealth accumulated while men decayed. "Enclosure" is the word for this, a cloud on the horizon when Richard Shakespeare farmed in Snitterfield, later a sign of the times.

Sheep still graze the meadows around Snitterfield and Stratford, and the landscape, closely shorn, is attractive to the eye. However, it tells a tale of depredation. Sheep brought a profit, not for their mutton, for their leather and fleece. Where grain rotted, you could store sheep's wool, holding it against a rise in prices. So farm land, supporting many, turned into pasture, enriching a few. Villages emptied out, sheep ate men, and a proverb of Shakespeare's time called the black sheep a biting beast. Modern historians of the Tudor period make light of enclosure, not a trouble in this time, they say, only later. But Shakespeare takes issue. In his late romance, *Pericles*, a straight man asks a question. How do fish live in the sea? "Why," says a sententious fisherman,

> as men do a-land; the great ones eat up the little ones. I can compare our rich misers to nothing so fitly as to a whale. A' plays and tumbles, driving the poor fry before him, and at last devours them all at a mouthful. Such whales have I heard on o' the land, who never leave gaping till they've swallowed the whole parish, church, steeple, bells, and all.

For Shakespeare this made metaphor, also giving him night thoughts. Not a sentimental man, i.e. hardhearted, he was like his hero Edgar, "pregnant to good pity." The plays record the pity, endlessly corrosive. Perhaps, being fallible, Shakespeare kept it to the plays. Near the end of his life and settled once more in Stratford, he made his peace with the local enclosers, a story that does him no credit. His last plays, breaking out in angry social asides, say that this compromise cost the man who made it, and an imaginative playwright in our time has him dying by his own hand.

Richard Shakespeare, not one of Breughel's peasants, eluded the land whale. Like his elder son and grandson, he rented land from others, leasing some himself. Part of his land, going down to the brook that runs through Snitterfield and feeds into the Avon, he leased from Robert Arden of Wilmcote. Robert had a daughter Mary, Shakespeare's mother.

An "ancient and worthy family" settled in Warwickshire before the Norman Conquest, that is how Dugdale, the old historian, describes the Ardens. They lived in Wilmcote near Stratford. This hamlet, a speck on the map in Aston Cantlow parish, lies in the valley of the Alne, divided from the Avon by low wooded hills. In the basin of the Alne, euonymus grows wild, also soft-leaved roses and viburnum lantana, "the wayfaring tree." Near the river is the church, late thirteenth century, where Mary Arden married John Shakespeare. Tourists, taking the bus from Stratford to Wilmcote, visit "Mary Arden's House" in Featherbed Lane. When John Shakespeare came courting in the 1550s, he used his legs. His way led across the fields, just over three miles.

Early in the 1560s, Richard Shakespeare died. He left the Snitterfield farm to his sons, John and Henry. Shakespeare's Uncle Harry farmed at Ingon, two miles from Stratford. In this western part of Hampton Lucy parish, the land slopes gently south to flat meadows bordering the Avon. The permanent meadows, called "ings," made up the bottom lands on the left bank of the river, dairy farm country today. Copdock

Hill, a long ridge, lay to the north, dividing the river valley from the Forest of Arden. Scotch firs on the hill made a landmark. On his valley farm, Henry Shakespeare harvested wheat and rye, oats, barley, and peas. A troublemaker, "Trojan" or bullyboy, he shirked his debts, fought with the neighbors, and ended up well to do like his father before him. Dying in 1596, he left money to his heirs, grain in the barn, and a mare in the stable.

John Shakespeare's story is different. Soon after his father's death, he let go his copyhold of the Snitterfield lands. Preferring trade to farming, he quit Snitterfield for Stratford. Had he not done this, his son, unlettered, would have died unknown, some village Hampden or mute inglorious Milton, keeping the noiseless tenor of his way.

By the middle of the century, John Shakespeare, glover, was living in Stratford. His seven years' apprenticeship, mandatory for all in his "mystery" or craft, lay behind him. In 1552, Stratford elders fined him for his midden, a dunghill or "laystow," heaped up on Henley Street in front of his house. In the east wing of the house, called the Woolshop, he made leather gloves, belts, purses, and aprons. A whittawer too, he dressed the whitleather, soft white and specially treated. The treating was "tawing." Tanning the leather, he soaked it in alum and salt. Later, says tradition, his son William assisted him. A reminiscence of John Shakespeare, set down a half century after his death, contrasts this clubbable parent, *l'homme moyen sensuel,* with the skeptical son, an impassive presence in the Woolshop. The "merry-cheeked old man" wants his visitor to know that the son, egregious-seeming, didn't differ from the rest. "Will was a good honest fellow," no tainted wether of the flock, "but he durst have cracked a jest with him at any time." "But," being inconsequent, makes the anecdote ring true.

Ambitious in worldly ways, John Shakespeare angled for office in the village corporation. Early on in Stratford, he began his climb, reaching for a place in the sun. This included Mary Arden, an heiress. She owned the family estate in Wilmcote, also the crop on the ground "sown and tilled as it is." Singling out a favored child, her father's will specified this. She couldn't read or write, though, and Mary Arden when she signed made her mark.

The Arden property was Asbies. Robert Arden, landed gentry, less than the best but better than the Shakespeares, kept oxen and bullocks, horned cattle, weaning calves, horses and colts, sheep, pigs, and poultry. The inventory of his household goods, taken after he died in 1556, noticed a deal of oak furniture, linen in the coffers, and battens and bacon in the roof. This middle-class man, not aspiring to tapestry, hung his walls with painted cloths, eleven of these. They showed scenes from

Scripture, comic-book style, not Gobelin. Balloons bearing words came out of the mouths of the pious. Falstaff knew a house hung like Robert Arden's. Bound for Shrewsbury and battle with the Percy, he leads his troop of soldiers "as ragged as Lazarus in the painted cloth where the glutton's dogs licked his sores."

Built in the sixteenth century, the house in Wilmcote, supposedly Mary Arden's, overlooks the village green on the north side of the road to Stratford. It rises two storeys with two stone hearths on each floor. Behind the wall that separates the house from the road, the boxwood is shaped in hedges. A gray stone foundation supports the walls, framed with timber from the Forest of Arden. This bleached oak timber is what is left of the Forest, a verdant memory in the suburbs. The gabled roof, cut with dormers, isn't thatched like Anne Hathaway's cottage in Shottery, familiar from picture postcards, but covered with hand-made tiles, red and weathered like the brick of the chimney. In front, the gabled cross-wing has herringbone framing, and the timbers are set close together. In back the spacing is wider, the white panels between the beams filled in with clay and wattles, poles intertwined with branches or reeds.

Mary, the child of a second marriage, was the youngest of twelve siblings, and they wrote above the lintel, "live and let live." In the "great hall," a common living room, this family jockeyed for place. Beside the hall was the kitchen, the floor paved with local stone, the windows leaded, and the raftered ceiling rough hewn from oak beams. Robert Arden owned an adze, and with this the beams were hewn, some of them chamfered, beveled at the edges. A quern for malt or mustard stood in the kitchen, also a kneading trough, milk pails, and vessels for brewing ale and beer. In Wilmcote, Stratford too, everyone was a maltster. Arden women made bread in the bake-oven next to the open fireplace. They drew their water from the pump beside the back door. Out in back, beyond the woodpile, barns and cowsheds ringed the farmyard, the barns stored with wheat, barley, and hay. Asbies had its dovecote, supplying food for the table, an apiary too. Shakespeare's people, drinking wine, liked to mix it with honey. Dominating the cider house, a large circular stone rotated on its rim in a circular trough. Crushing fruit in this trough, they made cider and perries, a drink fermented from pears. Perries, stimulating black bile, provoked melancholy, though.

The house, set in green fields flagrant with birdsong, suits the ancient worthy family. Mary Arden ought to have lived there, and already in the eighteenth century people said that she did. She and John Shakespeare married in the parish church of St. John the Baptist, still serving pious folk in Aston Cantlow. This was sometime between 1556, when Mary's father died, naming her in his will, and 1558, when their first child, Joan, was born. Joan was baptized a Catholic, a Catholic queen being on the throne. The Ardens were Catholic in private but in public followed the leader. "Erastian," they called this, the politics of submission. "God's true religion," the government told them, was "truly set forth by public authority."

Joan died, an infant. Margaret came next, born in 1562 and buried this year in Holy Trinity churchyard. Then came William, the third child. The Shakespeares' second son, Gilbert, born in 1566, followed his elder brother by two years. He died in 1612, a bachelor and childless. Another Joan was christened in 1569, the only one of four daughters to live beyond childhood, and excepting her brother William the only child of the Shakespeares to marry. Anne, their last daughter, born 1571, died before her eighth birthday. A son Richard, baptized in 1574, was buried in 1613. Six years separate Richard and Edmund, the last child, born in 1580. A professional actor, he took after his famous brother and went up to London. Edmund died at twenty-eight. Near his grave in St. Savior's church, in London on the Thames, pious Victorians placed a recumbent effigy of Shakespeare, a mild-looking shopkeeper with lymphatic eyes. So there were eight children, seven not much known to history, and all but the last are buried in Stratford.

Bubonic plague, intermittent and calamitous in Shakespeare's England, bred in muck-hills like John Shakespeare's on Henley Street. Plague has its important role in the fortunes of his son, the playwright. When a visitation closed the London theaters in the early 1590s, this playwright turned to poetry, writing *Venus and Adonis* and his *Rape of Lucrece*. Plague came down hardest on the very young and old. It visited Stratford in 1564. *"Hic incepit pestis,"* wrote Bretchgirdle, the vicar who baptized Shakespeare. "Here begins the plague." Two hundred people died in 1564, almost one-seventh of the total population. The burial register for the last half of the year shows interments up tenfold.

In the spring of this year, Shakespeare was born. Had he died in the cradle, the world wouldn't have noticed. The heavens, he said later, blazed forth the deaths of princes. Every loved child is singular, but his parents weren't to know how this one, only William, differed from the rest.

THE YEAR OF Shakespeare's birth, Michelangelo and Calvin died, Galileo was born, and Sir Richard Malory, mercer, was elected Lord

Mayor of London. English and French made a treaty at Troyes. Robert Dudley, elevated to the peerage, became Earl of Leicester, and Sir John Hawkins, an adventurer, brought back the first yams, sweet potatoes, from the New World. These events went unremarked in Stratford, not a backwater but having its own business.

The name Stratford describes it, a street or road coming down to a ford across a river. The river is the Avon. Rising in Northamptonshire, it runs westward through Warwickshire for almost fifty miles. It gets bigger as it goes, engorging tributary streams that drain the up-and-down farmlands. Thelesford Brook, draining the land in Snitterfield Richard Shakespeare leased from Robert Arden, is one of these streams. Along the river banks, forests of bulrush stand among the water lilies and yellow watercress. Otters, voles, and water shrew shelter in the meadow grass, and fishermen take "coarse" fish, dace and bream, also mud eels and silver eels. Before the advent of water locks and modern pollution, tench, the "fool gudgeon," and Shakespeare's "luce" or pike lived in the Avon, even trout, which you tickled if you wanted to catch it. A few miles north of Evesham, once a famous killing ground, the river falls into Worcestershire, leaving the Shakespeare Country behind.

Welsh *afon* is river. Meandering, the river resumes the long past. County place names, Combe, Welcombe, Luscombe, summon the dark *wealas*, strangers who were first on the land. Like the Titans, old gods thrust deep in the earth by the new dispensation, they suggest Shakespeare's dark underground, making credible his lights and orders. Celts, hearkening to prophecies, hid from encroaching English in the Weald. This was the Forest of Arden. Celtic *ard* is high or great, *den* is the wooded valley. Forest covered the land between the Avon and the site of modern Birmingham, extending south to the Cotswold Hills. Tradition says that a squirrel might have leaped from bough to bough across the county. By and by, the trees went down. English prevailed, and commonsensical Hotspur succeeded Welsh Glendower, whose head was crammed with "skimble-scamble stuff." Glendower, listening to his voices, is a survivor, though.

A mile above Warwick, the river passes Guy's Cliff. When English and Danes fought over Warwickshire, Guy of Warwick, a folk hero, rallied the defenders. He slew the Danish champion Colbrand. Shakespeare, ending his career, thinks back to this in *Henry VIII*. Warwick Castle, in his time, still preserved the hero's sword. "After he had done great victories," John Leland said, "he came and lived in this place like a hermit." Keeper of the King's libraries, Leland toured England in the reign of Henry VIII, looking for literary remains. Men showed him the cave where the hermit used to live, cut from a rock beside the river. On the track of old Britons, English, and Danes, came Shakespeare, an antiquary with a difference. He saw in his mind's eye the hiders-out in the Forest assailed by a "mighty power," then, stepping between them, the hermit, met providentially on "the skirts of this wild wood." To the hermit's cave, abandoned, he dismissed his Jaques, a "conver-tite," at the end of *As You Like It*.

Coming into Warwick, the Avon skirts the quadrilateral tower of St. Mary's, its gray stone black against the sky. This church, a reliquary, had a piece of the Cross, portions of the hair, milk, and garments of the Virgin, bones of more than thirty saints, and the ivory horn St. George carried in his baldric. Also it had the Burning Bush seen by Moses, anyway a part of this, part of the seat Abraham sat on, oil in which the Pentecostal fire fell from heaven, and a skillet or frying pan that belonged to St. Brandon. The relics are gone but in the chapel are effigies, among them the Kingmaker's. He was Richard Earl of War-wick, a "bug" or goblin who frightened them all in the Wars of the Roses. Fighting for the Red Rose of Lancaster, this Warwick fell at Barnet and Shakespeare wrote his valedictory:

> Why, what is pomp, rule, reign, but earth and dust?
> And, live we how we can, yet die we must.

A massive tomb in the chapter-house hearses the bones of Fulke Greville. Ten years Shakespeare's senior, he wrote poetry too, crabbed, didactic, sometimes powerful, and his best lines regret our wearisome condition, "Born under one law, to another bound." Living near Strat-ford on the southwestern edge of the county, he got possession of Warwick Castle in the reign of King James. This made him Shake-speare's overlord, if the old ways still held. A seventeenth-century annalist has him saying that he wanted to be known as "Shakespeare's and Ben Jonson's master." His tomb bears the legend: SERVANT TO QUEEN ELIZABETH COUNCILLOR TO KING JAMES AND FRIEND TO SIR PHILIP SIDNEY. The *beau idéal* of the age, Sidney died in the Low Countries, fighting the Spaniards. Romantics think that "Sargeant Shakespeare," enlisting in the army, fought at Sidney's side. This was in the Lost Years, before he journeyed to London. Some say that Greville boosted young Shakespeare out of Stratford and put him on the London road, knowing how this local poet wasn't born to blush unseen. Outliving Shakespeare by a dozen years, Greville died violently in his old age, stabbed by a disappointed servant. Avon white water tumbles over a little dam below the walls of Warwick Castle. Peacocks, gorgeous to look at, hideous when they cry, patrol the castle grounds, and the flag on the tower flies the Kingmaker's emblem, a Bear and Ragged Staff.

Before reaching Stratford, the river flows through Charlecote, home of the Lucys, local gentry. Beyond the gate house, flanked by octagonal turrets of pale red brick, the Elizabethan manor dominates a pretty park. Fallow deer graze the park, fenced with split oak saplings, hewn once upon a time in the Forest of Arden. William Lucy, lord of the manor in the 1540s, brought John Foxe to Charlecote as tutor for his children. Later this Foxe wrote a famous "Book of Martyrs," remembering the Protestants burned for their faith in the reign of Bloody Mary. The flames encircled Stratford, and men were burned at Coventry, Banbury, Lichfield, and Wotton-under-Edge. A woodcut in Foxe's book shows the burning of Master Laurence Saunders at Coventry, 8 February 1555. Lashed to a stake with the faggots piled around him, Saunders is saying: "Welcome life." Queen Elizabeth, coming to Charlecote in Shakespeare's early time, stayed with Thomas Lucy in his new house by the Avon. Honoring the Queen, they built the house in the shape of the letter "E." Shakespeare, growing up and getting beyond himself, is supposed by some to have poached deer from this Sir Thomas.

Swans sail the Avon where it arrives at Stratford, and there are ducks on the water below Hugh Clopton's bridge. Clopton, a Stratford boy, went off to London a hundred years before Shakespeare, seeking fame and fortune. He made his fortune in textiles and, knighted, became Lord Mayor. But this successful mercer remembered his roots. Meaning to spend his last years in Stratford, he built a large brick and timber house, New Place. Later Shakespeare, ambitious like Clopton, lived in this house. Across the street from New Place, the local guild had its chapel. A confraternity, it admitted both men and women. Clopton adorned the chapel with paintings. One showed St. Helena, Constantine's mother, divining the whereabouts of the True Cross. St. Helena was English, English people thought. The bridge over the Avon was Clopton's work, walled on both sides and carried on fourteen great arches. He built it in the reign of Henry VII and his useful work spans the river, going on five hundred years later. Leland, admiring, said it allowed people who feared for their life "to pass commodiously at such times as the river riseth." Shakespeare passed this bridge, coming and going from London. Masons, repairing it in 1546, got the lias stone they needed from the quarries in Aston Cantlow where John Shakespeare married Mary Arden.

2

The Town

SHAKESPEARE growing up, lived in Stratford "borough," for almost a millennium property of the bishops of Worcester. In 1553, the last year of the reign of Edward VI, short-lived son of Henry VIII, the borough received its Charter of Incorporation from the King. It enacted its own bylaws and chose its own bailiff. He governed through a council, fourteen burgesses and fourteen aldermen. To this influential circle, John Shakespeare aspired. In time he made his way in, becoming *primus inter pares,* and this was the crown of his life.

The "parish" of Old Stratford encircled the borough. Ten hamlets made up the parish. Shottery, where Anne Hathaway lived, was one, Luddington, where some say she married, another. Holy Trinity church, replacing a Saxon monastery, lay outside the borough too, in the area still known as Old Town. Like the belly in the body, "cupboarding the viand" or victuals but not doing much else, the borough got fat on its "incorporate friends." Rehearsing First Citizen in *Coriolanus,* local people thought so. Though they lived in the "out towns," they had to pay taxes to relieve the borough poor, a blight in Stratford, over seven hundred poor, maybe half the population. But men of means in the borough had their onerous duties. If chosen for office, they couldn't decline. Fines punished absence from sessions of the Council.

Folk in Old Stratford got excused from these duties. Also the law didn't reach there. The borough justices, very sore at the "horrible disorders being at all times committed about the church," were powerless to stop this. London in the 1580s, when Shakespeare came up, was like borough and parish all over again. Aldermen in the city didn't like plays, performed in the suburbs outside the walls. Their writ didn't run in the suburbs, however, lucky for Shakespeare and his fellows.

The Stratford Borough Shakespeare knew was bounded on the north by the highway called Gild Pits, Guild Street today, on the west by Grove Road and Arden Street. To the south lay the Old Town. Hall's Croft fronts on the street that bears this name. Tradition says Shakespeare's daughter Susanna lived on this street with her husband, Dr. John Hall. The Avon made a natural boundary on the east. Sheep and cattle, swine too, provided they were ringed, used the common or Bankcroft on the town side of the Avon, below Clopton Bridge. In the Butt Close near the common, archers practiced their skills, important for defending the realm. John Shakespeare, when he was bailiff, encouraged them to do this. Further south on the river, the collegiate church of Holy Trinity, topped by its wooden spire, looked over Stratford. In the eighteenth century the wood gave way to stone, but otherwise the church in externals remains the same. An avenue of limes leads up to the entrance, and a sanctuary knocker, cast in the thirteenth century, hangs on the inner door. Criminals, reaching this knocker before the law laid hands on them, claimed sanctuary for thirty-seven days.

Beyond the church, the weir or milldam by the village mills scooped out a deep pond, full of perch, pike, and eels. Millers owed tribute to the manor lord, paying part of this in malt. In older days the bishop accepted payment in eels, a thousand every year. A "cucking stool" on the bank, like an exercise machine operated by ropes and wheels, took order with crooked tradesmen, also termagant women. Speaking when they shouldn't got them ducked in the river. An excellent thing in woman, Shakespeare's people considered, if her voice was soft, gentle, and low.

Three principal thoroughfares moved out from the river to the center of town, Bridge Street, Sheep Street, and Chapel Lane. Henley Street continued Bridge Street, running northwest to the Birmingham Road. On the north side of Henley Street, Shakespeare was born. Two brooks flowed through town, the larger passing his house. This brook or "mere" kept the house from burning when fire burned much of Stratford in 1594. Making a grid, Waterside, Chapel Street, and Rother Street bisected these thoroughfares at rough right angles. "Rother" is cattle, an Anglo-Saxon word. "It is the pasture lards the rother's sides," says Timon, called "of Athens." In the Middle Ages the weekly market was held on Rother Street. The grid it makes with the others still shows on a bird's eye view.

At the junction of Bridge Street, Henley Street, and High Street rose the High Cross, emblem of popery, metamorphosed in Shakespeare's time to a square structure topped by a cupola and clock. Leather buckets for hauling water, a ladder, and a firehook hung beneath the floor. For Stratford people the eccentric pairing seemed right, not ill-assorted, and they located their place of punishment next to the Cross. In the pillory, offenders stood, their head and hands thrust through holes in the frame. A paper over their heads said what they were there for. Sometimes the offender was nailed to the frame by one of his ears, sometimes they cut off his ears or slit his nose. Rogues and vagabonds sat in the stocks, "cruel garters." If they broke Stratford's bylaws, they sat for three days and nights, their legs drawn through holes in a board. Tied to the whipping post, these petty felons were whipped until their backs were bloody. Prostitutes got whipped at the cart's tail while men, following the cart, beat on metal basins to bring out the crowd. Elizabethans liked noise, a good spectacle too.

A pleasant town in Shakespeare's boyhood, leafy with ash, willows, and elms, Stratford supported roughly fifteen hundred people. The King's Commissioners gave this figure in their survey of gilds and colleges, 1546. King Henry, sending the commissioners out on the roads, meant to plunder the old religious houses. Like surveyors in the forest, these forerunners sized up the trees, then others followed, cutting them down. Part of the plunder, Stratford's College adjoined the churchyard on the west. This "ancient piece of work," inspected by Leland, was built of hewn stone, square in shape, the corners or wings angling out from the facade. In the house lived a chapter or "college" of priests, five in number. Their warden served as rector of Holy Trinity too, making it a collegiate church. The priests chanted daily mass, praying for the founder, his family, the kings of England, and the bishops of Worcester. Four choir boys did the dogsbody work, waiting on tables and learning to sing. A fifteenth-century warden, establishing the boys, left instructions regulating their conduct. Before they put off their clothes at night, they had to say *De profundis* "with a loud voice." This remembered the warden.

A great prelate, John of Stratford, founded the chantry more than two hundred years before Shakespeare was born. Later, John's nephew Ralph, Bishop of London, summoned ten masons and ten carpenters from his bishopric to build a mansion for the priests. John and Ralph

were called "of Stratford" in the days before modern nomenclature
got settled. Dugdale the historian tells how the College came to ruin.
The dissolution of the monasteries, an ill wind blowing good to some,
blew away the priests and boys but made the fortune of Shakespeare's
acquaintance, the Combes. John Combe, the manor lord's bailiff for
the borough and parish, acquired the College, dying there in the Armada year, 1588. His son was John, also a moneylender. This John
bought up lands in Hampton Lucy, Ingon, and the two Stratford
manors. Shakespeare's friend and some say the butt of his humor, he
became Stratford's richest man. A great litigator, he died in 1614, two
years before Shakespeare, leaving sixty pounds for a sumptuous tomb.
The College passed to John's brother Thomas, then to a son William,
encloser of common lands. William made a good Roundhead in the
Civil War. Combes being as like each other "as a crab's like an apple,"
this tale of fathers and sons holds no surprises.

One of the two best houses in town, the College shared that distinction with New Place, imposing on the corner of Chapel Street and
Chapel Lane. Cloptons meant to live there but in a Protestant reign
this family stayed Catholic, and a local speculator, "subtle, covetous,
and crafty," got title to the house. Dealing with the speculator, Shakespeare bought New Place in 1596. Also he bought land in Old Stratford
from John Combe. The land earned him income, and he lived in the
house, "a king among the meaner sort," when he wasn't writing his
plays. Long since demolished, the College survives in an early nineteenth-century sketch. John Combe, usurer, was buried beside it in the
northeast corner of Holy Trinity chancel. An artist and impartial,
Gheeraert Janssen made his monument, later making Shakespeare's.
Tradition says that Shakespeare hung satiric verses on the usurer's
tomb: "Ten in the hundred the Devil allows, but Combe will have
twelve he swears and vows." Shakespeare wore his singing robes
lightly.

STRATFORD ROOTS went deep, fostering clannishness, a reservoir
of strength. This had another face, complacence. Ignorant of Jews,
blackamoors, and Turks, Shakespeare's people knew they didn't like
them. "Mislike me not for my complexion," says a black man in
Shakespeare, but nobody is listening. English, said a German traveler,
had their generous side. "If they see a foreigner, very well made or
particularly handsome, they will say, 'It is a pity he is not an
Englishman.' "
Stratford being a way station on the old Roman road from South

Wales, people hereabouts still turn up bits of tesserae and coins stamped with an emperor's likeness. Imogen, Shakespeare's heroine in *Cymbeline,* took this Roman road to Milford Haven in Wales, his hero Posthumus too, bound for Italy and a fall from grace. Italy for English was synonymous with this. Traveling there, they brought home "nothing but mean atheism, infidelity, vicious conversation, and ambitious and proud behavior." In his *Description of England,* Harrison said so, never traveling himself north of Oxford or east of Kent. Insular Shakespeare held with this, and his Iachimo in *Cymbeline* is everybody's flashy Italian. *Cymbeline,* a wild romance, celebrates Britain's victory over the Romans. Caesar "made not here his brag/Of 'Came, and saw, and overcame,' " Britain proving more than a match for the "hooknosed fellow" of Rome.

A provincial point of view, encountered often in Shakespeare, this distresses modern readers, whitewashed of prejudice and mostly innocent of roots. No nonpareil for once, universal Shakespeare is first of all Stratford's son, singing the praises of doughty English, e.g. the "band of brothers" we hear about in *Henry V.* Like his sententious rustics, mumbling platitudes and swearing by "God's little liggens," he knows what he knows. Who doesn't weary of his dialect jokes, meant to be funny, jokes about leeks, the Irish ("rough rugheaded kerns"), the "weasel Scot" on the border, the "French disease," etc. Then there are the apostrophes to England and St. George, work for the National Poet. Sometimes he leans forward, wagging a blunt finger. "Naught shall make us rue,/If England to itself do rest but true."

But complacent Shakespeare, cracking jests with the rest of them in the Woolshop on Henley Street, swears under his breath "by two-headed Janus." This is his quiddity, singling him forth. "I have no brother, I am like no brother." A "prodigy" and Shakespeare's mouthpiece, Richard of Gloucester says this, soliloquizing so no one will hear him.

Shakespeare had his friends in Stratford, their names surviving in local archives. Richard Quiney, the bailiff's son, later bailiff himself, read Latin and made sure his son did. Probably he and Shakespeare were together at school, and years later, writing Shakespeare, he addressed him as "loving good friend." Shakespeare wrote no letters or they were merest laundry lists and nobody bothered to save them. Quiney died in a vulgar quarrel, trying to keep the peace, just as Shakespeare was coming into his force.

Hamnet Sadler, the baker, kept a shop on the High Street. In 1584 a lawsuit entangled him with one of Sir Thomas Lucy's people, and the squire of Charlecote intervened to settle this. The baker is called

Hamlet in letters and wills. "I would Hamlet were at home," wrote Abraham Sturley when Sadler left town on business. Sturley, local lawyer and puritan, had a good opinion of Shakespeare, not the play-wright, the entrepreneur. Shakespeare named his only son for Hamnet Sadler, and Sadler's son is William, probably named for Shakespeare. Regarding this namesake, Shakespeare is silent.

Richard Field the tanner's son, three years older than Shakespeare, went up to London at eighteen, following the printer's trade. He married his master's widow and did Stratford credit in a long and successful career. Renowned for his skill in printing Greek and Latin texts, Field was competent in French, Italian, Spanish, and Hebrew. Shakespeare's first fruits, *Venus and Adonis* and *The Rape of Lucrece*, came from his press. Biographers imagine these two country mice thrown together in the great metropolis, and for a while they were neighbors, Field living on Wood Street in Cripplegate ward, just around the corner from Shakespeare. But Shakespeare never mentions Richard Field.

Boyhood acquaintance, William Reynolds and Richard Tyler appear in Shakespeare's will. Reynolds, a Catholic, got in trouble lampooning the neighborhood vicar. Tweaking the nose of authority, he set up a Maypole near his house. The Sanhedrin weren't amused. But Reynolds had "a most noble father," well-to-do and respectable, and indulgent Shakespeare left him money to buy a ring. Tyler, a real-life butcher's boy, lived near the Bankcroft. He was son of William, John Shake-speare's colleague when the two served as chamberlains. In the Armada year he volunteered to go as a soldier, the town equipping him with dagger and sword. Not a soldier, much less a volunteer, Shakespeare, armed cap-a-pie for his roles in the theater, wore a dagger of lath, make-believe. Tyler subsequently made an unlucky marriage, excit-ing the wrath of his father-in-law. Some, likening the angry father to old Father Capulet, see in Tyler and his Susanna local versions of Shakespeare's star-crossed lovers. Unromantic Shakespeare sympa-thized with the father, though. Rewriting his will, he cut out Richard Tyler.

These were some of Shakespeare's friends in his nonage and later. But "friends" overstates and none of his acquaintances were allowed to get close. Shakespeare didn't draw their portraits and didn't tell their stories, not "compositions," only life at its messy work.

SHAKESPEARE'S ACQUAINTANCE lived in timbered houses, the flat white plaster walls stitched with old dark beams, set crossways. From some houses, a narrow roof or "penthouse," running along the facade above the ground floor, jutted out like the brim of a hat. Underneath the penthouse, petty traders displayed their wares. Mere matter of fact, this furnished imagery for Shakespeare. If you were melancholy, he thought, you pulled your hat "penthouse-like" over the shop of your eyes.

This behavior, "semiotic," serves Shakespeare in comedy, where the soul of a man is his clothes. Getting the clothes or accoutrements right told the audience all it needed to know. A domineering father was the "old pantaloon," the fop had his perfume box, held " 'twixt his finger and his thumb." Histrionics, formulaic or conventional, were like this. Meaning to tear a passion to tatters, a woman came on stage "with her hair about her ears." Elsewhere, however, character shows depths, unexpectedly turbid. The Prince of Darkness is a gentleman, unmarked by the cloven foot. Superficies don't detect him, and tragic Shakespeare dispenses with signs.

Stone flagging, Wilmcote limestone, friable and easily cracked, covered the lower floors in Shakespeare's house. Other houses made do with clay. Carpets were for walls and the floors were strewn with rushes. Erasmus, coming to England, looked unhappily at the rushes, sometimes untouched for years and harboring spittle, vomit, fish bones, beer thrown over the shoulder, and "the leakage of dogs and men." Used to cosseting, Erasmus shivered in his drafty quarters, the wintry draft making nothing of the oiled linen cloth in the casements. Partial to the great outdoors, some English today still have louvers, stuck permanently open, in their windows. Meaner houses, omitting chimneys, got rid of smoke through a hole in the roof. This cured the householders like hams in a smokehouse, a blessing in disguise, parson Harrison suggested. Smoke, nature's medicine, kept "the goodman and his family from the quack."

Mostly, roofs were topped with thatch, washed over with lime, a crude fire-proofing. Conservatism enjoined this. In 1582 Shakespeare's neighbor, Walter Roche, the local schoolmaster and strong for the old ways, took out the tile roof and put back the thatch in his house on Chapel Street. Thatch was picturesque but a recipe for disaster. Twice in the 1590s fire, ravaging Stratford, almost burned it to the ground. This happened, said a preacher in Evesham, just over the county border, "chiefly for profaning the Lord's Sabbaths." The Corporation prescribed the use of tile or slate, and instructed its constabulary to see that men of means had their leather buckets ready at all times. Water carriers or "cobs" like everyone else, aldermen had two. John Shakespeare was sworn as constable in 1558, along with three others, and this bucket brigade was how they coped with fire.

Stratford nights were dark, a pitchy mantle. People went to bed with the birds. In winter every alderman and "capital" burgess had to "have a lanthorn hanging in the street before his door, and there a candle burning to give light." They snuffed the candle at 8 P.M. Country air notwithstanding, Stratford smelled to heaven. The Corporation prohibited the keeping of swine "in the open street of this town," i.e. swine roamed the streets. Stratford, where nightingales sang, had its useful population of hawks, jackdaws, kites, and buzzards. Scavengers, they rid the streets of offal and garbage. In ditches and gutters dug before the houses, householders dumped their slops. They weren't supposed to do this, and in 1558 John Shakespeare "stood amerced," punished by fine for failing to scour his gutters. Capulet's bully boy keeps clear of the gutters, walking on the inside of the sidewalk. This was "taking the wall," sometimes a bad idea. From the windows above the wall, "jordans," chamber pots, were upended.

Efflux of men and animals polluted the water. Food turned rancid and they ate it anyway. Most, like Shakespeare's siblings, died young. King Edward, in agony, died at sixteen. "Oh, Lord God, free me from this calamitous life," he said. Living on intimate terms with disease, Shakespeare's people, fatalistic, said how death "will come when it will come." In *Troilus and Cressida*, Thersites gives a short list of what ailed them: guts griping, catarrhs, lethargies, cold palsies, raw eyes, dirt-rotten livers, wheezing lungs, bladders full of pus or "imposthume," sciaticas, arthritis ("limekilns i' the palm"), boneache (syphillis, if "Neapolitan" boneache), also "the riveled fee simple of the tetter." This was when eruptions, endemic in the body, puckered or "riveled" the skin.

Tenure being fee simple, the eruptions were there for good. Physicians like Shakespeare's son-in-law battled for health against odds. Dr. John Hall ministered to young George Quiney, troubled with a "grievous cough," but this patient died, aged twenty-four. Frustrated and resigned, the physician wrote in his case-book: "Many things were tried in vain; peacefully he slept with the Lord." Physicians bled and purged their patients, dosed them with ancient nostrums, some tried and true, and kept a thoughtful eye on the stars. Checking the "humors," sanguine, choleric, melancholic, and phlegmatic, they looked for imbalance, seeking to correct it. Petruchio, taming his shrew when she sits down to dinner, "throws the meat, etc. about the stage." Overroasted meat, he tells her, "engenders choler, planteth anger." The two of them didn't need this.

Four elements made up the natural world, air, fire, earth, and water. Each combined qualities peculiar to itself, earth combining cold and dry, water cold and moist, etc. In the body, a microcosm, the elements showed as blood, yellow bile, black bile, and phlegm. Two elements, blended, gave a man his humor. Nature, casual like Fortune, often got the balance wrong. John Shakespeare, merry-cheeked, had a sanguine humor. Shakespeare's Uncle Harry was choleric, having more than his share of yellow bile.

A rule-of-thumb psychology, the theory of humors went in for type-casting, not favored by Shakespeare. He liked the oldfashioned "coincidence of opposites," where different things got together in an outsize container. This was true for the life, in the work too. Shakespeare's tragedy, a doleful "dump" or ditty, is merrily set down, and his actors, jacks-of-all-trades, play many people in one person. Shakespeare in the life, shuttling without ado from poetry to business, keeps one eye on a sonnet, the other on the tithes of Old Stratford. Buying tithes was his investment, not taken lightly. Devotees of the humor theory, honoring decorum, liked their categories discrete. Vexed by ambiguity and impatient of grace notes, they looked for the heart of the matter. This let them know where to have you. All the world's a stage, they thought, where life, enacted, made a puppet play like the commedia dell' arte.

Before Shakespeare wrote his *Hamlet*, English knew about Hamlet, a stereotype, familiar on the London stage. Reduced to type, he mixed air and earth in rough-and-ready proportions, producing an overplus of black bile. This Hamlet's wit was diseased. Lapsed in melancholy, he showed all the signs, folding his arms morosely, plunging hands in pockets, and pulling his hat, penthouselike, over his eyes. Characteristically lethargic, he didn't stir in his business, and his father, in a hurry, got on him for this. Shakespeare's old King Hamlet does that too.

Mostly characters in Shakespeare, growing under his hand, elude classification. Their center is identical with their circumference. In his bad strokes, Brutus, an ambiguous hero, gives good words. He has his humor, stoical, or you could call it phlegmatic. "No man bears sorrow better." This doesn't stick the heart of Brutus, however. Winding up *Julius Caesar* in his "noblest Roman of them all" speech, Antony tells them how Brutus made a man, the elements being "So mixed in him." This is generally read as straightforward panegyric. But much is wrong with Brutus, a mix of good and evil. That is Antony's double meaning and says why Brutus is a man.

Equivocal like Shakespeare, Stratford looked to the past, Catholic and easy-going, also forward to the modern world, Protestant and fierce. It still observed "the rite of May," a medieval survival, hateful to Puritan professors. An Englishman's home wasn't yet his castle. In spirit, houses faced outwards, not turned in on themselves like those modern semidetached "villas" that stretch in their thousands and tens of thousands from north London all the way to Waltham Cross. In Shakespeare's time, different from modern times, English were social. Why should a man whose blood was warm within sit like his grandfather, carved in alabaster?

Out in back they planted gardens, sometimes orchards or vineyards. In *Measure for Measure,* Angelo has his garden "circummured" with brick and backed on one side with a vineyard. Shakespeare's garden at New Place furnished a model. Fifteen years after his death, neighborhood people were still commending the vines, probably grapevines. John Parkinson, chauvinist and gardener born three years after Shakespeare, distinguished between "English" and "Outlandish" flowers, partly a moral distinction. Stratford favored English. Shakespeare's eye is keen for growing things, and his plays run through a list of flowers, the sweet briar or eglantine rose, a favorite in cottage gardens, pansies, his "love-in-idleness," long purples "that liberal shepherds give a grosser name," daisies, cowslips, daffodils, others. Stratford today, rich on the tourist trade and possibly enervated, cultivates outlandish blooms, but in Avon marshes and meadowlands and on verges by the wayside, Shakespeare's flowers still poke up, spring and summer. Hedges, privet or whitethorn, bordered the gardens. They still do in Hall's Croft. On the foundations of New Place, Shakespeare's home, restorers in Stratford have set out white camomile, sweet-scented when you crush it. "The more it is trodden on the faster it grows," Falstaff said.

A medicinal herb, camomile soothed the joints. Apothecaries pushed its "virtue," this word for them meaning power, as often for Shakespeare. Friar Laurence, filling his wicker basket with flowers and weeds, finds many excellent for a host of virtues, "none but for some." A herbalist, the Friar personifies Nature, making her his end and beginning, womb and tomb. He gets his strange lore, both healing and malignant, by "sucking" on her bosom, a vivid way to put this.

Philip Rogers, apothecary, stood in for Friar Laurence in Stratford. Shakespeare, selling him malt lent him money too. Not getting it back, he filed a claim against Rogers in the Court of Record. Like a modern Small Claims Court, this court settled disputes involving no more than £30. In his shop on the High Street the apothecary sold decoction of roses, liquorice, aniseed, oil of vitriol, turpentine, corrosive sublimate, and tobacco. Tobacco smoke gave pleasure, also killing pain and getting rid of bad smells, useful in this smelly place. John Hawkins introduced it, the same who brought back the first yams. The rose, distilled, quickened heart beat. Stirred with aniseed, it comforted pains in the head. Liquorice was for lungs, oil of vitriol, a bleach, turned the hair chestnut red, and turpentine plus powdered brimstone banished eczyma. For this, sublimate was more efficient but ate away the flesh, leaving scar tissue, blackened teeth, and "shakes" or palsy.

Plants in Rogers' stock were "signed," each having its arcane property, specific for particular disorders. Decoction of adder's tongue, a fern with a narrow spike, possibly tonguelike, cured the bite of an adder, and the quince, ingested, cured falling hair. This fruit was hairy. Like astrology, the doctrine of "signatures," a medieval hangover, located man in his natural context. Asserting correspondences, it tied things to things. The body, a little world, declared these correspondences, and men saw them in the macrocosm too. The stars, like theatergoers who took a hand in the play, commented "in secret influence" on man's life. "Disasters" in the heavens—like Shakespeare's "bad revolting stars" in the first lines he wrote for the theater—were meant for demonstrations "Unto our climatures and countrymen" below. A skeptic, Horatio said this. The demonstrations were weird, like the apothecary's crazy equations. Each pseudoscience had its core of wisdom, though, saying that men don't keep the universe alone.

The Middle Ages, when whimsy and terror made a mix, bizarre but cordial, lived on in Stratford. In the Gild Chapel on Church Street, St. Thomas Becket died gruesomely, hacked by assassins. Near him on the west wall, Sir Jonathus the Jew, a medieval heavy and the butt of miracle plays, insulted the Eucharist. Knowing their plays, Shakespeare's people, two parts horrified, one part tickled, looked forward to his comeuppance. Death, a grinning antic, postured on the walls, and a Day of Doom, terrific, admonished the congregation. It had its required Hell Mouth, the gaping jaws lined with teeth and ominous with flames. Lost souls, unwilling, went into the flames, hustled by demons. One, horned and winged, shook a pointed ax. He came out of nightmare, like the Seven Deadly Sins, but was also a figure of fun.

Marlowe in *Dr. Faustus* mounts a parade of the Seven Deadly Sins, and as this tragedy ends the peccant hero is swallowed up in the Hell Mouth. This never happens in Shakespeare. Of Heaven and Hell Shakespeare knows nothing, and his plays stop this side of the grave. Hamlet's father, in Purgatory, says his sins are purged by fire. But that is undiscovered country and you have to take his word.

The misericords in Holy Trinity church, made for the old chantry priests, read a lesson to Shakespeare's people, not easily parsed. When they stood before the choir stalls, they turned up the hinged seats of the stalls for support. Beneath the seats on narrow ledges called misericords, monsters confronted them, carved in the wood. They saw coiled serpents, a fool with a snaky tail, monkeys in chains, a mermaid and merman, a man riding a bestial woman, beating her hindquarters, a monk, part man, part beast. Brandishing a saucepan, an angry woman attacked a bearded man, her free hand tugging his beard. He perhaps was a soldier, sent by King Herod to slaughter the innocents, and the woman, Rachel, reproached him for this. Familiar from the mystery plays, this scene was comic and tragic, not by turns but both together, blending immiscible things. Shakespeare's art is like that. "My mother cried," says Beatrice in *Much Ado About Nothing*, "but then there was a star danced, and under that was I born."

St. George, a real presence, left his mark on Shakespeare's town. He was patron saint of England, thanks to John of Stratford. This Bishop of Winchester, promoting St. George, had his temporal side. In the fourteenth century, he pulled down a king and helped set up another. Marlowe tells the story in *Edward II*. But like Clopton the benefactor, Stratford's John remembered where he came from. Rebuilding Holy Trinity, he added the wooden spire, chapels honoring the Virgin and Thomas the Martyr, and an alabaster tomb for himself. St. George, painted by a local master, looked down from the ceiling. Triumphant on horseback, he skewered the dragon in Stratford's annual pageant. However, his Christianity was only skin deep, and in 1547 Reformers put a stop to the pageant. Later they ejected St. George from the church. But some houses in Stratford, their facades adorned with semigrotesque human masks, still evoked the older time, half Christian, half pagan. The Harvard House was one, now No. 26 on the High Street. Built by the maternal grandfather of John Harvard, the house is called for this founder of Harvard College.

Numbering houses, a modern convention, didn't occur to Shakespeare's people, and painted signboards, hung from brackets, told them whose house or shop this was. A bush declared a wine shop (but a good wine, said the proverb, needed no bush or sign), a garland an alehouse. The lattice windows of a tavern were red. Glass was newfangled, and country houses favored lattice, made of wicker or fine rifts of oak. Taverns were called for the bear, swan, or falcon, sometimes the dragon slayer, glimpsed by Shakespeare's Faulconbridge sitting "on's horseback at mine hostess' door." Ale and beer were mother's milk. Thatched malt houses, scattered through town, kept it flowing, alehouses too, thirty in Stratford. The malt houses were tinder boxes, and John Shakespeare, constable, had his hands full with tipplers. Amiable tradition makes Shakespeare a tippler, drunk at Bidford-on-Avon, five or six miles away. Before the pub at Broom, a nearby hamlet, the signboard shows him sleeping it off under a crabtree, "Shakespeare's canopy."

Just outside town, the open fields began. In stubble heaths to the north, men and boys coursed the hare. Shakespeare tells about this in his *Venus and Adonis,* where the "timorous flying hare," cranking and crossing to throw the hounds off their scent, hides in the "musits," gaps in the hedges. In the end, the hounds are on him, though. Knowing how it will end, "poor Wat" the hare grieves like "one sore sick that hears the passing bell." The red rust of suburbia presses on the modern town but mostly the fields remain open. The yellow flowers that look like alyssum are mustard. "That same cowardly, giantlike ox beef hath devoured many a gentleman of your house," Bottom says to "Master Mustardseed," a fairy. From the mustardseed comes oil, the leaves go for fodder, and the dead stalks, ploughed under, rejuvenate the land. "Champaign" land, i.e. flat and open, Leland called it, "fruitful of corn and grass." Against the green grass, the mustard shows bright as sulphur.

A FARMING COMMUNITY, also a trading depot, Stratford in the 1560s had its weekly market, held every Thursday. Butter, cheese, and meat were offered in the market. Skinners sold raw hides, tanned by the tanners. The hides came from the shambles in Middle Row, where the fleshmongers got their meat. Brewing beer and ale was Stratford's principal business, and trade in barley was brisk. Segregated by crafts, Stratford tradesmen like John Shakespeare were specialists and prickly about this. They were nailors, drapers, dyers, collarmakers, ropemakers selling funicles, little cords, shoemakers called corvisers, tin workers called whitesmiths. Like Abhorson the hangman in *Measure for Measure,* they looked with contempt on the jack-of-all-trades, not wanting to discredit their "mystery."

Fairs and festivals, coming round each year like clockwork, mixed business and pleasure. The big fair that honored Sts. Peter and Paul, beginning June 29, continued for more than two weeks. On Trinity Sunday, Stratford people held a wake, not gloomy but festive, celebrating the dedication of their parish church. Over these pastimes, said a Puritan writer, a great lord presided, "namely Sathan, prince of hell." Shakespeare served this prince, following "good counsel" as his flesh determined. In his young man's time he acted a young man's part, or he made a good observer, watching others play their parts. One way or another, Stratford doings absorbed him, grist for the theater to come.

If his memory served, they ran greyhounds on Cotsall hills, baited bears like famous Sackerson, battered each other at Dun-in-the-Mire where a heavy log or "dun," pushed and prodded, simulated a cart horse. Also they capered, danced the jig, high lavolta, and coranto, like Shakespeare's rejuvenated king in *All's Well*. The five-step galliard or cinquepace was part of their repertory, giving a joke to Sir Toby. He wouldn't make water unless in a cinquepace. This drunken knight knew the pavan too, dignified and Spanish. "Every pavan has its galliard," said the old proverb, a version of our "mingled yarn," joy after woe, sunshine after hail. For Shakespeare, this made "a day of season."

Shakespeare's Stratford had its blue laws, often honored in the breach. Alehouses were supposed to shut their doors on holy days, businesses too, but old customs died hard and the Puritan Sunday, not yet accomplished, waited on the next hundred years. Hatred of the theater, growing more envenomed in Shakespeare's younger time, was still a "baby figure" of the mass of things to come. Folk in Stratford went to plays, popular, not highbrow. Over the county line in Gloucestershire, a local boy born the same year as Shakespeare saw one of these plays, "The Cradle of Security." He stood between his father's legs, noting how the three young ladies drew the hero from sermons, "good counsel and admonitions." More or less tempting but not otherwise distinguished, these three were vices personified, Pride, Avarice, and Lust. Disembodied too, the hero stood for Everyman. Dandling this generic hero, the ladies rock him to sleep in a cradle, then cover his face with a swine's snout. Transformed by swinish passion, he goes to Hell in the end. Whose fault was this? Only the hero's, "that would make his will lord of his reason."

Expressionist Drama, the morality play lights up a great divide between Shakespeare and his forebears. Partly his plays are always moralities, a tug of war between reason and will. His heroes look like responsible agents. On the other hand, as they say: "Who can control his fate?" Often he tags them with allegorical names, e.g. Fortinbras or "strong arm," adequate for a one-dimensional man. Romeo's friend Benvolio means well, and Aguecheek in *Twelfth Night*, lily-livered, shows this in his face. The Seven Deadly Sins, abstract cartoons much favored by older playwrights, still live for Shakespeare, Marlowe too. Unlike Marlowe and the others, Shakespeare fleshes them out. More than their names, they survive as wrathful Lear, gluttonous Falstaff, envious Iago, lecherous Cleopatra who loves an inch of raw mutton better than an ell of fried stockfish. Hamlet, holding his fire, is duller than "the fat weed that roots itself in ease on Lethe wharf." This Hamlet stands for Sloth. The equivalence is inexact, though, and Bottom, not a type but indigenous, is Shakespeare's version of the man in the swine's snout.

Mysteries, another legacy to Shakespeare of the medieval drama, were still playing in Coventry, northeast of Stratford. Attentive to parochial things, they showed him the man in his habit as he lived. This meant ambiguity. Sinister King Herod, a famous villain in these pieces, is reprehensible but comic too, not so different from Falstaff, "a Herod of Jewry." "I rant, I rave," cries the king when the Magi escape him, "and now run I wode." "Wode" is mad, and the baffled tyrant, jumping down from the stage, tears a passion to tatters. "Here," says a direction from the Coventry play, "Herod rages in the pageant and in the street also." It isn't clear from this direction where jest breaks off and earnest begins.

On the pageant wagon, a moveable stage, the show moved from place to place, wherever the crowds assembled. Shakespeare, part of the crowd in Coventry, watched the Slaughter of the Innocents, bloody tale of Herod's revenge. He saw the naked infants spitted on pikes, while the maddened mothers, wives of Jewry,

> Do break the clouds . . .
> At Herod's bloody-hunting slaughtermen.

Meaning to be sure of his men and their purpose, the king has them swear on their swords. Shakespeare remembered this when Hamlet, in a grimly comic scene, swears Horatio and his fellows to silence. "Come on," says the antic prince as the ghost cries beneath the stage—

> you hear this fellow in the cellarage.
> Consent to swear.

Panoramic like Shakespeare's art and bound to get everything in, mystery cycles, combining playlets, dramatized the whole of man's story. Beginning with the Creation, cycles ended with the Harrowing of Hell. The wagons started off at four or five in the morning. It was dark again when Jesus descended into Hell, entering by a Hell-Mouth. Hell was in the cellarage, under the stage.

Cycles, performed by artisans from the local crafts or mysteries— glovers, chandlers, cappers in Coventry—celebrated the advent of spring and new life. A prime time was Whitsunday, early summer, "When all our pageants of delight were played." In Coventry the Corpus Christi Play, performed each year in June, lived far into the reign of Elizabeth. Then a new and strait religion, not liking antinomies, bad men who were funny, sheep stealers whose petty story was like the coming of the Lamb of God, decreed an end to the mystery plays.

.   .   .

SHAKESPEARE, escaping the Rule of the Saints, had a taste of it in boyhood. Stratford's establishment, his father included, leaned to the Puritan side. John Shakespeare's colleagues—"chief rulers in the synagogue," a local satirist called them—preferred Christ with a sword to the benevolent Christ, lamb of God. "Puritan," a portmanteau word, meant different things. Most thought it meant lugubrious. Malvolio in *Twelfth Night,* pulling a long face, "is a kind of Puritan," they say. But this does Puritans less than justice. In Shakespeare's last years, a Puritan preacher, sermonizing in Stratford, turned up at New Place. Convivial, he took his fee in sack and claret. Sir Toby's "cakes and ale" jibe, retorted on Malvolio, falls in his case to the ground.

Some Puritans spoke their mind on matters of state. That was lese majesty and people called Puritans disloyal. Disliking the Queen's suitor Anjou, French and foppish, John Stubbes wrote a pamphlet. It gave offense and he had his hand cut off, the one that held the pen. As the ax came down, he clapped off his hat with the other hand, unoffending. "God save the Queen!" this loyalist said. Straitlaced, seditious, or none of these things, Puritans had one thing in common. All called our human nature depraved. At the other end of the spectrum, "eupeptic" men, looking forward to Jean-Jacques, said we were naturally good. Montaigne, Shakespeare's contemporary, was one of these men. He thought evil, an imposition, came in with society. Later, Shakespeare in *The Tempest* crossed swords with this French essayist. For the present, young Shakespeare kept his eyes and ears open. An empiricist in Stratford, he worked out a psychology, mediating between radical positions.

In Shakespeare's part of the world, Puritans looked for strength to Robert Dudley, Earl of Leicester. Zealous patron of the leftwing Protestant cause, this lord of Kenilworth Castle was many other things, none lugubrious. The famous party he gave the Queen in 1575 went on for eighteen days, costing him £1000 a day. Over the party, pagan deities presided. Bacchus poured out "full cups everywhere, every hour, of all kinds of wine," also ale and beer, seventy-two tuns' worth. Far from the sea, Neptune offered fresh sea-fish, mullet, herring, salmon, oysters, and conger eels. Jove shot his thunderbolts, handed up by his lame son and firemaster, Vulcan. Twenty miles away, people saw the fireworks and heard the pealing cannon. A tumbler, casting himself into "many forms and fashions," presented Proteus, the mutable god, emblem for "protean" Shakespeare.

In the hottest July in memory, John Shakespeare and son, coming over from Stratford, watched the goings-on. The eighteen-foot mermaid, swimming in the man-made lake, seized and diverted young Shakespeare's imagination. Type of lustiness, the dolphin carried Arion the poet safe to shore. Sebastian, Viola's brother, turns up later as the boy on the dolphin, and the mermaid, saluting the "fair vestal" Elizabeth, gave Shakespeare's fairy king some good lines:

> Once I sat upon a promontory
> And heard a mermaid, on a dolphin's back,
> Uttering such dulcet and harmonious breath
> That the rude sea grew civil at her song,
> And certain stars shot madly from their spheres
> To hear the sea maid's music.

Arion had a speech, addressed to the Queen, but making too free of the silver wine pots misspoke it. In despair, triumphant too, he pulled off his mask, crying: "I am none of Arion, not I, but honest Harry Goldingham." This is Bottom or a piece of him, boorish and invincible.

Robert Laneham, one of Leicester's men, reported these Kenilworth nights and days. He said how the torchlight pageant of "Hombre Salvaggio," a Wild Man, brought the spectacle close to disaster. Meaning to abase himself before the Queen, the Wild Man came from the woods, an apparition "all overgrown with moss and ivy." In one hand he held an oak tree, plucked up by the roots. This made a tableau, beauty and the beast.

Like a man but not nurtured, "unaccommodated man," the "woodwose" haunted the imagination of Shakespeare's contemporaries. A medieval survival like much in Shakespeare's England, he lived in desolate places, up to no good. Knowing their enemy, Elizabethans took him in, the better to see what he was up to. He grimaces from title pages in their printed books, like the "mad pranks and robberies" of Gamaliel Ratsey, a notorious highwayman hanged in 1605. Not easily laid, "Ratsey's Ghost" presents the Wild Man, an ignoble savage unlicked by art or nurture. "Brought near to beast," his hair matted, face grimed with filth, the Wild Man found a place in civilized interiors. Elizabethan great houses, giving him house room, made him bear the weight of the ceilings. A foreign traveler, impressed, saw these bestial "termini" at Theobalds, palatial home of the Cecils. If he went away wiser, this was the intention.

Kenilworth's Wild Man, not tractable to any print or impression of goodness, fell like a shadow across the festive scene. Breaking his tree asunder, he cast the top from him, "it almost lighting on her highness' horse's head." Horrified, the Queen's footmen looked to the horse and rider. For once, though, tragedy misfired. " 'No hurt, no hurt!' quoth her highness," an affable guest. This made a high point, hard to climb down from, and the rest of the evening was anticlimactic.

For young Shakespeare it sponsored conclusions. Sticking in memory, "Hombre Salvaggio" is never absent for long from his work. Recollecting this epiphany on a summer's night in Warwickshire, he saw how disaster, averted today, waited on tomorrow, the Wild Man being himself, type of all ill. "Stripes" or the lash might move him, not kindness. Caliban, anagram for the cannibals celebrated by Montaigne in a goodnatured essay, is one version of the Wild Man, the Bedlam another. He eats the old rat in the fury of his heart. No Jeremiah, Shakespeare differed from Puritans, not taking this monstrous part for the whole. Not sentimental either, he didn't discount it. At the end of *The Tempest,* Prospero, his artist-hero, Apollonian man, discovers the relation between light and dark. Confronting Caliban, he tells them: "This thing of darkness I/Acknowledge mine."

The pageant of the Wild Man, Laneham considered, was like a tragicomedy where virtue, assaulted, gets reprieved. Much edified, he called this the best part of the play. Afterwards he wrote about it in a letter to a friend of his, citizen and mercer of London. A real-life version of Shakespeare's pedant Holofernes, he cultivated bizarre spelling, reflecting the speech of the tribe as it should be. The spelling makes the letter hard going but the point of view is simplicity itself. Festivities at Kenilworth winding down in late July, Laneham went away on the Earl of Leicester's business, the royal progress moved elsewhere, and Shakespeare and son returned to Stratford.

PRIVILEGED IN STRATFORD, John Shakespeare pitched his stall at the Market Cross under the clock. Stratford being a center of the gloving industry, the men of his craft, seven in the brotherhood, set up for business there on market days and fair days. A local success story, John Shakespeare prospered, the visible sign of grace. By 1552 he was living in the big double-house on Henley Street. This is the Birthplace, a reliquary for modern people. The three-gabled house, now a single unit, was two houses then. On the west stood a third house, burned in 1594. John Shakespeare lived in the "middle" house. In 1556, adding to his property he bought a freehold in Greenhill Street, now More Towns End, also the eastern wing of the Birthplace. This he turned into the Woolshop, his place of business. The easternmost room of the middle house is the Birth-Chamber, a holy of holies. On the windows, low ceiling, and plaster walls, pilgrims, going back a long way, wrote their names. Washington Irving was here, also Sir Walter Scott.

Built in the late fifteenth or early sixteenth century, these two houses showed their age when Victorians restored them, following an eighteenth-century sketch. The eastern bay of the Birthplace, on the right if you stand in front, has a single large gable, opened out to make an oriel window and two smaller wing-windows, one on either side. Two tall gabled dormers define the roof on the west, and the back wing, self contained, projects into the garden. Chimneys rising from the "ground-sill," a beam atop the stone foundation wall, hold the oak superstructure like a pair of bookends. A third chimney in the center ties the two houses together. Lower and upper storeys contrast with each other, the vertical studding below, close-timbered, changing to rectangular panels. Above the upper story is the solar or "cockloft," an attic. The outside walls between the beams are packed with lath or "winding," wattle work, daubed with clay. "Pargetting" covers the clay, this rough plaster mixing lime, chalk, and dung. Rooms in the solar went straight up to the roof. If you were conspiratorial, the rafters made a good place to hide things.

Burgesses in Stratford, recognizing one of themselves in John Shakespeare, set his feet on the road that led to Stratford's highest office. Starting on this journey, he is like that "scarfèd bark" resplendent with pennons Shakespeare tells of in *The Merchant of Venice*. Much later the bark returns, weather beaten. In 1557, about the time John Shakespeare married, he became ale-taster or "conner." The local court leet, held by the manor lord to hear complaints of false measure, instructed him to fix the price of ale and bread. He weighed the bread and saw to it "that all brewers do brew good and wholesome ale and beer." Tasting this, he determined the "assize" or top price per gallon. Then a wooden hand went up before the alewife's house, beckoning for custom. First, though, the taster had to give his approval. In *The Taming of the Shrew*, Sly, drunk on "sheer" or pure ale, rails on Marian Hacket, "the fat alewife of Wincot," a hamlet near Stratford. Real-life Hackets lived there. This one poured to her patrons from earthenware jugs, "no sealed quarts" stamped by the conner, and Sly vowed to have her up before the leet.

A year after his stint as conner and again in 1559, John Shakespeare served as constable. This made a study for his son the playwright, little pitchers having big ears. Dogberry, clown and constable in *Much Ado About Nothing*, being "most senseless" is fit for the job, irreverent Shakespeare thinks. "I am a wise fellow, and which is more, an officer, and which is more, a householder, and which is more, as pretty a piece of flesh as any is in Messina." In Stratford and "Messina," the constable, a killjoy, put down dicing, cards, even loggats. Playing at loggats, you stuck a bone in the ground and knocked this over with a bowling ball. Hamlet remembered, his bones aching.

Games of chance were like life, a reason to keep them under surveillance. Some card sharps, mistrustful, wore a ring set with a mirror. This detected cheating. Card games were Gleek, a three-handed game, Triumph, like modern Whist, and Primero. The Queen, not a spoilsport, was good at Primero. Each player got four cards, the principal groupings, as in poker, being flush. Prudent players, waiting for the right moment, reserved their stake or "rest." Hazarding this and losing, they forfeited the game. Romeo, not prudent, sets up his "everlasting rest," a metaphor from Primero, staking all at the end of the play. His suicide is imminent, Juliet's too, but at the tragic climax this hero commits a pun and Shakespeare lets him do it.

Stratford churchwardens assisted John Shakespeare in his role as custodian of public morals, more selfconscious than they used to be. Shakespeare's son-in-law Hall, when he served as churchwarden, brought parishioners to book "for late coming to church" or "being abroad, seen by the constable, at sermon time." Gentry and the well-to-do, whose land yielded an income of £100 a year, were exempt from the constable's attention. He tugged his forelock and passed on. At "vagrom men," he looked harder. He had the keys to the stocks, clapping up vagabonds, night walkers, and beggars, and he raised Hue and Cry if they wouldn't go along. Night walkers, even the Prince, were open to the law, but "not without the Prince be willing."

In Stratford things fit or were made to, as in their game of ticktack, fitting pegs in holes. The manorial court legislated for most offenses. Where it didn't do this, its "affeerors," four of them, levied fines on offenders who fell between cracks in the law. Also the affeeror, witnessing minutes of the leet, stamped them with his approval. Scotland under Macbeth, a tyrant but legally invested, can't get out from under, Shakespeare's character says bitterly. "The title is affeered" or confirmed. Affeeror was John Shakespeare's job in 1559. After this he was burgess. As chamberlain, he collected revenues, supervised the borough property, and made up the yearly accounts. A scrivener helped him or he had one at need. John Shakespeare signed with his mark, a pair of compasses, this glover's tool being used to make or measure perforations in the leather. Once he signed with the glover's stitching clamp, a "donkey."

Shakespeare, for whom nothing is sacred, has fun with this in *Henry*

VI, Part Two. Jack Cade, rebel and boor, addresses the Clerk of Chatham: "Dost thou use to write thy name? Or hast thou a mark to thyself, like an honest plain-dealing man?" Literate but not quick on the uptake, the Clerk is pleased to tell them he can write. This is confession and gets him hanged, his pen and inkhorn around his neck. Perhaps John Shakespeare was literate, like some others in Stratford who signed with a mark. Many have been anxious to say so, not wanting an unlettered parent for the Bard. But schooling and what comes of it seem off the point for his story.

Itemizing his chamberlain's account for 1563, Shakespeare's father entered the sum of two shillings, "paid for defacing images" in the Gild Chapel. The images, pious work of Clopton's, remembered the benighted time before the new learning. Becket, dying, was indigenous, and Solomon and Sheba, St. Helena too, had their local habitation and a name. This affronted the zeal of Reformers in Stratford, "pneumatic" men, obsessed with spirit. They hated the carnal world, province of John Shakespeare's son William. Zealous like the others or merely doing his job, John Shakespeare mutilated the frescoes. Then he had them whitewashed, and no one saw them again for more than two hundred years.

Elected alderman in 1565, plain John Shakespeare became Master Shakespeare. Like a stick figure in an old play, he had his signs and hallmarks, presenting the eminent man. The Vice in old plays had a dagger of lath, and John Shakespeare the badges of office, a black gown faced with fur, also the alderman's seal ring. Agate stone, cloudy colored, it showed on his forefinger, Mercutio said.

Then in 1568, he was bailiff. He stood atop Fortune's hill, another Clopton, Stratford's epitome of the self-made man. At meetings of the Council, he presided on his special footstool, the hourglass running beside him. It told time and pointed a moral. Justice of the peace, he dealt with malefactors and convened bimonthly sessions of the Court of Record. The bailiff had another function, speaking for Stratford in its back and forth with the lord of the manor, Earl of Warwick. Fifteen years before Shakespeare was born, the Earl bought title to Stratford Borough, succeeding the lords of the church. Where the bishop was King Log, this secular prince was King Stork. He made an avaricious landlord, jealous of his prerogative. In Stratford he chose the vicar, the schoolmaster too, and could reject the townsmen's choice of a bailiff. Once at least he did this, and they had to talk him over. The bailiff did the talking. Strong for local privilege, he appealed to London against the manor lord. Who had the bestowal of the office of market toll-gatherer, the lord or the village corporation?

In 1590, Edward Greville, son of Lodowick, Fulke Greville's cousin, secured the lordship of the borough and manor of Old Stratford. This happened by chance. A second son without expectations, Edward Greville in his youth shot an arrow in the air. Falling, it killed his elder brother. Lodowick, impressed, said it was "the best shoot he ever shot in his life." This heartless anecdote made a point, Shakespeare thought. His Claudius, a villain who wants to be good, says how our arrows are "too slightly timbered." The arrows are intentions. Seized by the wind, they fall where it wills, not where we want them to. Sometimes, reverting, they fall on our heads. Hamlet, a homicide, didn't mean any harm. He says he shot his arrow over the house, hurting his brother. Random shooting, this issues in tragedy. Sometimes the issue is lucky, as for Shakespeare's hero in *The Merchant of Venice*. Penniless Bassanio wants to marry an heiress, so applies for a loan to his rich friend, Antonio. This looks like throwing good money after bad. But the young man has his reasons:

> In my school days, when I had lost one shaft,
> I shot his fellow of the selfsame flight
> The selfsame way with more advisèd watch,
> To find the other forth.

Venturing both arrows, Bassanio finds them both, fortunate for him. Moralists in Shakespeare's time, dismissing luck or fortune, sponsored tragedies of character where the fault was in ourselves. Many suppose that Shakespeare followed their lead. How cause related to effect teased him out of thought, however. Assessing the relation, he saw that men, autonomous, were also "slaves of chance," flies or feathers on the wind. For what they wildly did, "the unthought-on accident" was guilty.

The sixties, years of Shakespeare's nonage, were troubled times in Stratford. In his father's term as bailiff, Northern earls, Percys, Nevilles, and Dacres, rose against the Crown. Rebels in Durham, celebrating Mass, hurled the English Bible and the Book of Common Prayer to the floor. Cowed by thirty years of strong royal government, most in Shakespeare's England kept their heads down, and only a skirmish of tenants followed their lords to the field. Last-ditch protest of the waning Middle Ages against the modern world, the Northern Rising was doomed but nobody knew this. Mary Queen of Scots, a scorched serpent, still potent, had her eye on the throne, and the Privy Council in London instructed John Shakespeare to check on men of doubtful allegiance. An efficient delator or spy, he did as told. Also they told him to increase the muster rolls. Chamberlains' Accounts for his year in office list payments for making weapons and "dressing" harness, pikes, and bows. The Crown's good servant, he kept the peace and swelled the coffers.

In church on Sundays, he sat with his wife in the front pew on the north side of the nave. Buff-uniformed sergeants carrying silver maces escorted him to church and brought him home again. When he went to the Gild Hall for Council meetings, the sergeants went before him, a guard of honor. This was distinction. Otherwise, assimilated to type, he doesn't show as different from the rest on Stratford's Council. In his son's phrase, "there went but a pair of shears between them."

Shakespeare's father failed of reelection. Robert Salisbury, brewer, served three terms as bailiff, John Shakespeare only one. Seduced by the "glimpse of newness," he liked his perquisites too well, or, too hot to command, he let them feel the spur in Stratford. One way or another, he didn't give what was wanted. They kept him on the Council for a long time. In 1571 he had a term as Chief Alderman, deputy to their new bailiff. The last three decades of his life record his failure, however, a long running down.

On a facile view, the failure makes him interesting, not the success. Seeing how things were, he got rid of the hourglass, etc. Less truth than poetry, this is matter for John Shakespeare's son, the playwright. Managing epiphanies, the son rubs spittle in the blind man's eyes. But John Shakespeare's eyes weren't opened, and the failed and successful man differ only in externals. Successful, he was all vitality, all debility in failure. Where the son, combining both, keeps a perilous balance, the father, radical or "humorous," runs all one way.

He began to miss Council meetings. He got in debt and left his creditors unpaid. He mortgaged his wife's property, losing some of it for good. Churchwardens reported his absence from church. He couldn't meet his alderman's assessment for support of the local soldiery. When the Council reduced this, he couldn't find the smaller sum either. Aldermen were supposed to pay a weekly tax toward poor relief, but the Council, knowing their man, excused "Mr. John Shakespeare." After 1576, with a single exception he went no more to meetings. Looking over his shoulder, he said he lived in "fear of death and mutilation." Four Stratford men were after him, one of them bailiff in 1582. This looks drastic. Later, he made it up with the bailiff.

Some, detecting a man of principle, lay John Shakespeare's fall to religion. He was a Puritan, Zeal of the Land Busy, or else a "recusant" Catholic, stubborn for the faith of his fathers. Either way, he stood outside the pale. A century and a half after he died, his spiritual testament turned up in the house on Henley Street. Repairing the roof in 1757, workmen found it where he left it, hidden between the rafters and tiling. A profession of faith in fourteen articles, the small paperbook, handwritten in English, consisted of six leaves stitched together. It seems to say that John Shakespeare died a Catholic.

The Testament, beginning, invokes the Holy Trinity, the Blessed Virgin, and the host of archangels, angels, patriarchs, prophets, evangelists, apostles, saints, and martyrs. In the presence of this celestial company, Shakespeare's father, emboldened, speaks his mind: "I, John Shakespeare, an unworthy member of the holy Catholic religion . . . do . . . ordain this my last spiritual will." He made the will or endorsed it, afraid of being "cut off in the blossom of my sins." This is like old Hamlet, murdered, telling his son how it was with him. Purgatory to come oppressed Shakespeare's father. Expecting a long stay, he besought friends, parents, and kinsfolk to labor his release, "especially with the holy sacrifice of the Mass." Why he cited his parents, long dead and no help now, has bothered some. But John Shakespeare's "Last Will of the Soul" is formulaic.

Composed in Milan by St. Charles Borromeo, a prelate-soldier of the Counterreform, it came to England in 1580 with Father Edmund Campion, Jesuit and martyr. Campion worked the Midlands, Shakespeare Country. As he told the Privy Council in a defiant "brag," he had a mission: "to cry alarm spiritual against foul vice and proud ignorance, wherewith many of my dear countrymen are abused." Once he came close to Stratford, sheltering with Sir William Catesby, twelve miles away. At the house of this local recusant, John Shakespeare received his testament from Campion's hands. Anyway, the opportunity offered. Then, taking the testament back to Henley Street, he left it in the rafters, light under a bushel.

Campion died at Tyburn, December 1, 1581, hanged, drawn, and quartered. Two companions died with him. To the packed jury that brought in its required verdict, he said: "In condemning us you condemn all your own ancestors, all the ancient bishops and kings, all that was once the glory of England." In this wholesale condemnation, John Shakespeare plays his part. With ancient glories and loyalties, he had little to do. Custom, his son's holy word, was "the dust on antique time." Like Coriolanus, the hero as barbarian, he undertook to sweep it away. When they told him to deface the old church monuments in Stratford, he did this. Later they sent the rood-loft the way of the frescoes, broke the stained glass windows, and took the altar from the Gild Chapel. The copes and vestments were disposed of, old clothes. Alderman Shakespeare, not demurring, gave his soul's consent. Shakespeare in the plays confronts his type many times. "Do not stand on

quillets," they tell him, i.e. no hemming and hawing. "My commission," he tells them, "Is not to reason of the deed, but do 't." Perhaps
he was timorous, perhaps indifferent or inured. Long before, in 1559,
he had voted with the others to oust Roger Dyos, the Catholic curate
of Holy Trinity. This Dyos, a year earlier, had baptized his first child.

John Shakespeare's colleagues, their patience exhausted, removed
him as alderman in 1586. He "doth not come to the halls," they said
morosely, "nor hath not done of long time." By then or a little later,
his son, not delinquent, self-delighting, had departed from Stratford.
Shakespeare's father lived on for another fifteen years. Serving his class,
he hoped for preferment but failed to achieve it. Shakespeare, a success,
in his deepest place served no one, hoping for nothing. In this tale of
Father and Son, he stands to his father like Hamlet to old Hamlet, a
strenuous hero smiting them left and right with the poleax. John
Shakespeare died in September 1601, an old man in his seventies. The
stone that marked his grave in Holy Trinity churchyard disappeared a
long time ago, gone with the dust of time.

3

"I, Daedalus"

SHAKESPEARE LIVING when he did, his skeptical bias comes as a surprise. The Elizabethan Settlement meant to form a different man, loyal to the throne and his bread. Prescribed by the throne, education wore down rough edges and composed points of view. Shakespeare had his share of this, attested by the plays where point of view is often elusive. A product of the system, he has an empty air about him, and the staring eyes in the Janssen bust look on nothing.

But Shakespeare, bereft of conviction, is emancipated too. His formal schooling, stifling dissent, awoke in this young scholar disbelief in all shibboleths and creeds. Where the boys who studied with him, faithful sons of prosaic fathers, had their useful careers in business, law, or trade, he kept his distance in Stratford, reading a different lesson in the orthodox curriculum. He began to read this lesson the year John Shakespeare served as bailiff. Imaginative biographers see him getting up at five or six in the morning and creeping like a snail unwillingly to school. For a fact, he found little to praise in his school days.

The "small Latin and less Greek" Ben Jonson allowed him he got from the King's New School, Stratford. Nicholas Rowe, sentimental playwright and Shakespeare's first editor, records this in his edition of 1709. Getting off on the right foot, Rowe's Shakespeare goes to gram-

mar school, acquiring "that little Latin he was master of." Then his
father, in straits, calls the son from his studies, wanting a helping hand
in the Woolshop. Likely, though, Shakespeare was glad to drop from
school—

> Small have continual plodders ever won,
> Save base authority from others' books.

Useful to plodders, school is no place for genius. The registers for
Stratford pupils in Shakespeare's boyhood, kept on parchment, have
crumbled, and the entry that might tell of his pupilage is lost. But this
acquisitive man who lived mostly by osmosis shows the stigma of
formal training, a point of departure, sometimes a crucifixion.

Letting them know what he knows, young Shakespeare has "eat
paper . . . drunk ink." Spendthrift, he disposed an exchequer of words,
more than the matter needed. (His clowns, cousins of Mrs. Malaprop,
get the words wrong, "your old vice still," they tell him.) "Figures
pedantical" tickle this learned playwright, hyperbole, for instance, laid
on with a trowel. Shakespeare has a different image, "three-piled" like
thickest velvet. In his prentice work, schoolboy Latin waits its turn.
"*Gelidus timor occupat artus,*" says one of Shakespeare's characters,
brought up on the classics. Cold fear seizes his limbs, not likely.

Kowtowing to the academy, Shakespeare is his own banner bearer.
Later he got rid of this self-proclaiming style and, enacting a familiar
paradox, became his own man. Even at the end of his career, though,
he remembers his schooldays, the cask smelling of the wine that steeped
it first. Prospero, saying goodbye to his art in one of Shakespeare's
sincerest speeches—"Ye elves of hills, brooks, standing lakes, and
groves"—is harking back to Ovid in the *Metamorphoses,* a grammar
school text. But Shakespeare, who used to be an acolyte, is a conqueror
now. Absorbed lock, stock, and barrel, the art no longer shows.

In grammar school, not child's play, Shakespeare made acquaintance
with the Roman poets, historians, and orators. He cut his teeth on
Latin, for some of his authors a dead language. Boys read Prudentius,
who bears the onus of creating the allegorical Christian epic, Boethius
on the consolation of philosophy, "good old Mantuan," fifteenth-
century Latin poet boosted by a donnish pedant in *Love's Labor's
Lost.* Here and there in this wasteland, Shakespeare picked up an
eagle's feather. Palingenius, whose "Zodiac of Life" ran to nine thousand Latin hexameters, gave him a line: "All the world's a stage."

He wasn't a scholar, contemporaries agreed, not John Selden, the
genuine article and a pillar of learning in this age, not even Ben Jonson,
a gifted amateur in learning. "Nature only helped him," said Leonard

Digges, stepson to an overseer of Shakespeare's will. By her "dim light" he went a long way, not borrowing from Greeks or imitating Latins. Milton, sketching the well-known portrait of Shakespeare the naif, called him "fancy's child." Poets weren't made but born, they said, and Shakespeare proved the rule. "Indeed, his learning was very little."

This "indeed," a stately word, has something to back it, not much. Shakespeare, remembering Ovid, a favorite poet of his, "honest Ovid among the Goths," remembers him mostly from an English translation. Lackadaisical students won't find this surprising. But he had the real thing at hand when he wanted to use it, validating his ambitious love poem, *Venus and Adonis,* with a Latin couplet from the *Amores,* or mustering Virgil for an early history play. "Can such anger dwell in heavenly minds?" This sounds better in Latin and Shakespeare supplies it.

He got his five-act structure from Terence and Plautus, expert farceurs. Plautus might have written *Twelfth Night* without heart or soul. Horace came in handy to Shakespeare at sonnets, and *Titus Andronicus* has an aphoristic villain who read him too, "in the grammar long ago." Trained rhetorician, logician, and orator, Shakespeare takes first place for artifice even in an "artificial" age. Describing him on this side, scholars have a battery of technical terms, mostly Greek. *Anaphora, epizeuxis, anadiplosis.* Whether or not he knew these jawbreakers by name, he deployed them adroitly, for instance in *Julius Caesar* where the rhetorician, deceiving others, fools himself. "As Caesar loved me, I weep for him; as he was fortunate, I rejoice at it; as he was valiant, I honor him. But as he was ambitious, I slew him." Shakespeare didn't get his due from Jonson and knew it. In the old story he stands godfather to a son of Ben's, giving the boy a dozen good "latin" spoons (i.e. brass). This, he said, was for Jonson to translate.

Not an early study for Robert Burns behind the plough, Shakespeare, going to school, learned sufficient. What he learned bears its part in what he did later, and his endings declare his beginnings. The distance between them is vast, though. Horace, a great Cham to Renaissance schoolboys, told him not to mix hornpipes and funerals or put a monster's head on a man. A refractory scholar, he did what Horace said he shouldn't. Life, he thought, made a *discordia concors,* "hot ice and wondrous strange snow."

Reading the Roman historians, e.g. Livy and Sallust, he learned that history, like his Aesop's fables, made exemplary sense. It showed "fine things to take as models," Livy said, "base things, rotten through and through, to avoid." Building on this, Shakespeare wrote history plays, dramatizing a contest between good and evil. Prudentius called this contest a spirit war or "Psychomachia," and Shakespeare, "continual plodder," made a note. But his history plays spoil the exemplum, and good, warring on evil, infiltrates it too. Jonson's *Catiline*, true to history as polemic, is clear as clear, i.e. coarse. Shakespeare's version of *Catiline* is *Julius Caesar*, a "speculum" or mirror where we see as through a glass darkly. The tyrannicide, a hero, is partly a villain, and the tyrant partly "the noblest man/That ever livèd in the tide of times."

Unlike Marlowe, older by two months, Shakespeare was spared the university, so never studied the *quadrivium*, arithmetic, music, geometry, and astronomy. His lot was the *trivium*, first or "trivial" part of the medieval curriculum, still in vogue. This meant grammar itself, "mother and foundation of all the sciences," logic, and rhetoric. If Shakespeare enjoyed his studies, that was a bonus. Art for its own sake had yet to be heard from, and the end of his education was moral. Latin and Greek, bedrock of the curriculum, increased "knowledge and worship of God," said John Colet, famous humanist, also "good Christian life and manners in the children." Children not minding their manners got expelled, thickheaded children too. Detecting a dullard, "the master giveth his friends warning and putteth him away."

Shakespeare's schoolmaster, probably Thomas Jenkins, Oxford M.A., had an ax to grind. Teaching boys the New Testament, he confuted "all such sentences and opinions as seem contrary to the Word of God and Christian religion." The government told him to do this. Sometimes confuting failed and the boys, growing up, turned to beggary, thieving, and murder. That was when the master shirked his job. Let him bring up the boys "in some good literature," said King Henry in a royal injunction. Then they would profit themselves and others "to the great commodity and ornaments of the commonweal." The premise, unspoken and perhaps unexamined, held that literature, a moral enterprise, saved souls. Many still read Shakespeare's plays, cornerstone of a liberal education, under this practical aspect.

Here pedantic Shakespeare, connoisseur of tropes and taffeta phrases, takes leave of the academy. His plays, adventures in esthetics, teach nothing instrumental. Dr. Johnson, Shakespeare's best critic but not always admiring, sees how the offhanded manner lacks purpose. "His precepts," said Johnson, "drop casually from him," so don't put us on the road to salvation. In Shakespeare's time, schoolmasters and their humanist friends understood this. Sir Thomas Bodley, founding his great library at Oxford, declined to clutter it with plays, and Shakespeare was dead and canonized before the catalog admitted his name. *Hamlet*, says the title page of the first edition, has been acted "in the two universities of Cambridge and Oxford," but this is a puff, disingenuous. Touring companies like Shakespeare's put on their plays in town. Masters barred the college halls against *Hamlet* etc., sensing in plays and players their natural antagonists.

Shakespeare's masters, six of them in Stratford during his school days, covered the territory in politics and religion. One was brother of a missionary priest, another, joining the Society of Jesus, died in Rome. Others were Anglican clergy. All appealed against experience to "base authority," saying how truth was truth, indivisibly itself "to the end of reckoning." In August 1572, Paris streets ran red with Huguenot blood. Just after this Massacre of St. Bartholomew's Day, boys in Shakespeare's school, perhaps making a scapegoat of their Romish master, Simon Hunt, broke the windows and plaster in the schoolroom. Chamberlains' accounts for the year following itemize the cost of repairs. Some biographers have a patriotic Shakespeare joining the protest, but his plays, though sometimes patriotic, sometimes make you feel that patriotism is the last refuge of a scoundrel.

John Shakespeare, ending a term as deputy bailiff, no doubt brooded on the massacre, matter of State and Faith. But St. Bartholomew's Day meant little to his son, except as it made a vivid altercation. Eleven years later, John Somerville, a Warwickshire man, set out from his house near Stratford to kill the Queen. Failing, he hanged himself in Newgate prison. Young Somerville, a despairing Catholic, was kin to the Ardens, but Shakespeare is silent on the connection. Not Protestant or Catholic, he appealed to the "dependency of thing on thing," discovering his truths, a myriad of them, between the "endless jar" of right and wrong. This discovery makes him an ungrateful scholar. Where Mozart, his only peer among artists, shows himself step by step the product of thoughtful nurturing, Shakespeare, rejecting the nurture that meant to form him, realized his genius against the grain.

SCENE OF his young man's rebellion, undercover and "mining all within," Shakespeare's schoolhouse stood behind the Gild Chapel on Church Street. The lower storey served for a town hall where John Shakespeare met with members of the village corporation. Upstairs his son, a "breeching scholar" old enough to be flogged, fed of the dainties bred in a book. Mostly brambles and thistles, they were dished up by "mutton-heads" like Holofernes. "What is a, b, spelt backward, with the horn on his head?" This is Holofernes, keeper of the schoolhouse in *Love's Labor's Lost*. Schoolmasters provide Shakespeare with the stuff of odious comparisons. Malvolio, blown with self-conceit, is like "a pedant that keeps a school i' the church."

Parishioners in "Navarre" or Stratford made much of the master, and Sir Nathaniel, a dim curate, tells why. "Their sons are well tutored by you, and their daughters profit very greatly under you." Anyway, says Holofernes, "If their daughters be capable, I will put it to them." Stratford daughters and sons started out together but the daughters soon fell by the way. An elementary education did nicely for them. Acquiring this, they plied their needlework at home, not going to school with young Shakespeare.

Built almost a hundred years before Shakespeare was born, the King's School remembered the Guild of the Holy Cross. In the older time, this medieval foundation saw to daily life in Stratford, both joys and sorrows. George, Duke of Clarence, an unlucky brother of the king, was among its members. Shakespeare tells how 1st and 2nd Murderer took him over the head with their sword hilts and "chopped" or chucked his body in a butt of malmsey. Afterwards they regretted this or one of them did, nagged by conscience. Men and women of the Guild had their eyes on heaven, so made a better habitation on earth. Endowed by a wealthy guildsman, a priest taught "grammar freely to all scholars coming to him, taking nothing for their teaching." In hard times, the Guild saw to the town's usual charges. It cared for poor parishioners in the almshouse at the south side of the chapel, ten of them living there when Leland came through. Well-to-do parishioners contributed alms, the Guild recompensing this with forty days' indulgence. Members were their brother's keeper. At Easter, the brothers and sisters kept a love-feast. Banners flying, they marched in procession to the Gild Hall, each bringing a tankard. Filled with ale, these tankards were poured out to the poor.

The Dissolution of religious houses put an end to the banners and tankards. For Shakespeare, however, things changing remained the same. The Guild disappeared, its property going to the King's Exchequer, but the guild school, rechristened, went on as before. King Edward's royal charter, setting up the municipal corporation, authorized a "free grammar school, to consist of one master and teacher, hereafter forever to endure." Four hundred years later, the square tower of the chapel still overlooks the school, a quarter of a mile from the Birthplace on Henley Street.

Shakespeare with satchel and shining morning face ascended by a stone staircase, open to the weather and covered with tile. In the big room at the top of the stairs, haloed saints, much diminished, looked backwards to the Middle Ages on the plastered south wall between the studs. Carved bosses in the middle of the roof tied the chamfered oak beams together, and painted roses and hearts taught a lesson, political.

The red rose of Lancaster showed a white heart. Conciliating differences, the heart of the white Yorkist rose was red. Boys froze in this schoolroom, bitter cold like most public rooms in England. At the head of the room sat the master, enthroned, at the other end his assistant. Shakespeare blew on his fingers, making false Latin. "Dunghill for *unguem.*"

He started off in "petty school," prescribed by statute and lasting two years. The "petits," first formers, sat down with the older boys, doing different things. Summers, school began at 6 A.M., an hour later in winter. It ended at dusk. Boys recited on an empty stomach, not breaking fast till mid-morning. In the afternoon they had playtime, fifteen minutes for this. They wrestled, leaped, ran, or practiced shooting the long bow, but frivolous sports like bowling were out. Fortune smiling, they got a day off, called a "remedy." Masters discouraged this, saying that "Many remedies make ignorant scholars." Thursdays and Saturdays, school recessed at noon. Sunday was free. Twelve months of the year, though, no day was wholly free, and boys went to church on free days, supervised by the master. After church he quizzed them, wanting to know about the sermon.

Sometimes in Stratford, schoolmaster and vicar were one and the same, not a conflict of interest. Vicar Bretchgirdle, christening Shakespeare, instructed his seniors in Latin. Merging church and school, he promoted obedience in weekly sermons and "homilies." God was an Englishman and the sovereign His deputy, "elected by the Lord." Prefabricated for all churches, homilies stressed this connection, coming down hard on dissent. At Morning and Evening Prayer, Shakespeare listened to the Bible and Psalms, all the Psalms repeated monthly. He heard the New Testament, Revelations excepted, three times a year. Reading from the Old Testament, the vicar passed over the drearier parts but got through a lot of this too. In II Samuel, Shakespeare heard: "With the pure thou wilt show thyself pure; and with the froward thou wilt show thyself unsavory. And the afflicted people thou wilt save: but thine eyes are upon the haughty, that thou mayest bring them down" (22: 27–28). This was poetic justice.

Attentive but considering, Shakespeare thought back to these preachments when he came to write history plays. In *King John*, for instance, the "rude eye of rebellion" dares to look at the king, and civil tumult, impious, overwhelms the kingdom. Shakespeare is glad when the rebels go home again, resuming their proper bounds or banks like an abated flood. In the meantime, the king isn't worried. "Our strong possession and our right for us," he says smoothly. Tentative and Shakespeare's surrogate, the queen mother amends this.

Your strong possession much more than your right,
Or else it must go wrong with you and me.

"History" having its own imperatives, things turn out badly for the
Lord's anointed. Rough justice is served but not poetic justice, and
homiletic sayings get their quietus.

Shakespeare took his place in school at the age of four or five.
Presiding over the lower form was the usher or *abcedarius,* called for
his function, teaching the ABCs. Sir William Gilbert, alias Higges,
served as Stratford's usher when Shakespeare was a boy. Later he
became curate and that is why he is "Sir," the respectful title allowed
a priest, sometimes mock-respectful. His nickname or alias distinguished him from others with the same surname. Richard Shakespeare
of Snitterfield was Shakestaff, not to be confused with other Shakespeares in Warwickshire, and Sir William Gilbert was Higges. Knowing
Latin, he flaunted this, stuffing the parish register with esoteric terms.
Still vivid in the register, he looks a little "overparted," i.e. not up to
it when he put on airs. Ushers weren't long on competence, resembling
Sir Nathaniel, the "hedge priest" of *Love's Labor's Lost.* Some such
"foolish mild man" as this one taught Shakespeare to read from the
hornbook. "Absey-book," they called it, primer for the ABCs. The
Bastard in *King John,* posing questions, expects answers, pat "like an
Absey book." Partly this means that the answers were ready even before
the questions were posed.

The hornbook, made of oak and shaped like a cutting board, went
with young Shakespeare to school. A leaf of paper or parchment,
fastened down with metal borders and covered with a transparent layer
of horn, it showed him the alphabet, Lord's Prayer, and *In nomine,*
"In the name of the Father, Son, and Holy Ghost." Before the alphabet
stood the sign of the Cross. From this "Christ-cross row" Shakespeare's
King Edward, doting on prophecies but getting them wrong, plucks
the letter "G," ill-omened. "G" is for George, Duke of Clarence, he
thinks, and his brother's death in the Tower is a sequel. The handle of
the hornbook, pierced with a hole, had a cord running through it.
Shakespeare, coming and going, tied the cord at his girdle or looped it
around his neck. Coming from school was better than going.

Love goes toward love as schoolboys from their books,
But love from love toward school with heavy looks.

Romeo says this, more truth than poetry.

Repetition, dear to Shakespeare's masters, wore down obdurate
students like water drops on stone. One of his Two Gentlemen of

Verona, the less disagreeable one, falling in love sighs like a schoolboy "that had lost his ABC." But masters knew what they were up against, and a short catechism, general issue, reprinted the hornbook leaf. Instilling faith and morals, the catechism dogged Shakespeare from one form to the next. Prayers and psalm singing framed his school day. Singing, delightful, was useful exercise too, "good to preserve the health of man." Strengthening the breast, it opened the pipes and remedied "stuttering and stammering in the speech." With these words, William Byrd, England's best composer, justified his choral music.

Boys when they sang enunciated clearly. Not doing this got them whipped with the black bill or "list." This rod, said one pedagogue, was "the sword that must keep the school in obedience." The heart was desperately wicked, especially a child's, but "the rod of correction" drove wickedness far from him. Whimsical pedagogues specialized in "jerks," sudden strokes raining down without notice. Holofernes, a punster who teaches boys the hornbook, says that Ovid is the man, not least for his "jerks of invention." Wielding the rod like a broom, masters swept their living from the posteriors of little children, Jonson said.

Initiating his children in the mysteries of Christian religion, the usher led them through the Lord's Prayer, Hail Mary, Creed, and Ten Commandments. Versions were canonical, just this one, no other. King Henry's *Primer* established the canon. "Supreme Head of the Church of England," the king wanted "one uniform manner or course of praying" throughout his dominions. His successors wanted this too, and under Elizabeth the Act of Uniformity, June 24, 1559, insured that they got it. But England, homogeneous by fiat, allowed for diversity at home. The best of both worlds, this fostered strength without stultifying, and the monolith, having a safety valve, didn't crack. Gypsies, recusants, some Jews, and other "outlandish" persons lived in Shakespeare's England, but honored public mores and bowed to the Anglican God. Whether they believed or not, nobody asked. The letter mattered more than the spirit, a lesson in priorities, useful to Shakespeare.

"Begot in the ventricle of memory," learning was by rote. Sound assisted sense, sometimes preempting it, like the "choughs' language" baffling the comic villain in *All's Well That Ends Well.* Combinations of the vowels with b, c, and d followed the alphabet, giving the rudiments of syllabification. The first row ran: "ab eb ib ob ub! ba be bi bo bu." Sheepish Holofernes, baaing or bleating, comes from the syllable row. Shakespeare, petty scholar, said his syllables out loud, corrected by the *abcedarius,* "a domineering pedant o'er the boy." No one in his time anticipated posterity's interest in Shakespeare, and no curriculum survives for the school where he studied. But Stratford's course of study followed the rule, everywhere the same in Elizabeth's reign. Having mastered his ABCs, Shakespeare memorized the catechism. He learned the first ten numbers and grace before and after meals, for good measure six graces. Next came calendar, almanac, and penitential psalms. Like the deadly sins, they were seven.

Students, conning this material, practiced "prosodia," the art of pronouncing words, and "orthographia," how to write. Some botched the job, Holofernes complained, saying "dout" instead of "doubt," "det" for "debt," etc. This was "abhominable" which they called "abbominable." Others racked their orthography, like Hamlet, obstreperous. He thought it "baseness to write fair" and tried to forget that learning. Later, though, it did him yeoman service. Students wrote cursive script, free flowing. This was "secretary hand," standard in Shakespeare's England. Richard Quiney, Shakespeare's Stratford acquaintance, addressed his friend in this hand, and Shakespeare, if he wrote the part often assigned him in *Sir Thomas More,* used it too. Compositions like this history play didn't commend themselves to petty school teachers. Innocent of Renaissance, their emphasis was all on Reformation. Hortatory verses, bucking up the prospective scholar, declared this:

> Come, little child, let toys alone,
>   and trifles in the street:
> Come, get thee to the parish clerk,
>   He's made a teacher meet.

Putting away foolishness, Shakespeare at seven addressed himself to Latin grammar. The *abcedarius* got him started, declining nouns and conjugating verbs. This was the "accidence," painful to Shakespeare. In *Henry VI,* Part Two, his Lord Say, erecting a grammar school, is accused of corrupting the youth of the realm. He has men about him "that usually talk of a noun and a verb," words no Christian ear could endure. Boys studied endurance, though, having no option. Speaking and writing went on in the Latin tongue, lapses being punished by flogging. An older boy, company spy, reported lapses to the master. Reading "colloquies" by humanists like Erasmus (Dutch but looming large in the lives of English schoolboys), Shakespeare made his own dialogs, epistles, and themes. "Vulgaria," sentences in the vulgar tongue, English, matched with their Latin equivalents, helped him do this. One, anecdotal, pointed a contrast between home and school. "I was wont to lie still abed," the breeching scholar says. "But now the world runneth upon another wheel. For now at five of the clock by moonlight I must go to my book and let sleep and sloth alone. And if our master hap to awake us, he bringeth a rod instead of a candle." Boys who stayed the course had seven years of this.

William Lily, sixteenth-century master of St. Paul's School, London, wrote the textbook. For the next three hundred years, his *Short Introduction,* Cerberus before the portals, confronted young English starting out. Like Latin mottoes on sundials, Lily's *Grammar* made simple sayings sound deep, for example, "*homo* is a common name to all men." Shakespeare's Gadshill, a sententious thief, recites this schoolboy tag, impressing his partners in crime. The *Grammar,* promoting new Calvinist morality, said how "it is most healthful to get up early." This came home more profoundly in Latin and Sir Toby quotes the Latin in *Twelfth Night.* A drunkard, he went to bed with the sunrise.

Illustrating the *Grammar,* a woodcut showed little humanists coveting fruit on the tree of knowledge. Shakespeare offered his own version in *Love's Labor's Lost* where things look up when study leaves its "bias." Berowne, a truant hero, burns candles to Love, "still climbing trees in the Hesperides." Not a humanist, he gives his voice "for barbarism," and the golden apples he covets aren't the same as study's fruit. The fruit was different for Shakespeare, his colleagues and masters. "What is the end of study?" Shakespeare at school wrote this question in his "tables," addressing it later.

Always on the lookout, magpie Shakespeare picked a comic scene from the *Grammar.* In *The Merry Wives of Windsor,* he brought the grammar school master on stage. Sir Hugh Evans, Welsh and comical, makes fritters of English. This mattered less, Lily being his text. "The Vocative case," he read, "is known by calling or speaking to: as O magister, O master." Catechizing his student "William," Parson Evans has this by heart. "Come hither, William," the master begins. "Hold up your head. Come." Mistress Quickly, left over from Shakespeare's Henry plays, is his straight man.

> EVANS. What is the focative case, William? (At "focative," the audience rolled in the aisles.)
> WILL. Oh, *vocativo,* O.
> EVANS. Remember, William. Focative is *caret.* (I.e. Latin "missing," also "carrot" for "penis")
> QUICK. And that's a good root. ("Penis" again)
> EVANS. 'Oman, forbear. . . . What is your genitive case plural, William?
> WILL. Genitive case!
> EVANS. Aye.

WILL. Genitive—*horum, harum, horum.*
QUICK. Vengeance of Jenny's case! [I.e. "pudendum"] Fie on
her! Never name her, child, if she be a whore.

Ignorance, wiser than learned clerks, wins this contest. It happens
all the time in Shakespeare's plays, an enclosed garden where he got
his own back. In Shakespeare's school, annexed to the real world, the
clerk rode roughshod. Complementing the *Grammar* with books of
moral precepts culled from choice authors, he bore down on the class
with these *Sententiae pueriles,* saws and sayings for little boys, often
puerile. The Privy Council didn't want him to teach heathen poets,
"from the which the youth of the realm doth rather receive infection
of manners than advancement in virtue," but he saw a way to get
round this. Witty Ovid, metamorphosed under his hand, turned into
moral Ovid, leading boys "to the temple of honor and virtue." Poetry
filled this role if it expected a hearing. Otherwise it was nonsense,
"guards on wanton Cupid's hose."

"Moralized Ovid," a pious fraud perpetrated by the Christian Middle Ages, Shakespeare saw through at once. He liked his Ovid jaunty,
a little overripe. This mock-serious poet turns up often in the early
work, and one reader, taking notice, said how his sweet, witty soul
lived again in "honey-tongued" Shakespeare. For instance, *Venus and
Adonis:*

> She vailed her eyelids, who, like sluices, stopped
> The crystal tide. . . .

This is everybody's Ovid, a superficial presence. The famous "love-
duet" from *The Merchant of Venice* brings before us another Ovid,
unguessed at by Shakespeare's colleagues and masters, indifferent
scholars. Versed in out-of-the-way learning, this Ovid is a magus, like
his witch Medea or Ovidian Shakespeare, and his dark magic is potent
for good.

> In such a night
> Medea gathered the enchanted herbs
> That did renew old Aeson.

Great poet of renewals, essential Ovid is Shakespeare's possession
alone, unexpectedly the fruit of study. Shakespeare didn't read his
schoolbooks cover to cover. Pulping them, he found their quiddity,
though. Sometimes the books were trots, but for this scholar, pene-
trating to the heart of the matter, "small Latin" puts it too low.

Greek, as Jonson said, he had less of. Queen Elizabeth read Greek,

translating Euripides, and Erasmus, much gratified, knew of clever
English schoolboys who turned out Greek epigrams. Shakespeare
wasn't among them. Writing his sonnets, he leafed through the pages
of the Greek Anthology, but mostly was like his Casca who hears
Cicero speak Greek. "Those that understood him smiled at one another
and shook their heads; but, for mine own part, it was Greek to me."

Ignorant of Greek plays, Shakespeare, like Keats pondering the Elgin
Marbles, worked out "the Greek thing" for himself. He didn't know
Aristotle, master of those who knew, but learned how drama had to
demonstrate sequence. Making love to their bad employment, Shakespeare's villains lose "on account of this," *propter hoc,* as Aristotle has
it. His heroes win, keeping a bosom "franchised" or free. Not *post hoc*
or "after this," action in Shakespeare happens for cause. Often, though,
cause seemed remote from effect. Hippolytus in the Greek play isn't at
fault but Phaedra is, Theseus too, bad luck for the hero. Dangerous,
Shakespeare thought, when the baser nature came "between the fell
incensèd points of mighty opposites." Then this "classical" playwright,
looking deeper, saw how we are destroyed simply as we are human.
"Alas, our frailty is the cause, not we." This was what it meant to be
classical in spirit.

For Shakespeare the schoolboy, "two truths" are told, as for the
heroes he wrote about later. One says that school was something he
got through. But this needs the other side of the coin. "What is the end
of study?" Kicking against the pricks, Shakespeare worked out his own
position, "egregious." He was maverick cattle, no part of the herd. Or
school gave him hints and he encrusted them, working his sea change.
Not a born poet, he made himself a poet. The stunning truth about
him is that his scholarship was profounder than anyone else's.

TWENTY-EIGHT BOYS were christened in Stratford the year Shakespeare was born. One went to the university, matriculating at Oxford, aged eighteen. He was William Smith, Shakespeare's grammar-
school contemporary, otherwise unremembered. Universities offered
training for the learned professions, law, medicine, and divinity, and
most boys enrolled at fifteen. Marlowe, also born in 1564, went to
Cambridge at seventeen. Studying Dr. Faustus, he enrolled in divinity, another dawn-to-dusk regimen like his grammar school and Shakespeare's. This course of study took him six years. En route to the
priesthood, scholars spent much time on their knees. Creature comforts
they dispensed with, not always by choice. Some, before they went to
bed, were "fain to walk or run up and down half an hour to get a heat

on their feet." University statutes governed conduct and appearance, one providing "that no scholar do wear any long locks of hair upon his head."

Shakespeare skipped the university. Necessitous or consulting his pleasure, he chose instead to "go to the world." That is, he got married. He was eighteen, Anne Hathaway twenty-six. Always let the woman "take an elder than herself," says Orsino in *Twelfth Night,* knowing that men's fancies are giddy and unfirm. But sentimental Orsino isn't Shakespeare, a dramatic artist, and the failure of Shakespeare's marriage didn't turn on difference in years.

The brass marker in the chancel of Holy Trinity, commemorating Anne Hathaway's death in 1623, says she died at sixty-seven. So Anne was born in 1556, most likely in Shottery, a mile west of Stratford church. A little stream waters the country around, some of it farmland, some pasturage for sheep. Part of the manor house, built of Arden sandstone, goes back to the fourteenth century. North of this is the village, a scattering of half-timbered cottages, thatched with wheat straw or roofed with handmade tiles. Shottery village in Shakespeare's time stood on the edge of the Forest of Arden. The house his wife grew up in, called Anne Hathaway's Cottage by eighteenth-century tourists, lay west of the village, "down in the neighbor bottom." Celia in *As You Like It* reports this, drawing, some say, from the life.

Picture-perfect amid gardens, roses, herbs, and clipped box, the fifteenth-century farmhouse evokes rural England in old days. Twelve rooms in all, it makes a narrow rectangle four times longer than deep. Thatch crowns the high-pitched roof and the paneled walls are cut with tiny latticed windows. Timber frames the walls, wattle and daub finished with plaster. Looking older than it is, the mellow brickwork came later. Inside, a pair of "crucks," curved oak timbers pegged together at the top, carry the roof. Six chambers on the upper floor served for bedrooms or storage. In the principal chamber, the one at the head of the staircase, the "Hathaway bedstead" takes up most of the room. Below, when Hathaways lived there, was the buttery or dairy. This family stored its farm produce behind the "buttery bar," a half door with a ledge. "Bring your hand to the buttery bar and let it drink," says Maria in *Twelfth Night,* inviting Sir Andrew to a flirtation. Simpleminded, he misses his cue.

Shakespeare was more responsive or Anne showed him the way. Tour guides point to his "courting chair" drawn up to the stone fireplace in the living room or "hall." On the narrow wood settle, they say the lovers sat together. The fireplace, eight feet wide, is spanned by its ancient bressumer, a massive horizontal beam, chamfered oak.

The original bake-oven dominates the kitchen, beside it the "salamander," a flat utensil for baking bread. Living in fire, the salamander, impervious, took the heat. Hathaways, thrifty, made lye soap from the ashes. Anne Hathaway's Cottage had an orchard, babbling brook, and a resident shepherd. Do they know a sheepcote on the edge of the Forest, Oliver, a prodigal son, asks the girls. "The rank of osiers"— willows—"by the murmuring stream . . . brings you to the place," Celia tells him.

Shakespeare, coming over from Stratford on visits, followed a grassy pathway, still trodden today. He came to Hewlands Farm, as it was then, the substantial holding of Richard Hathaway, husbandman. Before the middle of the sixteenth century, Hathaways in Shottery were farming two "yardlands," an indeterminate measure, between forty and ninety-two acres. Either way, this made an estate. Marrying twice, Richard Hathaway sired seven children who outlived him. All were his legatees and he left them well set up. On a small scale, Anne Hathaway, like Mary Arden, was a catch.

Hathaways knew Shakespeares, an old connection frayed or cemented by the marriage of their offspring. When Shakespeare was two, his father stood surety for Richard, involved in a lawsuit. Elizabethans litigated, driven back on their rights by enclosers, grabbing landlords, and pettifogging attorneys. "The first thing we do," says Shakespeare's character, "let's kill all the lawyers." John Shakespeare, often plaintiff or defendant in the Court of Record, evidently liked going to law. Law made an expensive pastime, though, and later he was called on to pay Richard Hathaway's debts.

Anne's father, a supernumerary, setting the scene for others, passed from it in the summer of 1582. He left a widow, Joan, who outlived him by almost two decades. Sir William Gilbert, known to young Shakespeare as *abcedarius*, lately Stratford's curate, wrote the will. Joan farmed Hewlands with two sons and her shepherd, Thomas Whittington. Careful like old Adam, Orlando's faithful retainer, this shepherd laid his wages by against bad times coming.

> I have five hundred crowns,
> The thrifty hire I saved under your father,
> Which I did store to be my foster nurse
> When service should in my old limbs lie lame,
> And unregarded age in corners thrown.

Bequeathing some of his store to poor folk in Stratford, Whittington the shepherd died in 1601. His will directed "Anne Shakespeare, wife unto Mr. William Shakespeare," to see to the bequest.

She was Anne or Agnes, interchangeable names like Hamnet and Hamlet. Usher Gilbert married Agnes, buried nineteen years later as Anne. A faded drawing in a copy of Shakespeare's Third Folio purports to give her likeness. The woman in the drawing is someone to reckon with. Over the hair, smoothly pasted down, her sixteenth-century cap makes a prim fit. The head, severed from the body by the starchy ruff, floats above it like John the Baptist's on its platter. Like Shakespeare, this Anne has a high forehead. The eyebrows are severely plucked, the nose strong and fleshy. Expressionless but wide awake, the eyes show nothing behind them. The lips, sensuous, are compressed, the chin heavy and decisive. Verses in the Folio, paying tribute, say that this is "Shakespeare's consort."

Most of his married life Shakespeare lived apart from his consort, the marriage, hugger-mugger, suggesting why. Wanting a license to marry Anne "with once asking of the banns of matrimony between them," Shakespeare went down to Worcester, seat of the diocese, Thursday, November 28, 1582. This was cutting it fine. Law required a reading of the banns in church on three successive Sundays before marriage. On payment of a fee, the bishop might abridge this for couples in a hurry. Banns couldn't be read, though, from Advent to Epiphany, a season off limits for marriage. Advent Sunday falling December 1, there was barely time to call the banns on the last day of November, St. Andrew's. With these lovers time didn't amble, Anne being three months gone. Applying to the Ordinary, a lawyer exercising the bishop's jurisdiction, Shakespeare got his waiver, special but not all that special. Many others before him were dispensed in this way, including Henry Heicroft, Stratford's vicar. After a single declaring of the banns, this Heicroft, in a hurry, married Emme Careless.

Some, discounting the need for haste, have Anne and Shakespeare pledging troth without benefit of clergy, like Tobias and Sarah in the Old Testament story, one of the Apocryphal books of the Bible. "Hand-fast" marriage, Shakespeare's people called this, more or less auspicious depending on whose opinion was asked. Most, if asked, thought the auspices were good. Thomas Russell, the overseer of Shakespeare's will, was living as husband with his second wife before these two got married. No one objected, and the angel in the Book of Tobit was glad to stand surety for Tobias. Sixteenth-century murals in an old house by the Mere-side in Rother Market showed the meeting of Tobias and the Angel. Today these paintings, uncovered, glorify Stratford's White Swan Hotel. Shakespeare saw them when they were fresh. What did he think? In *All's Well That Ends Well*, his ruttish hero Bertram, exchanging rings with Diana, means to lie with her the way Tobias did with Sarah. The exchange of rings is mere pretext, though, the coupling felt as sinful, and Bertram is only fleshing his will.

In Stratford, the year Shakespeare's First Folio was published, another William and Anne made a handfast marriage. He gave her a token, bent sixpence, gloves, or fruit, then took her by the hand. "They be man and wife before God and the world," said a sympathetic friend to the vicar. Gratuitous, the vicar didn't officiate, and Florizel in *The Winter's Tale* doesn't need him either. "Contract us 'fore these witnesses," says the hero, impatient, taking his mistress's hand. But Polixenes, not so hot, comes between them. This father wants a proper nuptial and Shakespeare, obliging, holds the young lovers in check.

Under twenty-one when he married, Shakespeare was technically an "infant." He needed the consent of parents, but a mark scrawled on a paper satisfied the authorities and he didn't bring his parents along. Giving his age, he disclaimed impediments, nearness in blood, or a precontract with others. Shakespeare's word was only as good as his bond. If he misrepresented, the bishop claimed the bond, forty pounds, a large sum. Two sureties, friends of Anne's, stood with Shakespeare in consistory court. They posted the indemnity, dictating its terms. In the event of legal action, Shakespeare had to pay court costs. Also the bond provided that Anne Hathaway, maiden, shouldn't be married without the consent of her friends. Shakespeare's sureties were Fulk Sandells and John Richardson, Shottery farmers, brothers-in-law, and neighbors of Richard Hathaway, recently dead. Trusty friend and neighbor, Hathaway called Sandells in his will.

A mysterious entry in the Bishop's Register has suggested to some that Shakespeare, a reluctant suitor, needed to be told what he was there for. On November 27 the clerk of the court, recording an application for a marriage license, entered this in the name of "William Shakespeare and Anne Whateley of Temple Grafton in the County of Warwick." The next day, however, license to abridge the banns is entered for "William Shakespeare and Anne Hathaway of Stratford." To err is human, and elsewhere the Worcester clerk, stumbling over names, wrote Barbar for Baker, Bradeley for Darby, etc. But Whateley for Hathaway seems more than a slip of the pen. One biographer, imagining another William Shakespeare, brings him to Worcester to marry another Anne. Not a plausible suggestion, it has its odd propriety, like saying that someone else named William Shakespeare wrote the plays.

Haunting the edges of Shakespeare's story, Anne Whateley is a ghost but her surname is real. Whateleys lived in Stratford, Henley-in-Arden too, and records of the Worcester diocese disclose a William Whateley, vicar of Crowle. Perhaps his surname, remembered, crept into Shakespeare's license where it had no business being. Perhaps the vicar had a daughter Anne, Shakespeare's first intended, chaste unlike the other one and a forsaken victim of his unlucky liaison. This libidinous Shakespeare, with one bird in hand, another in the bush, is like his seducer in *A Lover's Complaint*. He had "a plenitude of subtle matter" in him, using it for "cautels" or tricks.

Proper marriage in Shakespeare's time, highly ceremonious, went forward step by step. A phrase for this is "cold gradation and well-balanced form." The first step was betrothal in the house of the bride. A priest conducted the ceremony, and in *Twelfth Night* a priest describes it—

> A contract of eternal bond of love,
> Confirmed by mutual joinder of your hands,
> Attested by the holy close of lips,
> Strengthened by interchangement of your rings.

After the betrothal a decent interval followed, tormenting concupiscent flesh. Time "trots hard with a young maid between the contract of her marriage and the day it is solemnized," says Rosalind in *As You Like It*, knowing what she means. Consummating marriage before the wedding day took off "the edge of that day's celebration," however. Ardent couples paid for this, "sour-eyed disdain," says Prospero, being their portion.

Spenser, Shakespeare's contemporary, hymned a proper marriage in his "Epithalamion." The day having come at last, they wake and dress the bride, "clad all in white." She wears her hair loose about her, token of virginity. Before her father's house the groom appears, bringing bachelor friends. First of all this day was sexual but ordered by its rules, and later the friends took away the bride's garters, trophies convention allowed them. "Set all your things in seemly good array," they tell the groom. This included music, pipe, drum, and trembling viol. Shrilling loud but not discordant, it made a harmony without breach or jar.

Shakespeare's people, unsentimental, got married in church, not in the open air like beggars under a bush. "Get you to church," says Jaques to Touchstone, "and have a good priest that can tell you what marriage is." An honorable estate, it wasn't "to be enterprised, nor taken in hand unadvisedly, lightly, or wantonly." Death or love or fortune's wreck were all potential in marriage, and King Edward's

Prayer Book took cognizance of this. "For better, for worse." Occasion for thought, marriage was sobering but never lachrymose and rarely sober. A wedding was a "bride-ale," the bride drinking from her cup with the others. At the bridegroom's house they drank not by cups but by the bellyfull, carousing "full measure to her maidenhead." Explicit in first and last things, Shakespeare's people weren't sniggering, and the bride, though chaste, wasn't snowbroth.

"Now night is come," Spenser bids them in his tactful poem, "now soon her disarray, And in her bed her lay." To this bower came the groom, anticipating "the triumph of our victory." Friends undressed him and brought him to bed. Then, sewing up the sheets, they departed. This was Tudor marriage, not Shakespeare's.

Wherever Shakespeare wed Anne, it wasn't in his home place. He makes no appearance in the marriage records of Holy Trinity church. No records exist for smaller chapels in Stratford parish, Luddington three miles west, or Bishopton north of Shottery. Local people insist that Shakespeare married in Luddington, referring skeptics to an "ancient tome" that used to record this. But the Luddington register went to the fire a long time ago. On a cold day the curate's housekeeper burned it, fuel for her kettle.

Temple Grafton had a vicar John Frith, "an old priest and unsound in religion," i.e. Romish. He took care of hurt hawks but couldn't preach or read well, and Bishop Whitgift in Worcester made him post bond not to solemnize marriage out of season. A local version of Sir Oliver Martext, Vicar Frith looks like the priest for Shakespeare. "This fellow will but join you together as they join wainscot," wooden paneling, says Jaques. "Then one of you will prove a shrunk panel, and like green timber warp, warp." Five miles from Stratford, Temple Grafton lies just south of the high road to Alcester, home of Fulke Greville. The village, shaded by maples and built on rising ground, commanded a view south and west to the Cotswolds. Beyond the hills, at Oxford, the London road begins.

No subject has more inflamed Shakespeare's readers than his marriage, source of bitter expostulation or chivalrous protest. In modern times readers have begun to calm down, but theirs is largely the calm of indifference. Making love is only "untrussing," etc. Certifying Anne's behavior and affronted by Shakespeare's, some cast her as Ophelia to his misogynous Hamlet, disposer of the second-best bed. An eighteenth-century biographer, acquitting them both, thought it only natural to impute charms to a woman "who could engage and fix the heart of a young man of such uncommon elegance of fancy." Victorians and Edwardians tended to a stronger line. One, dismissing

"any strictures that have been offered in regard to Shakespeare's early
relations with Anne," imagined "a maiden free from reproach" inspir-
ing the playwright "with the pure and noble passion that irradiates all
that is best in his plays." Another supposed that "if the antecedents of
Shakespeare's union with Miss Hathaway were regarded with equa-
nimity by their own neighbors, relatives, and friends," it ill became
carpers to "impugn the propriety of their conduct." He hoped that
nothing more would be heard of "the insinuations that have hitherto
thrown an unpleasant shadow over one of the most interesting periods
of our author's career."

Shakespeare in the plays seems to insinuate a doubtful opinion, in
Measure for Measure, for instance, where jumping the gun smacks of
"too much liberty." Claudio, the hero, has a metaphor for this, dis-
turbing in its violence.

> Our natures do pursue,
> Like rats that ravin down their proper bane,
> A thirsty evil, and when we drink we die.

The hero, a little feckless, getting possession of Julietta's bed "upon a
true contract," says how only the proclamation of "outward order" is
lacking. He thinks this order, merest form, is drapery or flourishes.
Sign and flag of the heart's truth, form for Shakespeare participates in
the content it betokens. Sometimes it creates what it betokens. Lucio,
a libertine indifferent to forms, is Shakespeare's antihero in *Measure
for Measure*, among the persons of the play the only one he can't find
it in him to pardon.

Guardians of the playwright's good name bristle at the image of
"woodman" Shakespeare, overlusty at legs. For the National Poet they
want a whey-faced Shakespeare, begot between codfish. But the man
who wrote the plays has his vivid sense of "the fire i' the blood" or
"blade of youth,"

> When oil and fire, too strong for reason's force,
> O'erbears it and burns on.

This sense is the earnest of his point of view and makes Shakespeare
for once an apprehensible figure, somebody readers can take hold of.

"Natural rebellion," Shakespeare's familiar, agitates Lysander in *A
Midsummer Night's Dream*. Wanting her lover to lie farther off, Her-
mia isn't a prude, and Prospero isn't a Victorian parent. Attentive to
Miranda's "virgin knot," he begets stunned surprise in modern readers.
Never break the knot, says this parent, dead serious, before

All sanctimonious ceremonies may
With full and holy rite be ministered.

"Sanctimonious" isn't hypocritical but sacred.

Marrying in haste, Shakespeare learned how contempt grew upon familiarity. "If there be no great love in the beginning," says a lackwit in *The Merry Wives,* "yet Heaven may decrease it upon better acquaintance." Early local tradition in Stratford tells how Anne, outliving Shakespeare, "did earnestly desire to be laid in the same grave with him." His bones weren't to be disturbed, though, on this he was adamant, and Shakespeare is buried alone.

NEWLY MARRIED and needing a roof over their heads, Shakespeare and Anne likely found this on Henley Street, moving in with his parents. On Trinity Sunday, May 26, 1583, Heicroft the vicar christened their first child, Susanna. Less than two years later came the twins, Hamnet and Judith. The vicarage had a new incumbent by then, and Richard Barton did the christening, February 2, 1585. The Shakespeares named their twins for Hamnet and Judith Sadler, neighbors who lived near the Corn Market. Three decades later, Sadler witnessed Shakespeare's will.

Shakespeare's daughters bear the names of Apocryphal heroines, not conventional in his time. The name Susanna first appears in Stratford registers nine years before Shakespeare's first daughter was born. Susanna is the one lusted after by the elders. Judith, the other one, comely but bloody minded, cuts off the head of Holofernes. Puritans liked the Apocryphal books, domestic and often ferocious. Enter Shakespeare, closet Puritan, sorting out names? This seems doubtful. Hamlet has his reasons, swearing by St. Patrick, and Richard III by St. Paul. Shakespeare's life differs from his art, however, pointing to nothing beyond itself until he dreams it. Turning pages in the Bible, he found his daughters' names and liked the way they sounded.

Mostly devoid of matter of fact, ten years separate Shakespeare's marriage and his surfacing in London. He was at home in August 1582, nine months before the birth of Susanna, again in November for his marriage, yet again in the early summer of 1584, nine months before the birth of the twins. He appears on the record in 1588, joining with his parents in a Bill of Complaint against his cousin Lambert, sequesterer of Arden lands. Otherwise these years are enveloped in shadows.

On the public stage big things were going on, but mostly Shakespeare ignored them or converted them to his own use. William the Silent, Dutch champion of the Protestant cause, died in 1584, struck down by an assassin. Four years later, Henri IV, a lapsed Protestant, came to the throne of France. He said Paris was worth a Mass. The murder of Dutch William left Shakespeare unmoved, also Henry of Navarre's qualms of conscience, if any. But this Henry, not a womanizer as he was in life, quite the reverse, turns up in *Love's Labor's Lost* with his real-life confederates, the Duke of Longueville and Biron-Berowne. Making a fourth in their little ensemble is the Duke de Mayne, a mortal antagonist, reconciled by Shakespeare.

The Armada, menacing England in 1588, is noticed by Shakespeare but from far off, beacons on the hills in *Henry IV, Part Two*, not warning England but "this little kingdom, man." In the Armada year, the Avon rose in Stratford, no flood in memory like this one. The church register of Welford, south of town, has an entry: "Old Father Porter, being 109 years of age, never knew the Avon so high by a yard and a half in the house." The storm broke the Spanish fleet, as later in *Othello* it scattered the Turks. Also it broke Clopton's bridge at Stratford, important to Shakespeare.

Abhorring a vacuum, Shakespeare's early biographers people his shadowy time with forms. Sir William Davenant, seventeenth-century playwright who liked to pass himself off as Shakespeare's by-blow, has Shakespeare, a London prodigal, holding horses for a living. Riding out from the city, playgoers went on horseback to the Theater and Curtain. On his uppers in Finsbury Fields, young Shakespeare awaited them, soliciting custom.

He knew horses, no doubt about it. See the "trampling courser" in *Venus and Adonis,* biting the flies in his fume, or the old nag Petruchio rides to his wedding, "possessed with the glanders and like to mose in the chine, troubled with the lampass . . . full of windgalls, sped with the spavins, rayed with the yellows, past cure of the fives, stark spoiled with the staggers, begnawn with the bots, swayed in the back and shoulder-shotten. . . ." And so on. This is circumstantial, putting it mildly, and Shakespeare in the lost years must have been an ostler.

He knew law pretty well and some imagine him a law clerk, coming up to London to plead suits in superior court. The first scene of *The Tempest,* thick with sailors' argot, says he knew seamanship, so must have sailed. One of his characters likens a round beard to a glover's paring knife, this simile suggesting that Shakespeare, glover's apprentice, put in grudging time in the Woolshop. Other accounts of his time rise from old men's memories. William Beeston, son of Christopher who acted with Shakespeare in the Lord Chamberlain's Men, makes Shakespeare "in his younger years a schoolmaster in the country," an irony too gross for art.

John Aubrey, seventeenth-century gossip, has heard that young Shakespeare exercised his father's trade, a butcher's, according to Aubrey. Remembering the Christmas pantomime in nearby Coventry where the mummers kill a calf, the butcher's apprentice killed his own calf "in a high style," making a speech. This introduces the Butcher Boy of Stratford and predicts the future actor. Polonius, accounted a good actor, played Julius Caesar, killed by Brutus in the Capitol. A brute part of Brutus, Hamlet-Shakespeare thinks, "to kill so capital a calf there." In the last years of the seventeenth century, a parish clerk and sexton of Holy Trinity church recalled how Shakespeare "was formerly in this town bound apprentice to a butcher; but that he run from his master to London, and there was received into the playhouse." Stitching together different traditions, this recollection puts Shakespeare on the road, possessed of the "opportunity to be what he afterwards proved."

Runaway Shakespeare, less chilly than extraterrestrial Shakespeare, meeting us on our own level, accounts for the stubborn currency of the deer-poaching story. The young man who thinks that venison is "nothing so sweet as when it is stolen" is such a man as we see in the mirror. One biographer, indulgent, likens him to that future Bishop of Worcester who in younger days enjoyed dancing, stealing deer and conies, and "wooing of wenches."

One of Diana's foresters, robbing by night, Shakespeare the poacher enters history with Richard Davies, a seventeenth-century clergyman. Rowe chimes in afterwards. Getting into bad company, "common enough to young fellows," Shakespeare, they say, stole venison and rabbits, in particular from Sir Thomas Lucy, squire of Charlecote. Worse, he hung lampoons, "the first essay of his poetry," on the gates of Charlecote's deer park. The lampoons were scurrile, equipping Lucy with the cuckold's horns, also punning on his coat of arms, "three silver pikes gasping" or rising to the surface. A pike is a luce and Lucy was lousy.

Remarking on this connection, Shakespeare, said his annalist, "was much given to all unluckiness." Out in the country, squires did what they pleased, and Shakespeare's neighbor William Combe, squire of Welcombe, locked up a tenant, Hiccox, who didn't show him the deference "it seemeth he looked for." Later Shakespeare, getting into the landlord class, put his boot to this same Hiccox. Just at present, however, he got better than he gave. Sir Thomas "had him oft whipped, and sometimes imprisoned, and at last made him fly his native country." Only the intercession of the Queen saved his skin, or was it Robert Dudley, Earl of Leicester, who interceded?

But the flight from Stratford had its silver lining. Shakespeare, exiled in London, nursed his bitter grievance, then turned it to profit in *The Merry Wives of Windsor*. As this play begins (but not as it gets going), Shakespeare pays attention to a foolish great man, Shallow, J.P. in the County of Gloucester. Justice Shallow owns a deer park, violated by Falstaff, and his coat armor bears the required luces, or rather "louses," says Parson Evans, becoming an old coat well. But Shakespeare the scapegrace isn't visibly there in *The Merry Wives of Windsor*, a cold-blooded farce, and his art, often savage, is never polemical. Part of the buried life, Lucy, others too, rest somewhere in the plays, supplying the playwright with a turn of phrase, "a foolish hanging of the nether lip," etc. Shakespeare's dramatic fiction not being allegory, the characters who people it won't come together again until Judgment.

Charlecote in Shakespeare's time had a warren but no deer park. Getting on without it, Shakespeare learned about deer, parading this in *Love's Labor's Lost*. Omniscient Shakespeare, jack-of-all-trades, is the artist, not the man, though. He had his antennae up, always circling, and what he knew for fact was less than what he let on. Also on his artistic side he was weirdly sympathetic, a condition approaching morbidity. For most, singleminded, "one fire drives out one fire—one nail, one nail." This is Shakespeare's Coriolanus, who doesn't move easily from war to peace, "the casque to the cushion." Shakespeare, quick study, equable, also proleptic, i.e. knowing states and psychologies before he confronts them, makes these transitions without ado.

In the lost years he began writing sonnets. Wordsworth thought that in the sonnets he left a key that unlocked his heart. But the heart is a maker's heart, tumid with other men's passion. Like the chameleon to whom he compared his first great stage villain, he changed colors when he wanted to. Or like the facile young man in his *Lover's Complaint*, he received "all strange forms," appropriate to women not less than men. Then he gave the forms back again, "burning blushes, weeping water, swooning paleness." This impressionable Shakespeare, overendowed with personality, leaves too many calling cards, each with a different address. But he wasn't an airborne spore, and though you glimpse him only rarely, you often hear or overhear him, music on the waters.

Like Othello, traveler among the cannibals, Shakespeare gains for the margin of unknown territory around him. Bigger than biography, he lived other lives on the edges of his own. An Italianate Englishman, he went to Italy in the lost years, meeting Giulio Romano there, toured Denmark with the players and saw the castle at Elsinore beetling over its base, mingled blood with Sidney on the fatal field of Zutphen. Air, playing about his life, compromises its clarity, making the likeness more nearly real.

One account of the lost years puts Shakespeare in Lancashire, teaching school and acting in plays. Real or imagined, the Lancashire story comments on ubiquitous Shakespeare. Immanent in the creation, he is like "adamant," a lodestone and inert but drawing all things to itself. Lancashire, magnetized, is part of his field.

Far to the north of Stratford, near Preston by the sea, lived Alexander Houghton, wealthy recusant and patron of players. In 1580–81 "William Shakeshafte" served this Houghton, and some merge him with William Shakespeare, seventeen when Houghton died. Shakespeare's age seems a problem, even for this precocious young man. Also he still had business nearer home, courting Anne and fathering children. Perhaps, riding hard from Preston, he was able to manage this.

Alexander Houghton, possible patron, died in 1581. He left his musical instruments and "play clothes" to a half brother "if he be minded to keep and do keep players," otherwise to his neighbor and kinsman, Thomas Hesketh, knight. His will, remembering William Shakeshafte, "now dwelling with me," and another servant, Fulk Gyllome, implores Hesketh "most heartily" to take these two under his wing. So perhaps Shakespeare, alias Shakeshafte, passed into Hesketh's service, stage one on the road to London and the theater.

Minded to keep players, Hesketh sent them on tour to entertain his friends. In 1587 they played at Knowsley, the Lancashire seat of the Stanleys, Earls of Derby. Among the guests this Christmas season, two catch the eye, Ursula, the illegitimate daughter of Henry, the fourth earl, and her husband Sir John Salisbury, later eulogized in *Love's Martyr* (1601). To this collection of poems, Shakespeare contributed his enigmatic *Phoenix and Turtle*. Like Hesketh, the Stanleys patronized players, sponsoring their own company, Lord Strange's Men. Shakespeare's *Titus Andronicus* was played by Strange's Men, and actors from this company formed the nucleus of his company, the Lord Chamberlain's, in 1594. London actors on tour stopped off at the Stanley seats, giving Shakespeare his heaven-sent opportunity to meet them. He had the chance to hobnob with their patron too, Ferdinando, Lord Strange, fifth Earl of Derby. Some, liking a near relation between the art and life, think this Ferdinando sat as model for Shakespeare's Ferdinand, King of Navarre.

Lancashire, Catholic and feudal, is part of Shakespeare's story. In 1599, helping to negotiate a ground lease for the Globe Theater, he dealt with Thomas Savage, one of two trustees. This London goldsmith came from Rufford in Lancashire, domicile of Sir Thomas Hesketh. Like his kinsman Houghton, Hesketh was Catholic. Brave or foolhardy, he had a priest hole in his house, and after he died his widow sheltered Catholics too. Walter Roche and John Cottom, Stratford schoolmasters, were both Lancashire men. Cottom got his job in Stratford via Thomas Jenkins, Shakespeare's chief instructor. This Jenkins, taking degrees at St. John's College, Oxford, hospitable to Catholics, had a fellow student, Edmund Campion. Arraigned with Campion, Cottom's younger brother died a martyr in 1582. "Really, universally, relations stop nowhere." This is James' great truth, luminous for Shakespeare's story.

Cottom, persona non grata in Stratford, resigned his mastership in 1581. He went home to Lancashire, ten miles from Lea Hall, estate of Alexander Houghton. The families knew each other and a John Cottom is named in Houghton's will. As this plot thickens, Shakespeare travels north with a letter of introduction, seeking service with Houghton, first as a teacher ("schoolmaster in the country"), then as a player. The player's role is the important one, and getting on at Lea Hall demanded his best performance. In Lancashire, "sink of popery," they wanted their Shakeshafte a Catholic.

Pieced out with conjecture, these are the facts, discrete like iron filings. Shakespeare, "hardhearted adamant," makes them coalesce. Finding sequences everywhere, he activates this tendency in his biographers. Was he a Catholic? Some of them think so. "He died a Papist," said Parson Davies, first begetter of the deer-poaching story. Deathbed conversion introduces another Shakespeare, sentimental like his father or his villainous Edmund, putting things right at the end of the play. Some good he meant to do, despite his own nature.

Lopsidedness makes the bowling ball run the way it has to, and elliptical Shakespeare, true to his nature, is like this. Wearing "ideas" easily, he found nothing to offend him in Catholicism, per se. Under Queen Mary, he would have been Catholic. (For the upcoming reign, he made no promises.) Hermetic but not a secret anything, not a convicted theist or atheist in his closet, Shakespeare went to church routinely, knowing what was good for him. Catholic Ben Jonson got in trouble for his faith, and Marlowe and friends, playing adolescent games, learned how to spell God backwards. Shakespeare didn't do either. Unlike Donne of St. Paul's he didn't pose in his shroud, and no one found him prostrate before the altar, like his near-contemporary, the poet George Herbert. Anglicans, middle roaders, worshipped a moderately pious God, not fire-breathing like Calvin's or Ignatius Loyola's. This suited "irenic" Shakespeare, peace-loving from boyhood on.

Holy Trinity, where he worshipped, was vandalized in his time, its carvings mutilated and the chancel with its misericords boarded off from the rest of the church. No comment, he said, when they asked him about this. John Shakespeare bore a hand in the vandalizing, and falling apart in later life, showed a backslider's bad conscience. Shakespeare, if he felt this deity in his bosom, never let on. The testament in the tiles begot no comment either, except for its language, "words, words, words." That was what he cared about, and the words crop up in *Hamlet*. Lapworth, Sir William Catesby's estate where Campion sheltered, lay just north of Stratford, but Shakespeare took no notice of the martyred Jesuit. (He noticed Catesby, though, potting an ancestor in *Richard III*.) His imperturbable temper fostered a great cold, and martyrs like Campion, even shifty Cranmer, were outside his ken.

When Shakespeare was seventeen, his Uncle Harry embarrassed them in Stratford, not paying his church tithes. Or he wore a hat to church instead of the plain "statute cap" required by law. Puritans jibbed at the law, and some call Uncle Harry a Puritan. Shakespeare's son-in-law Hall, Susanna's husband, showing his colors looks like a Puritan too. Susanna, Shakespeare's first child, fell foul of the authorities, not taking Easter communion. She looks like a Catholic. Shakespeare, wishing them all well, left them to their opinions. Law-abiding, he paid his tithes, took communion, and honored the dress code.

Richard Barton was Stratford's vicar in Shakespeare's young manhood. He came from Coventry, a hotbed of reform, and Puritans admired his zeal and godly fitness. For the men of reform, symbols were battleflags. They wanted English clergy to wear the black gown of Geneva. Anglicans detested this, and Barton when he officiated wore a proper surplice with sleeves. The Clown in *All's Well* hints that Puritans, conforming outwardly, hid a black heart with the surplice. His wit is impartial, though, no respector of creeds, and elsewhere he lumps Puritans and Catholics together. One eats meat, the other leaves it alone, but "howsome'er their hearts are severed in religion, their heads are both one," not stuffed with intelligence, furnished with horns. This likeness comprehends Anglicans too. Religious professors, different on the surface, didn't differ in last things, skeptical Shakespeare thought. All might jowl horns together "like any deer i' the herd."

A "SHALLOW PLASH" or pool, Stratford bred a restless Shakespeare. He was like his character who

> stands upon a promontory
> And spies a far-off shore where he would tread.

So far, this "would" was only inclination, and energy, unused, fusted in him. "Lost in a thorny wood," he sought a way but strayed from it,

"Not knowing how to find the open air." Characters in his early plays have a telltale habit, raising their eyes. They want to plunge in the deep, "see the wonders of the world abroad," or

> seek their fortunes farther than at home,
> Where small experience grows.

Setting off for Milan, Valentine, young gentleman of Verona, speaks a proverb: "Home-keeping youth have ever homely wits." Shakespeare, living dully at home, "sluggardized," taking the force of this. "Not being tried and tutored in the world," he couldn't be a perfect man.

Shakespeare's Stratford acquaintance thought they knew him well enough, the "good honest fellow" patronized by old Merry-cheeks. Letting them think so, he sketched for posterity the role of Sweet Will. Sometimes the mask slipped and they glimpsed the prodigal, a recurring figure in the plays, also the "prodigious son." Like his Shylock the Jew and Antonio the Merchant who doesn't know why he's sad, he stood outside their comedy, qualifying its ardors. Baleful Don John and melancholy Jaques are other roles of his, still unappeased when the rest go off hand in hand. A gifted mimic but passive, he carried mirth or anger the way the flint bears fire. If they rubbed or chafed him, he showed "a hasty spark," then went cold again.

In his first play, *Henry VI, Part One*, he made a better playwright than poet, and his poet's imagination was seized only once. This was when he invoked the story of Daedalus, fabled artificer, and his unlucky son:

> in that sea of blood my boy did drench
> His overmounting spirit, and there died,
> My Icarus, my blossom, in his pride.

As these first Henry plays end, the image of the artificer is still working in Shakespeare's mind. King Henry is Daedalus, anyway in hope. "I, Daedalus," he says, casting himself in this role. As it turns out, the role is beyond him, and Henry is a maladroit hero. Aspiring to flight, he fits his son with wings, but "the fool was drowned" and this Daedalus dies also, caught in the trammels. More devious or ruthless, Shakespeare made good his escape.

In 1569, the year of John Shakespeare's bailiwick, the players came to Stratford. Times being slack in London, they took their show to the country, like the cry of players who appear at Elsinore or practice on drunken Christopher Sly. The Queen's Men came first, then the Earl of Worcester's Men. A wagon traveled with them, hauling props and costumes. Nuance wasn't part of their actors' equipment, and like Termagant, roaring god of the Saracens, they sawed the air and split their lungs. Shakespeare, different from fastidious Hamlet, liked this robustious style. "It out-Herods Herod." Some biographers set him, goggle-eyed, before these touring players, guessing at his future vocation. For the man without "views," the player's role seems foreordained.

In the seventies and eighties, the players came back often. Led by James Burbage, builder of the first London playhouse, Leicester's Men played Stratford in 1573. A decade after this, Worcester's Men, touring the neighborhood, had with them young Ned Alleyn, a boy of seventeen. Later at the Rose in London he spoke Marlowe's mighty lines. In 1587 five companies came to Stratford, the Queen's Men among them. Specially chosen by the Master of the Revels from among the best actors in the land, men of this company, habited in scarlet coats, were servants of Queen Elizabeth. Richard Tarlton, a famous clown, made the troupe preeminent until he died in the Armada year. When the Queen was "out of good humor, he could un-dumpish her at his pleasure."

Players in Stratford performed in the Gild Hall. Occupying the southeast corner of the ground floor, the Council Chamber gave them their tiring-house. At the upper end of the chamber, they erected a temporary stage. Shakespeare's people, taking in the action, sat on wooden benches, athwartships in the Hall. They saw plays like *The Famous Victories of Henry V* where roistering Prince Hal, not yet Shakespeare's fishy hero, runs a crazy gamut from tavern brawler to king. Blood, supplied by a pig's bladder hidden under a doublet, drenched the stage. Urged on by King Cambises, actors in the Gild Hall, sparing nobody's feelings, cut out a little boy's heart. Muly Mahomet, heroic Moor, stood before the crowd with a lump of lion's flesh on the point of his sword. Orestes, not classical but a brutal English revenger, made mincemeat of his mother. This was Shakespeare's kind of play, blood-boltered.

William Knell, star performer in the *Famous Victories,* was one of the Queen's Men. He never made it to Stratford in 1587. As the troupe moved north, it paused briefly in Oxfordshire. There, on June 13, Knell, brawling with a fellow actor, took a sword in the throat. So the company, arrived in Stratford, needed a man to make up its full complement. Shakespeare, "tickle o' the sere," was twenty-three this summer, primed like a gun and ready for use. When the players departed, did he follow their wagon, leaving Stratford behind? His career in the London theater lay just over the horizon. It needs its beginning and this was a way to begin.

4

Shadows of Himself

H E WAS WONT to go to his native country once a year,"
said John Aubrey, Shakespeare's anecdotal biographer.
Nourishing soil to his weary Antaeus, Stratford set him
back on his feet. First, though, it was the place he had to
flee from. Having reached his majority, that is what he did, turning
away from wife and children. At the end, his plays all written or playing
out the play, he rejoined them.

Tourists from London, visiting Shakespeare's birthplace, make the
journey by rail in a matter of hours, even with a change at Leamington
Spa. Shakespeare's journey to London took him four days. He left no
itinerary and no letters home tell of his progress. But other travelers
before and after him fill in the blanks, and Shakespeare in the plays
functions as his own chronicler, filtering the life through art.

Going to London, he went "up." (Stratford, a hundred miles distant,
was "down.") Whatever route he took, it led over gullied highways,
slippery with mud and hard to pass at all seasons, worst in winter.
Farm wagons and the heavy springless coaches favored by the well-to-
do settled in the "cledgy" soil. Law of the realm required common folk
to spend six days each summer putting the roads of their parish in
order. Mostly, however, this statute, unhonored, stood like "forfeits"
in a barber shop, extracted teeth hung up for show. Men of property,

indifferent to commonweal, looked after their own, not looking to right or left. Surveying England's highways, William Harrison didn't like what he saw. "Such as have land lying upon the sides of the ways do utterly neglect to ditch and scour their drains and water courses for better avoidance of the winter waters." A traveler himself, he groused about this, saying how the rutted roads filled with standing water, "very noisome" or stinking "for such as travel by the same."

Most traffic up to London went by pack horse in the carrier's charge. Stratford carriers, their goods sacked in panniers, carried ginger roots, cured ham, and live turkeys, dropping their load at Charing Cross, a country village west of the city. Then the carrier took the road back to Stratford. Like the vault in Gloucester church, conveying whispers at a distance, he plucked the sound from your mouth in the Midlands and made it heard on the banks of the Thames. A hackneyman too, he let out horses to travelers. Men of means, pressed for time, hired post horses, but at three pence a mile this wasn't an option available to young Shakespeare.

Jounced up and down, travelers on horseback needed "brawn" buttocks and a stiff upper lip. The carrier, a petty tyrant, beat the roads "out of measure." Sometimes the purse-taker revenged this injury, and then, said a traveler, "the voyage miscarries." Rogues and vagabonds, flotsam of the wars or set adrift by enclosures, roamed the open country, rendezvousing at "bowsing kens," alehouses along the road. In proportion to the whole, there were more of them in Shakespeare's England than ever before or since. When he was a boy of five, sheriffs and their constabulary, sweeping the countryside, netted 13,000 of these "masterless men." This wasn't Robin Hood's England, and they took from rich and poor without distinction. "Young men must live," says Falstaff.

Hand in glove with the purse-taker, "setters" or spies kept an eye out for booty. On to their tricks, First Carrier in *Henry IV*, Part One is wary of these highwaymen, "St. Nicholas' clerks." Shakespeare, making entries in his table book, distinguished their degrees. Some were common footpads, "long-staff sixpenny strikers." Larding the lean earth, Falstaff went on foot, a reluctant "landraker" unhorsed by his confederates. Some, coming up in their profession, went booted and spurred like Gamaliel Ratsey, a brigand with a taste for stage plays, Shakespeare's *Hamlet* included. Nabbed by the law, all swung on the gallows. But fear never yet made a good deterrent, and solitary travelers, not wanting to be fleeced, rode with the carriers, looking for safety in numbers.

Shakespeare didn't do this. Befitting his chosen profession, he walked. That was how the players traveled, young Ben Jonson, for instance, glimpsed by a contemporary ambling beside the wagon, "lapped in a player's old cast cloak." Under the law, "strolling players" were vagabonds, lumped together with fencers, bear keepers, and minstrels. Sheltering beneath a great man's protection, they wore his badge or livery or carried his license when they went on tour. Otherwise, "stripped naked from the middle upwards," they were whipped in public until the lash drew blood.

Alone or in company, Shakespeare headed south into Worcestershire and Oxfordshire, or he took the road to Banbury and dropped down from there. Following Banbury High Road, he crossed the Vale of Red Horse, "fruitful and pleasant." (Dugdale, hunting antiquities, described it a half century later.) The vale got its name from the figure of a horse, cut in the red loam of the hills. This remembered the Earl of Warwick, Shakespeare's Kingmaker, who postures colorfully in *Henry VI*, Part Three. In the Wars of the Roses, he fought a famous battle at Towton to the north. The issue being doubtful, the Kingmaker plunged a sword in his horse's breast, vowing to fight on foot with the meanest of his men. He was one of Shakespeare's harebrained heroes, governed by spleen.

Going east, Shakespeare came to Compton Wynyates, an ancient pile of redbrick, yellow stone, and black timber in a hollow between the hills. Katherine of Aragon stayed in the manor house. This was in her salad days before King Henry, sated, put her away. Nearby was the field of Edgehill, its steep face barren of trees in Shakespeare's time and sharper in outline then than now. A battle nobody won began the Civil War at Edgehill, fifty years after Shakespeare passed through. Recording this for posterity, a revolutionary zealot said that "The Lord made the Red Horse of His wrath ride about most furiously to the ruin of our enemies."

Three crosses and a Maypole dominated Banbury, fifteen miles from Stratford. This market town was famous for its cream cheese, wafer thin. The crosses and Maypole, incensing relics of popery, were pulled down by Puritans in Shakespeare's young manhood. Silent on these godly men, he remembered the cream cheese. Bardolph in *The Merry Wives*, eyeing Slender disdainfully, thinks of this cheese.

In these eastern precincts of Warwickshire, stone farmhouses, grayish brown, are dark against the fields. Linnets nest in the gorsebushes, rooks build in the high trees, and the cuckoo, ominous to Shakespeare, sings all summer long. In country inns beside the road, this traveler broke his fast at the host's table, paying sixpence a meal. He paid a penny for his bed, lying in clean sheets "wherein no man hath been lodged since they came from the laundress or out of the water." Peripatetic Harrison liked these country inns, "very well furnished with napery, bedding, and tapestry." They weren't always like that, and a gloomy Shakespeare singled out one of them, "the most villainous house in all London road for fleas." No chamber pot in the bedroom, his traveler says, "and then we leak in your chimney, and your chamber lye"—urine—"breeds fleas like a loach." This fresh-water fish, infested with lice, resembled the lodgers and the chamber they lay in.

Just over the border in Buckinghamshire, a side road brought Shakespeare to the hamlet of Grendon Underwood. Putting up for the night, he lodged at the Ship Inn, a watering place for the locals. Tradition makes him say that only two people in the place were worth talking to. He pulped the two of them, however, getting hints for Snout the tinker and Starveling the tailor, "rude mechanicals." Aubrey pieces out this story, deferring Shakespeare's travels to a later time. On a lucky night in Grendon, malapropisms rained down on his head and he took delighted notice, finding "the humor of the constable in 'Midsummer Night's Dream.'" Shakespeare's art, reportorial, imitated nature, a one-to-one relation, Aubrey considered.

However, he got the play wrong. Conscientious biographers, setting him straight, opt for *Much Ado, Love's Labor's Lost,* or *Measure for Measure.* Each has its foolish constable, prone to "misplacing" words. A fool who stumbles on truth where the truth eludes his betters, he lives near the heart of Shakespeare's psychology. Meeting his foolish-wise man on the London road (he wasn't Dogberry, etc., brazen life being less costly than art), Shakespeare met him first in Scripture. As for Snout and Starveling, tongue-tied in their simplicity, Duke Theseus prefers them to the parroters of learned eloquence, saucy and audacious. He is saying that the heart of a fool is in his mouth but the mouth of the wise is in his heart.

Shakespeare coming up to London followed a well-traveled road. His schoolfellow Richard Quinley, a bailiff on a mission, took this road back to Stratford ten years or so later. Returning from Warwickshire fifty years before, Leland, King Henry's librarian, said what he saw along the way. Like Shakespeare, he came over the Chiltern Hills and through the Vale of Aylesbury, "tedious and ill to pass by" in wet time. Leland found the Chilterns full of enclosures. England, balanced on a tickle point, already inclined to the future.

At Uxbridge, twelve miles northwest of London Wall, the Banbury road merged with the road from Oxford, both still so called today. Where the Banbury road went straight on, the Oxford road, leaving Stratford, branched off to the right after Clopton Bridge. Shorter and more direct, it crossed a corner of Worcestershire, not much peopled in Shakespeare's time. Isolated cottages, wattle-and-daub, still emphasize the loneliness, and rounded gateways, some free standing, front on "bare ruined choirs." Unaspiring, these Norman arches remember Simon de Montfort, not humble himself but limited and knowing this. The broken buildings, their stones plundered by up-and-coming men, tell of the Dissolution of religious houses, recent history when Shakespeare left Stratford.

Refording the river Stour in southern Warwickshire, the London road entered Oxfordshire just beyond Long Compton. In this Cotswold country, more up and down than Shakespeare's, split sapling fences give way to stone, and dressed limestone, honey-colored, faces the houses. Between Long Compton and Chipping Norton, a Bronze Age survival, "Stonehenge of the Cotswolds," meets the traveler on his way south. The Rollright Stones, seventy of them forming a circle, stand like a comitatus, the King's Men. Summoning the long past, the burial chamber is the Whispering Knights. Just over the hedge in Warwickshire is the King's Stone, "nine feet high and upwards," an awed traveler said. Old legend reports that Rollo the Norwegian, a hammer of Englishmen, was crowned on this spot.

Bloody ground, it isn't special, even for its antiquity. Blood soaks the Vale of Aylesbury, lying athwart Shakespeare's other route to London. About Bernwood Forest, west of the vale, Danes and English slew each other, and Camden the historian rehearsed their encounters in his Latin history of the British Isles. Much of his history is sound and fury, first Romans, then Saxons, Danes, and Normans, then medieval English fighting internecine wars. In Shakespeare's boyhood mock Danes and Saxons, mumming for the lord of Kenilworth Castle, still banged each other like "rams at their rut." Reformers, the same who took order with Banbury, shut down this Hock-Day Play, decreeing a sour peace. But Cavaliers and Roundheads went at it again in the age after Shakespeare's. His time was an interlude, calm between storms. A peaceable man who doted on carnage, he made the most of this.

West of Rollright Stones is Barton-on-the-Heath, where Shakespeare's cousin Lambert lived, beyond it misty Gloucestershire. Falstaff and Shallow have a sentimental meeting there. After fifty years, they still recall "the chimes at midnight." At Pebworth in Gloucestershire, a bibulous Shakespeare stopped to wet his thirst. Doggerel verses, recorded in the eighteenth century, proclaim this. Tradition, doing its best for Shakespeare, says he "loved a glass for the pleasure of society."

East of Woodstock, its royal park numinous with ancient oaks and beeches, Shakespeare's road took in Oxford, where Protestant martyrs, their names hallowed to English people, died for the faith in the reign of Queen Mary. Endlessly vacillating, Archbishop Cranmer found his courage at the end. Latimer, best of the Reformers, bade the chaplain who died with him play the man. "Be of good comfort, Master Ridley," said Latimer at the stake. "We shall this day light such a candle by God's grace in England as, I trust, shall never be put out." The rhetoric is Shakespearean, the day 16 October 1555. Shakespeare, born nine years later, had reason to know it. He passed through Oxford many times on his way north and south, staying at the Crown Tavern in Cornmarket Street. A stone's throw away, the martyrs were burned. But Shakespeare left all that alone.

After Uxbridge, the traveler approached the city via Southall and Acton, "a pretty thoroughfare" connecting them. Shepherd's Bush was just a name, not a local habitation. Later, the center of gravity shifting, London moved to fill this vacuum. In Shakespeare's lifetime, its population doubled. His city still meant East London, however, not the great wen of today. The long Uxbridge Road, dividing Notting Hill from Kensington, ran along the northern edge of Hyde Park. Hereabouts the biggest landmark was the "triple tree" at Tyburn, place of executions. A year or two after his arrival in London, reminiscent Shakespeare milked it for a joke. In *Love's Labor's Lost*, his three young men make a "triumvery," the shape of "Love's Tyburn." Simpleminded, these three deserved hanging.

Where Tyburn brook flowed south, later hiding itself beneath Buckingham Palace, the Uxbridge Road, now Oxford Street, continued east to the city, passing through St. Giles in the Fields. A country village, it remembered the hanging and burning of Sir John Oldcastle, heretic or protomartyr, depending on who wrote the book. He gave Shakespeare much trouble with the powers-that-be. In *Henry IV*, Part One, an irreverent version of history, this Protestant hero shows up as a fat man, Lord of Misrule. (Martyrs, Protestant or Catholic, were only grist to Shakespeare's mill.) Descendants taking offense, a chastened Shakespeare rewrote his play, and "the fat knight, hight Oldcastle," turned into Falstaff.

Remote in St. Giles Fields, the "lazar house," a leper hospital, occupied the site where modern Charing Cross Road meets Shaftesbury Avenue. (Henry VIII dissolved the hospital, wanting its endowment.) Condemned men, chained together "two and two, Newgate fashion," rested in the fields en route to the gallows. Marched out from the ancient prison just inside London Wall, they drank ale from St. Giles'

Bowl, "their last refreshing in this life," then went west to their deaths. Death was by hanging but not all at once, and men dangled, still alive, at the rope's end. After an interval, the hangman disemboweled them with a neat thrust. Crowds at Tyburn watched the hangings, a popular diversion. Shakespeare, heading the other way, skirted Gray's Inn, celebrated for revels and masques. Early in the 1590s, a disorderly crowd, assembled in the great hall of this London law school, witnessed his *Comedy of Errors.*

Gray's Inn Fields, providing cover for coneys and game fowl, extended north from the Inn gateway to Kentish Town and Islington. Londoners hunted in the fields, today a concrete warren. Sir Francis Bacon, one of the "fellowship" of judges, barristers, and students, laid out the famous gardens and planted the catalpa tree, still green. This "new philosopher," Shakespeare's great opposite, pronounced on the truth of things, universal, not parochial. The world was unruly like old Typhon, a mischievous presence from the underground, but his adamantine net held it fast. Shakespeare, gifted in parody, might have written Bacon, at least until the exercise palled. But Bacon, of all men, could not have written Shakespeare.

Posts and chains at Holborn Bars, a brook or bourn in a hollow, separated London's suburbs from the city. Gerard the herbalist had a house in Holborn, between Staple Inn and Chancery Lane. In gardens around the house he grew his own tobacco, sovereign against cruddy vapors, also "apples of love," tomatoes. This exotic growth, brought over from the New World and prized as an aphrodisiac, looked like a bad bet in England's soggy climate but the herbalist, a cunning gardener, had a green thumb. Standing tall near his gardens, timbered houses at Staple Inn played tricks on the passerby. Each had two or three front doors and culminated in two or three gables. All one house inside, they faced the street like separate tenements, narrow and cramped. Behind the double or triple facade, well-to-do merchants lived in a high style, keeping this to themselves.

A palimpsest, Shakespeare's London showed the past through the present. Newgate wasn't new but first of all a Roman gate. Near the gate stood Grey Friars, an ancient monastery converted in Shakespeare's time to an asylum for orphans and "decayed" poor. George Peele, one of Shakespeare's forerunners in drama, grew up in this asylum, Christ's Hospital as it was then. Still walled when Shakespeare saw it first, the city proper began at Newgate. Through the archway that pierced the walls, he entered London, late in the 1580s. Nobody knew him when he came up. An inconspicuous man about theater, he was "Johannes Factotum," doing odd jobs. Later, this changed. Paying more than he promised, Shakespeare is like that Roman hero of his who covered discretion with a simpleton's coat,

> As gardeners do with ordure hide those roots
> That shall first spring and be most delicate.

Shakespeare remained in London for upwards of twenty years. This matches his youthful time in Stratford, preparation for things to come. A "crescive" or growing time, it had its rich harvest, so far unguessed at. Growing like "summer grass, fastest by night,/Unseen," Stratford Shakespeare hid his powers. Now it was time to enlarge them.

FIRST OF ALL a survivor, Shakespeare took strength from the city he lived in, also a thick skin and his unsurprised demeanor. His art, faithful to its context plus some other things, reflects this. Like Dr. Johnson, born and bred a provincial but citified in his bones, he shows more vividly when you place him, "bright metal on a sullen ground." For Shakespeare's London, "sullen" doesn't do justice, though. His flashes of humor, often coarse, sometimes cruel, tell of the dreadful-buoyant city. So does his "lower-case" psychology, a scandal to conceptualizers like his exact contemporary, Galileo. Indifferent to the heavens, no "optic glass" for him, Shakespeare keeps his eyes down, absorbed in "our terrene state," this parish on this side of the wall. Curiosity consumes him but begins at home. Shakespeare's readers will want to know the city that provoked it.

London in the 1580s, though insular, made room for difference. It wasn't yet centrifugal and the center still held. Afer Rome "the second city in Christendom for greatness," its name resounded in the four corners. To provincial Shakespeare Coventry looked big, but London, ten times bigger, gave him his "critical mass." When Elizabeth became queen, 100,000 people lived in her capital, at least twice this number by the century's end. Foreigners, making a pardonable mistake, thought it "the country and England but the city therein."

Most of Shakespeare's contemporaries squeezed into a narrow corridor running along the Thames from Shadwell down river to Westminster, the royal enclave, on the west. When Shakespeare came to Westminster to play before the Queen, the wherry that carried him passed the wall-begirt Temple on the north bank, once the London residence of the Knights Templars, below this the old Carmelite monastery of Whitefriars. Later a playhouse flourished in the ruined precincts, and outlaws called Alsatians sheltered there from the law. Players and outlaws went hand in hand, the law looking on both with disfavor. Beginning his career with *Henry VI*, Shakespeare set a famous scene in the gardens of the Temple. His murdered King Henry, much buffeted in life, is committed in death to Whitefriars.

Palaces, brick and freestone, lined the river's edge. Baynard's Castle was one, near the western end of Queen Victoria Street. Richard III, stagemanaging his henchmen, is offered the crown in this castle. "Play the maid's part," they tell him. "Still answer nay, and take it." Having energy to burn, he follows this counsel, touching a responsive chord in one aspiring playwright.

Behind the riverfront, a beguiling facade, seethed a pressure cooker, squat one-storey cottages, three-storey tenements built of loam and lath, shops, and parish churches, north of them the industrial quarter. Inside this finite space, Londoners, heated particles, collided in Brownian motion. They lived in twisting streets and alleys dating back to the Middle Ages, Fish Lane, Pudding Lane, Idol Lane, Bread Street, Friday Street, Milk Street. The Mermaid Tavern, drinking haunt of the Sons of Ben, stood on Bread Street, running south to the river from Cheapside. Francis Beaumont, poet and playwright, remembered this tavern:

> What things have we seen,
> Done at the Mermaid! heard words that have been
> So nimble, and so full of subtle flame,
> As if that everyone from whence they came,
> Had meant to put his whole wit in a jest
> And had resolved to live a fool the rest
> Of his dull life.

Often the jests were sodden. "Immoderate quaffing," a vice of English, plagued many in Shakespeare's London. Middlesex, London's county, accommodated almost 900 taverns. Shakespeare mined them for place names, and the Pegasus in Cheapside turns up in his *Taming of the Shrew*. Mostly, tavern employees get the back of his hand. He put little store in "a tapster's arithmetic" and thought a tapster's oath, like a lover's, synonymous with lying. In Eastcheap, known for tippling houses, hung the sign of the Boar's Head, sacred to Falstaff. Where he drank "sherris sack," London poor got drunk on "small" beer and ale, weaker than they liked it. Prince Hal, coming into his kingdom, thinks back regretfully to this small beer.

"Cheap," from an Anglo-Saxon word, meant to bargain, and "cheapening" or bargaining lit up dull lives in the great markets on Westcheap and Eastcheap. The one continuous passageway crossing the city, Cheapside paralleled the river between the Tower and St.

Paul's. South of this passageway dwelt the London cockney within earshot of Bow Bell, sounding from the church of St. Mary-le-bow. Cunning on his own turf, the cockney was the ultimate provincial. "Is charcoal made?" one asks another. "I had thought all things had been made at London, yet I did never see no charcoals made there. By my troth, I had thought that they had grown upon trees."

Elbowed by the locals, Shakespeare found London's streets hard going. Sanitation was a tradeoff, and this walker in the city picked his way with care. Lead-lined pipes, little aqueducts castellated on top, brought water to the city from Tyburn brook and elsewhere, outside the walls. Otherwise, Londoners drew from the river. Conduits, like the one in Hog Lane, washed the streets and people, but water from the conduits, carried in three-gallon tankards, had to be fetched by hand. Labor lost, Shakespeare's Jack Cade considered. Enthroned in Cheapside, he charges and commands that "the pissing conduit run nothing but claret wine this first year of our reign."

"Such a thundering" in the pressure cooker! Hammers beat in one place, tubs were hooped in another, pots clinked in a third, in a fourth water-tankards ran at tilt. At every corner, men, women, and children congregated in shoals, putting houses in peril. Posts were set up to strengthen the houses, "lest with justling one another . . . [the people] should shoulder them down." Coaches, once rare, now the mark of an elder brother, lumbered through the two-wheeled carts and barrows, "so as the streets of London are almost stopped up." Porters sweat under burdens, merchants toted their money bags, chapmen, "as if they were at leapfrog," skipped from one shop to another. Nobody ever stood still.

A tight fit and malodorous, Shakespeare's city clamored for attention. Like the boy who cried wolf, it did this too often, and Londoners, inured, wore flaps on their ears. Street cries split the air: "hot peas," "small coals," "new brooms, green brooms." From London's prisons, five in the city, came a different cry: "Bread and meat, for the Lord's sake, to the poor prisoners of Newgate!" Beggars, holding out a wooden bowl or clackdish, rattled the cover, crying for alms. Coster-mongers sold apples and balladmongers their sensational broadsides, like the ballad of a monstrous child born in Kent, God's judgment on its immoral mother. Whores, known as "traffic," inveigled men into brothels where the pimp, a "crossbiter," stole their money and clothes.

Giordano Bruno, an Italian visitor, not easily scandalized, made a journey by night through Shakespeare's London. He said the city could "boast of a lower population which in disrespect, incivility, coarseness, boorishness, and sheer savagery of nature" yielded to none in the world.

Up top in the sunlight stood Bruno's friend Sir Philip Sidney, "the glass of fashion and the mold of form," below him in darkness "a mixture of desperadoes, vagrants, scullions thrown out by their masters, jack-anapes, castaways, unemployables, the useless and the shiftless." This *lumpenproletariat*, Shakespeare's "general gender," is always just around the corner in his plays. The "beast with many heads," he called them. Ready for mischief, their cry is "Go fetch fire. . . . Pluck down forms, windows, anything." In one of the plays, overpeering their "list" or bounds, they tear an inoffensive poet to pieces.

"A NEEDY ADVENTURER" in the metropolis, Shakespeare scraped a living as he could. Tradition, supplying the details, says he got work as a printer's devil, reading proof or setting type for Richard Field, late of Stratford. Or James Burbage, theater builder, connected by some with the Burbages of Stratford, took him on as a hired hand in his livery stable. Dr. Johnson, building on hearsay, sponsored Shakespeare, major domo of the Horseboys' Brigade. Waiting at the playhouse door, he held the horses of gallants "too proud, too tender, or too idle to walk," doing his job so readily that "every man as he alighted called for Will Shakespeare." After a while, this entrepreneur hired others to wait under his inspection. They had their password: "I am Shakespeare's boy, sir." This, Johnson thought, was "the dawn of better fortunes."

But the dawn came on slowly and Shakespeare "lived for a time by very mean employments." Johnson's out-at-heels Bard resembles Robert Greene, prototype of the artist in his garret. The role doesn't suit Shakespeare, though, closer in type to his fellow countryman, John Sadler, grandson of a local alderman. Leaving Stratford for London some years after Shakespeare, this Sadler found his niche in Bucklersbury, home of grocers and pepperers. Shakespeare knew the shops, sweet-smelling, where the grocers "in simple time" sold dried herbs or simples. The grocer's apprentice, honoring his priorities, rose like a "nova," new star, in London's sky. Before he died he got title to much land in the New World. Hamlet, less respectful of the good life than Shakespeare, had a phrase for this: "Spacious in the possession of dirt." Meanwhile the Muses mourned Robert Greene, "late deceased in beggary."

Shakespeare, writing Greene's epitaph in the mid 1590s, was already a man of substance, far outstripping his rivals, the University Wits. Greene distinguished between him and these poets and playwrights, "quondam acquaintance." None of them, he said bitterly, would ever "prove an usurer." Did Shakespeare, studying Shylock, take "A breed for barren metal of his friend"? Some suggest that he did, and the suggestion, outrageous to Bardolaters, has the merit of accounting for his rapid ascent. In May 1592 "Willelmus Shackspere," looking for a mark in Cheapside, lent £7 to John Clayton, up from the country. Later he sued to recover his money, no mean sum. Few biographers mention this unedifying story, supposing that the money lender could not have been their William. Within a few years a man of property in London, Shakespeare appears in the Subsidy Rolls. Tax collectors, assessing him, rate the new arrival higher than his neighbors, Richard and Cuthbert Burbage, already famous in the world of London theater. In the next decade, a strolling player, commenting on his fellow actors, has heard "of some that have gone to London very meanly and have come in time to be exceeding wealthy." Many see Shakespeare in this tale of the poor boy made good.

In the Augustan Age, Alexander Pope, himself an outsider skilled in self preservation, looked at Shakespeare with a considering eye. Pope's Swan of Avon, called by others "the divine, the matchless,"

> For gain, not glory, winged his roving flight,
> And grew immortal in his own despite.

Intimating a piece of truth, the couplet is either/or in its psychology, however. For Shakespeare, poet in his closet writing sonnets to his mistress' eyebrow, plus hardheaded businessman speculating in "futures," the gain and glory went together. (The type, not uncommon, still has its exemplars, and perhaps Chaucer in the age before him was like that.) Shakespeare bears a part in the stories that present him, shadows of himself. But he lived along a wide spectrum where different imperatives asked his attention, and his rise is more spectacular than that of the single-minded man.

One way or another, London Shakespeare knew how to get on. This was his long suit, setting him apart from other great men, Mozart, for instance, down and out in Paris. "He is too sincere, not active enough, too susceptible to illusions, too little aware of the means of achieving success." Grimm, Mozart's patron, said this. "Here, in order to succeed, one must be artful, enterprising, and bold." Enterprising in art, not life, Mozart let money run through his fingers. For this protégé's sake, his patron wished him less genius, twice as much of the other thing. Adding halfpence to the pence, provident Shakespeare made the sums mount up. John Shakespeare's son, he knew what he didn't want to be.

One account, recorded early, makes him a "serviture," doing the bidding of actors in the playhouse. In this underclass were money gatherers, prop keepers, stage hands, and prompters. Reciting a stage tradition, Edmund Malone, Shakespeare's greatest scholar, says his first theater job was that of prompter's attendant or callboy. This job was what he made of it. Some in London's theaters, elevated subsequently "to the highest dignities," first came on stage "in the quality of mutes, joint-stools, flower pots, and tapestry hangings." So, perhaps, this Johannes Factotum.

He needed a passe-partout to the theater, and most likely the Queen's Men supplied it. This company, playing in Stratford just at the time Shakespeare came up, dominated London's theater world in the years of his apprenticeship. The Queen's Men had their competition, actors called for the Lord High Admiral and the Lords of Pembroke, Sussex, and Strange. Early Shakespeare, a freelance spreading the wealth, wrote for all these companies or none of the above. The records that ought to declare his allegiance went up in flames at Whitehall Palace, three years after he died. But the Queen's Men in the 1580s took first place among equals, playing at Court at least seventeen times. This looks like the company for Shakespeare.

The earliest full-dress account of his life, Nicholas Rowe's, has him "received into the company then in being, at first in a very mean rank." Unlike Marlowe, powerfully connected and university bred, he lacked credentials. His apprenticeship served him well, though, and where Marlowe remained a great poet, writing plays, Shakespeare, incidentally a poet, made himself a playwright.

He had at his disposal "his admirable wit and the natural turn of it to the stage." This, said Rowe, "soon distinguished him, if not as an extraordinary actor, yet as an excellent writer." The acting came first and he did it "exceedingly well." (Aubrey reports this, drawing on the recollections of William Beeston, son of Shakespeare's fellow in the Lord Chamberlain's Men.) He played a part in Jonson's first successful comedy, *Every Man in His Humor*. Jonson mocked him for his pains but he didn't take offense, later appearing at the Globe in Jonson's tragedy, *Sejanus*. His colleagues Heminges and Condell, preparing the Folio of 1623, placed Shakespeare's name at the head of the list "of the principal actors in all these plays." Sometimes he acted kingly parts, a contemporary said, and Rowe assigned him the Ghost in *Hamlet*. Tradition called this role "the top of his performance." It suits him, "crepuscular" Shakespeare.

Adroit in clapping on masks, the young man played old men. "In one of his own comedies, he wore a long beard and appeared so weak and drooping and unable to walk, that he was forced to be supported and carried by another person to a table." At the table aged Shakespeare sat "among some company who were eating, and one of them sung a song." After this cameo appearance he dropped from sight, having written himself out of the play. *As You Like It* was the play and the old man was Adam, left over from the antique world.

Rowe's Shakespeare, a "hireling," worked for a fixed stipend. Better than a common servant, he stood below the "sharers" who made up the acting company and split the daily take. Tutored in "swearing tragical and buskined oaths," assiduous Shakespeare, perfecting his craft, graduated to playwright. Fame was the spur, emolument too, and he hoped in time to be a sharer himself. Within two years of his first stage success, this hope was realized.

STILL MAKING his way, Shakespeare took lodgings in Shoreditch. Distinctly down to earth, this unsavory quarter attracted theater people, on the word of Puritans dissolute and hard drinking. Shakespeare, a "looker-on" like his Duke of dark corners, kept a clear head. That was how the writing got done. "He was not a company keeper," said reminiscent Aubrey, "lived in Shoreditch, & if invited to, writ he was in pain." Stay-at-home Shakespeare, avoiding "hot and rebellious liquors," isn't as good copy as Jonson and Sons. A countrified suburb housing the first theaters, Shoreditch lay just north of Bishopsgate, outside the walls. Not a prime location, it housed the brothels too. "Dwell I but in the suburbs/Of your good pleasure?" Portia asks Brutus, an uncommunicative husband. "If it be no more, Portia is Brutus' harlot, not his wife."

Déclassé Shoreditch was still suburban in our modern sense, i.e., not hemmed in. An illustration, dating from the 1590s and showing one of the theaters, has a man in the foreground driving a horse and plough. London needed its safety valve. Roughly a square mile in area, the city petered out in old monastic lands, Finsbury, Moorfields and Clerkenwell, below the river Southwark and Bermondsey, once the site of a Cluniac abbey. To the west were the hamlets of Chelsea and Battersea, above them Paddington and Mary le Bone, only a park and a brook. Further north and west was Barnet, where the Underground ends. Shakespeare's Kingmaker fell in battle there, a cedar yielded to the ax's edge.

Some Londoners, fleeing the plague, ventured out that far, like "Civis" and "Uxor" his wife, captured in a dialog the year Shakespeare was born.

UXOR. I never was so far from London in all my life. How far
have we ridden already, sir, I pray you?
CIVIS. Wife, we have ridden ten miles this morning.
UXOR. What town is this, I pray you, sir?
CIVIS. This is Barnet. . . . How like you this town, dame?
UXOR. A pretty street, but methinks the people go very plain. It
is no city, as I do suppose, by their manners.

Like most in Shakespeare's city, this husband and wife didn't know
what to make of "extramural" London, a savage Boeotia. Cockneys
and complacent, they hunkered down inside their wall, two miles long
and punctuated by battlements. St. Helena, Constantine's mother, built
the wall, Londoners told each other, asserting a lineage that went back
a long way. Around it, making sure, they dug a ditch, two hundred
feet wide. London's cloaca, its eastern arm was called Stinking Lane.
In Shakespeare's time, gardens grew in the ditch, shanty-dwellers threw
up houses there, hoi polloi and their betters used it for a town dump.
When the wall showed signs of crumbling, repairs were carried out of
old "with the stones taken from the Jews' broken houses." Rioters,
xenophobic, broke the houses. (London's accommodating side had its
limits.) By and by, however, few Jews were left, and what Shakespeare
knew of Shylock was mostly hearsay.

An irregular crescent, the wall, beginning at Fleet River mouth west
of St. Paul's, ended at the Tower of London. This royal palace had a
bad name and deserved it. A state prison for dangerous offenders (i.e.
men or women who stood too near the throne), England's armory,
national mint, and a treasure-house for the crown jewels, it served also
as a legal archive, storing records of the king's courts at Westminster.
The Tower housed a menagerie too, leopards, lynxes, an aged wolf,
and a trio of lions, king's beasts. A foolish hero of Shakespeare's,
before he fell in love, walked proudly "like one of the lions." In 1609,
King James came to the Tower to watch a combat, much touted,
between a lion and bear. The royal beasts, led out one by one, had no
stomach for a fight, and turning tail slunk back to their cages. Finally,
to please the king, dogs were set on the bear, baiting it to death.

Shakespeare's characters supposed that Julius Caesar built the
Tower, a vulgar error. William the Conqueror, raising the central keep,
meant to overawe the city. His White Tower, now a museum, has a
mincing portrait of Southampton, Shakespeare's patron, also Henry
VIII's military armor. The girth is enormous, a fifty-six-inch waist, and
the arms, pendulous, are like a gorilla's.

Some said that blood of beasts tempered the mortar cementing the Tower's stones. Blood of men was as likely. The "aspiring blood of Lancaster" sank in the ground when Henry VI was murdered there, "striked with a dagger by the hands of Richard of Gloucester." Shakespeare tells how this same Richard lured the Yorkist princes to their deaths in the Bloody Tower, "Rough cradle for such little pretty ones." Elizabeth, not yet queen, came to the Tower, a prisoner, in 1554. Moving men's hearts, she lived to tell about it, a glamorous exception, not the rule.

Through a covered channel under Tower wharf, prisoners entered the Bloody Tower from the Thames. They came in at Traitors' Gate, the iron grille closing behind them. Edward, Duke of Buckingham, an eloquent presence in Shakespeare's *Henry VIII*, made the journey in 1521. The greatest noble in the realm, he was old nobility, affronted by "butcher boy" Wolsey. (Shakespeare, a new man, bears comparison with Wolsey, Thomas Cromwell too, both mocked for their ignoble beginnings.) Condemned at Westminster Hall on a trumpery charge of treason, Buckingham took the water road to the Tower, imprisoned in his own ducal barge. He wouldn't sit on the splendid cushions and carpets. "When I went to Westminster," said this tragic hero, "I was Duke of Buckingham; now I am but Edward Bohun." In his story, art and life come together for once, and Shakespeare, reading up the sources, used these words almost verbatim.

Buckingham's execution took place on Tower Hill. On the site of the scaffold, now a grassy enclosure, young mothers perambulate with their charges. Most notables died on Tower Green, habitat of ravens, protected birds, and green in summer with plane trees and lime trees. Last of the Plantagenets, Margaret, Countess of Salisbury, made Henry VIII, a Tudor prince, uneasy. Her death sentence was a sequel but this old woman, obdurate, wouldn't lay her head on the block. The headsman, pursuing her, hacked her to death with his ax.

Anne Boleyn, Queen Elizabeth's mother, died five years earlier on Tower Green, followed many years later by the Earl of Essex, Elizabeth's great favorite. The dead were brought first to the little chapel near the Green, St. Peter ad Vincula, "in chains." (Snitterfield in Shakespeare's boyhood had a church that bore this name, remembering the apostle and his fabulous escape from prison.) Exeter, brother of Henry V, is buried in the chapel, surmounted by a prayerful effigy. He created "Exeter's Daughter," the rack. In a moving panegyric, Shakespeare's Henry at Agincourt tells about Exeter and his "band of brothers." Henry, prophetic, said the good man would teach their story to his son. A large wooden frame, the rack had rollers at either end. To ropes passed through the rollers, the victim's hands and feet were secured. Levers, increasing the tension, "toused" or tore him joint by joint until he talked or died.

A moat on the three land sides still surrounds the Tower, its perimeter glorified with bank on bank of spirea, daffodils, iris, and flowering dogwood. Just up river, London Bridge connected the city at Fish Street with Southwark across the Thames. One end stood in Middlesex, another in Surrey. Twenty stone arches supported the bridge, giving it a name, "Polypus," well furnished with legs. Water-mills, their great vans clapping noisily, harnessed the tide. Londoners found in this a similitude for a scolding woman. "The noise at London Bridge is nothing near her," says a character in Fletcher's comedy, *The Tamer Tamed*. In this good-humored version of Shakespeare's *Taming of the Shrew*, Petruchio, the tamer, gets his comeuppance.

Shops and houses rose on either side of London Bridge, like a street in the city. Coming together at the top, the houses shut out the light, and much of the passage was dark. Four ancient cornerstones bore the name "Jesus," between them the drawbridge, once raised for high-masted ships. Above the gatehouse at the south end, the heads of traitors, stuck on spikes, were shown to the crowd. Some of Shakespeare's dramatis personae ended up on the gatehouse, Jack Cade, Thomas More, and rebellious Lord Bardolph among them. In *Henry IV*, Part Two, this nobleman jumps the wrong way. The heads, admonitory, had medicinal virtue, or Shakespeare's people thought so. In the 1560s, taken down by permission, they were hollowed into drinking cups. Metal workers in Tower Mint, suffering from noxious fumes, drank from these cups. A number found relief, "though the most of them died." In Visscher's famous "view" of London, 1616, the heads show like onions on toothpicks.

Until the mid-eighteenth century, London Bridge stood alone. Today a modern bridge, Blackfriars, spans the river on the west where Fleet "Ditch" emptied into the Thames. Beside the Fleet stood Bridewell Palace, converted in Shakespeare's time to a House of Correction. Covered over two hundred years ago, the Fleet crept along languidly, "not so much for age as the injection of city excrements wherewith it is obstructed." Into this muddy stream went

> grease and hair of measled hogs,
> The heads, hooves, entrails, and the hides of dogs.

On Fleet Street above the river, today a "street of ink," headquarters of London's sensational press, waxworks and puppet shows—"motions," Shakespeare calls them—played to "holiday fools." Hucksters exhibited "prodigies" or freaks, good for a laugh or ironic speculation. Shakespeare's character remembered one of them, the "strange Indian with a great tool." Nearby were London's four law schools, the Inns of Court. Francis Collins, Shakespeare's lawyer, studied at Clement's Inn, a training ground for the law schools, still imposing on the corner where Fleet Street turns into the Strand. Justice Shallow was once of Clement's. An old man and doting, he thought they talked there "of mad Shallow yet."

In the Strand then and now stood the Savoy, a ducal palace in early days, lately a guest house for men with business in the law courts. Rising sheer from the river, it hugged itself to itself. Poor folk weren't welcome there. "Pull down the Savoy," Shakespeare's Cade bids the rebels. The Strand, an elegant ligature, tied London to Westminster. Physically, the two were twain and legal theory confirmed this. A state within a state, London admitted the Queen when it wanted to. First, she had to ask. This remains true and the second Elizabeth, wishing to enter the city, waits on the Lord Mayor's invitation.

On either side of the Strand, noblemen and gentry lived in battlemented mansions, set amidst terraced gardens. Behind them, going north, the country lay empty. At river's edge "great oneyers" had their pleasure boats, like limousines, moored at private stairs. Some of these great ones still lived in the city, among them Sir Thomas Gresham who said how bad money drives out good. Mostly, the city Shakespeare knew was left to merchants, distinguished by pelf but otherwise unimportant. Men of genuine consequence wanted to be nearer the throne. The nearer they got, the more it sucked their marrow. Burghley, the Queen's Secretary, i.e. her first minister, lived in the Strand, also the ill-fated Earl of Essex. Essex Street marks the spot, angling north from the river. Up this rise, on a cold Sunday in 1601, came Essex, Cuffe, and Southampton, rebels with their heads in the clouds.

The Royal City of Westminster, seat of England's government (London being the center of its business and trade), housed the Queen's palace, her Parliament, and law court. One chronicler of Shakespeare's London imagines him walking the streets of Westminster, returning from a ramble in the northern countryside. Up there off the map were Highgate and Hampstead. Descending to St. Pancras' village and St. Giles in the Fields, he passes through Long Acre to the "Convent Garden," once the garden of Westminster Abbey. A grassy footpath brings him west to St. Martin's, also "in the Fields," a recurring phrase in place names. He looks in on the "mews" that used to house the royal falcons, in his time the stables for Her Majesty's horse, then walks on through St. James's Park, coming to the Tilting Yard, now

the Horse Guards Parade. Men in gorgeous armor ran at tilt in the
yard, honoring the Queen on her Accession Day. Chivalry was dead
but the Tudors liked to pretend, a way of dressing up their shaky title
to the throne. Shakespeare remembered the punctilio of tilting, faintly
absurd, in the first act of *Richard II*.

The royal palace was Whitehall, a twenty-three acre sprawl of Tudor
gothic south of Charing Cross. Cardinal Wolsey, creating Whitehall,
knew it as York Place. King Henry's great minister, he trod the ways
of glory, sounding the depths and shoals of honor. This cardinal's pride
broke beneath him, though, and he fell like Lucifer, not to rise again.
"You must no more call it York Place," says a tactful character in
Shakespeare's *Henry VIII*. "That's past."

In Wolsey's Great Hall and the Banqueting House, the court mustered for plays, among them "The Moor of Venis," credits going to
"Shaxberd." The Queen built the Banqueting House, a mean shed, her
successor said, and Inigo Jones, architect and scene designer, consulting
his own taste rebuilt it. For elegance and airiness, nothing in London
touched his white and gold confection. Allegories on the ceiling, work
of Peter Paul Rubens, showed the king's apotheosis, assisted by a
cherub. Both Jones and Rubens were Shakespeare's contemporaries,
each a little junior. Between these "modern" artists, ruthlessly subor-
dinating every part to the whole, and egalitarian Shakespeare, prone
to byways and meanders, a universe opens. Whitehall Palace burned
down three hundred years ago, except for the Banqueting House and
Cardinal Wolsey's wine cellar, now a lunch room for the Ministry of
Transport.

In Westminster Hall, Parliament sat and the Queen's Courts of
Justice determined civil lawsuits. Star Chamber, convening there, tried
cases the Crown didn't want the courts to handle. No one appealed
from Star Chamber. Nearby in the abbey church of St. Peter, famous
poets were buried, Chaucer, Spenser, and Jonson, not Shakespeare. A
bust commemorates him, though, and on a scroll are lines misquoted
from *The Tempest*. Queen Elizabeth and her arch rival, Mary of Scots,
lie together beneath the floor. Already a necropolis when Shakespeare
arrived in London, Westminster Abbey hearsed the bones of kings and
queens, beginning with Edward the Confessor. From pulpits sealed
with dust, they preached the vanity of human wishes, "Since the first
man died for sin."

To St. Margaret's church on the north side of the Abbey came the
body of Sir Walter Ralegh, beheaded for treason, in 1618. His ghost,
said Trevelyan, pursued the House of Stuart to the scaffold. A traveler
to the round earth's imagined corners, Ralegh loved London best. In

all the universe, he said, two things were unmatched, the sun in heaven and the Thames on earth.

Before Ralegh's time and Shakespeare's, London's wall ran along Thames Street but "the fishful river" wore it away. A highway to the world, wealth and glory of the city, the Thames used its strength for commerce. "Well-conditioned" or tractable, a patriot called it, unlike "some tyrant rivers in Europe." This mingled true and false. Meat and drink to Londoners, the Thames gave them their water, brought up by force-pumps, also their daily bread, a never-failing harvest. Men drew salmon from the river, swans, protected, sailed its surface, and on festival days it glittered like a moveable pageant. Some days it put on mourning, as for great Leicester, dead in the Armada year. Then its barges and boats were hung with black.

Quitting the city, the river made for the ocean, thirty-five miles away. Tidal water, it floated great merchantmen from France, the Netherlands, Sweden, Denmark, Hamburg, and new worlds beyond the sea. Inbound ships discharged their cargo at watergates, sheltered ports or "hithes" in the river wall of the old Roman city. Ripa Regina, the great gate, survives as modern Queenhithe, its protected harbor still there in Upper Thames Street. Smaller boats harbored at Billingsgate, later London's fishmarket, synonymous with ribald abuse. Over their sprats and whitings, fishwives talked "Billingsgate," igniting the air around them.

Making the river their road, travelers hired wherries, small boats like taxicabs. At public stairs along the banks, watermen, a licensed fraternity, vied for custom. Expert in chaffering, they had their familiar cries, echoed by Shakespeare's heroine in *Twelfth Night*. "Then westward ho!" says Viola, pushing off for home. Shakespeare, leaving Blackfriars, the private theater on the north bank, hailed a wherry at Puddle Dock. Crossing to Bankside, he disembarked at Paris Garden Stairs, near the Falcon Inn, or he used the landing stage at Horseshoe Alley. Opposite the alley, on Park Street, a narrow passageway brought him to the site of the Globe. John Taylor, doggerel poet and one of Shakespeare's "witnesses," said that 40,000 travelers-by-water lived between Gravesend and the bridge at Windsor. A self-publicist who craved the limelight, he nearly drowned sailing a brown-paper boat on the Thames.

It wasn't always "sweet Thames." From autumn through spring the river turned nasty. Sometimes a sudden swell in the North Sea, racing south, caught a high winter tide. Wind, meeting this surge tide, whipped up the water, white between the arches under London Bridge. The Thames "seems to complain at the bridge," said a respectful Londoner, "because it hath intruded into his bowels." That made the river roar, and men died shooting the arches. Today a retractable flood barrier, like the portcullis suspended in the gateway of a medieval castle, commands the Thames at Woolwich, eleven miles southeast of Charing Cross. In Shakespeare's time, nature, imperious, shrugged off constraints. John Stow in his *Survey*, the best account of Shakespeare's London, tells how a young man, leaping Dowgate channel where it entered the river above London Bridge, "was taken by the feet and borne down by the violence of that narrow stream." He brought up against a cartwheel in the watergate, "before which time he was drowned and stark dead." Battling a tide in the affairs of men, Shakespeare's Duke of York likens himself to a swan on the Thames. Against the overmatching waves, his strength is bootless.

Between Deptford and Greenwich, the river rounded the Isle of Dogs on the north bank. Some name this headland for dead dogs, rolled down river from London. A marshy peninsula dotted with windmills, it kenneled the King's hounds when the court, always moving, took up quarters at Greenwich. Jonson and Thomas Nashe, one of the Wits, called a play of theirs after the Isle of Dogs. Full of "seditious and slanderous matter," it sent Jonson to prison. More than the famous classicism, this unquiet spirit separates him from Shakespeare. On the Isle of Dogs the windmills have gone, replaced by giant earthscoops and decaying warehouses. Behind them in Limehouse rise modern council flats. But fog, a prestidigitator, still summons England's past when "the limbs of Limehouse," common rowdies, got Shakespeare's attention. Hanged in chains at Wapping Old Stairs, pirates and some land-thieves rotted at water's edge for three washings of the tide. "There's a waterish tree at Wapping," said Taylor the Water Poet, "Whereas sea-thieves or pirates are catched napping."

On the south bank at Deptford, the *Golden Hind* lay at anchor until it fell to pieces. Sir Francis Drake sailed around the world in this vessel, and kneeling on its deck received his knighthood from the Queen. Drake died a disappointed man fifteen years later, on an unlucky voyage to the West Indies. At Madame Bull's, a Deptford tavern, Christopher Marlowe met his death, stabbed through the eye at the age of twenty-nine. Opposites attract, and Shakespeare in *As You Like It* remembers this "dead shepherd."

Deptford had a famous son, Thomas Tallis, the composer. Not flamboyant like Marlowe and not a man of action, he lived for a long time, surviving triumphantly on a wild and violent sea. Ejected from Waltham Abbey after the Dissolution, Tallis, a Catholic, consulted his wit. When King Edward came in, he wrote music for the English liturgy, switching to Latin under Queen Mary. Elizabeth gave him the monopoly for printing music and music paper, a lucrative concession that freed him for the work he was born to. Rendering to Caesar, this opportunist rendered also to God, turning out his music on demand, as they liked it. The yield for him, others too, was pleasure and profit. A "clerk" or singing man, not a modern artist, he looks back to the craftsmen who carved the choir stalls in Stratford, forward to "atavistic" Shakespeare. Tallis died, well-to-do, in 1585, and is buried in St. Alphege church where he played the organ.

SHAKESPEARE, citizen of London, first appears on the tax rolls in 1595. A householder in the parish of St. Helen's, Bishopsgate, he lived near the terminus of the great northern road. Travelers from the north came in through this "episcopal" gate, Marlowe, another young hopeful, among them. In July 1587, quitting the University, he took the turnpike that led from Cambridge to Bishopsgate. Dazzled by the skyline, a serried row of church steeples, he said the sight of London was as "Elysium to a new-come soul."

Seven gates cut the wall, two of them remembered by names of stations on the Underground. Shakespeare, standing in Bishopsgate on the northern perimeter, had Aldgate on his right hand, Moorgate, Cripplegate, and Aldersgate on his left. Through Aldgate in the east, traffic entered the city from Whitechapel, Mile End, and Bow. Once a year on Midsummer Day, the trained bands, London's National Guard, sorry soldiers like Falstaff's, practiced infantry drill in the fields at Mile End Green. Shakespeare's Captain Dumaine, a Frenchman domiciled in England, "had the honor to be the officer at a place there called Mile End." Practiced in insult, Parolles reported this, and the groundlings fell about in the pit.

In fields outside Moorgate, the trained bands held their yearly parade. "Is this Moorfields to muster in?" an irascible porter in *Henry VIII* inquires, beating back the crowd. Carcasses of dead animals lay unburied in this swampy wasteland, drained by the Moorditch, a stinking canal. Shakespeare's character, holding his nose, rued "the melancholy of Moorditch." Once cripples begged in Cripplegate. Then reformers, their brother's keeper, cast a cold eye on the mendicant life. Rational men, they enacted Poor Laws, turning Bridewell Palace into a "hospital" for the morally deformed. Something new beneath the sun, their social activity announced the modern age. Shakespeare, social in his art but without an eleemosynary bone in his body, stood apart.

Only a postern in the walls, Cripplegate opened on a country village and the parish church of St. Giles. In 1607 Shakespeare's younger brother Edmund buried his bastard son in St. Giles Cripplegate. Famous Dick Whittington, type of the outsider who finds his way in, made the water conduit in the churchyard. West of the church, near Aldersgate, place names remembered the "burhkenning," a baronial fortress. From the top of the tower its master, surveying the city, looked into Kent, Surrey, and Sussex, far afield. In the older time, however, a prudent king, one of those efficient kings commended by Shakespeare, took thoughtful notice. Cutting off the heads of fast-growing "sprays" or sprigs that looked too lofty in his commonwealth, he destroyed the watch tower and filled up the ditch that enclosed it. The tower was the Barbican and the ditch was Houndsditch.

Shakespeare's way into London, Newgate looked west. Beside the gate was the prison, near it the slaughterhouses, St. Nicholas' Shambles. Prisoners in Newgate had the privilege of "standing dumb at the bar." Found guilty, they forfeited their goods to the Crown. Trials couldn't proceed without a plea, however, and accused who didn't plead kept their goods intact for their families. This required stoicism, submitting to the ordeal of "pain forty dure." Stretched out on spikes, the prisoner lay face up with legs and arms extended. Above him on a board, weights were piled, one by one. "Pressing to death," Shakespeare's characters called this. One, with a sense of humor, said it was like marrying a prostitute or "punk."

Last of the seven gates, Ludgate evoked for some a Celtic king who gave his name to the city, Lud's Town or London, before history began. Just east of the gate rose old St. Paul's, not Wren's, a gothic version. "The land's epitome" or lesser isle of Great Britain as it used to be, this medieval church mixed Babel and Sodom. The south aisle was for usury, the north for simony, the font, tombs, and rood loft for changing of money, "the horse fair in the midst." In 1600 a dancing horse, Morocco, climbed the blocky tower, "while a number of asses stood braying below." Shakespeare, missing nothing, has his word on dancing horses.

Cockeyed "inventions" (panaceas) were advertized in Paul's, "and not few pockets" were emptied. Nips and foists emptied the pockets, the foist, more genteel, using his hand, where the nip, like a common tradesman, used a knife. In this den of thieves and easy livers, not congenial to the austere Christ who drove the profaners out of His temple, butchers, ale sellers, and fishmongers competed for trade with whores and their "apple squires," pimps. "The ears' brothel" and a mint of lies, Paul's attracted "delators," professional informers, lawyers on the prowl, and "fantastics" like Shakespeare's Lucio, keen for the latest slander. Looking for service, masterless men like Bardolph set up their bills. "I bought him in Paul's" says Falstaff.

They met in the middle aisle, "Duke Humphrey's Walk," and Shakespeare has a word on this too. First in the long line of his tormented heroes, Humphrey, called the Good Duke, dies violently in *Henry VI, Part Two*. His former almsmen, at a loss for their dinner, regret this. You went without your dinner, said a proverb in Shakespeare's England, if you dined with Duke Humphrey. On one side, that was what tragedy came down to.

Little of the old remains in new St. Paul's, rebuilt from ashes after the Great Fire of 1666. Tourists walking the ambulatory are still brought up short, however, by the grisly statue of John Donne in his shroud. More modern than Shakespeare, this sensitive poet agonized at every pore. He had a vision of the body, "Bedded and bathed in all his ordures." Our "rotten world" dejected him, and like many in his time he preferred the world over yonder, tabernacle of a comelier truth. A child of the time, Shakespeare reflected this new spirit in his plays. But he had two faces, one turned backwards to the age before his own, not especially hopeful, so not often dejected. Blessed with good digestion and innocent of "truth," he must have seemed a callous Shakespeare to many.

IN THE LATE WINTER OF 1592, Shakespeare opened to big crowds at the Rose on Bankside. Chronicle history plays were in and he gave them what was wanted, a panoramic history completed in three parts. (Later he added a coda, the tragedy of *Richard III*.) Philip Henslowe, theater manager and diarist, recorded the event, also the takings, uncommonly large. Shakespeare's *Harry the Sixth* had a cast of thousands, personated by "three rusty swords,/And help of some few foot-and-half-foot words." The contemptuous phrase is Ben Jonson's. Duelist and bully boy, he liked his art verisimilar, reserving implausible business to life.

Shakespeare's pieties chiming with the crowd's, he took for his theme the Wars of the Roses, still as vivid as yesterday. Edward Hall and Raphael Holinshed, official historians who rendered to Caesar, furnished the matter of fact. But he had his own sense of the prime movers, Henry VI, roi fainéant, his wicked queen Margaret, the good Duke Humphrey, the bad Cardinal Beaufort. Glamorous cartoons, all were picked out in arras cloth at Coventry, near Stratford. The tapestry still hangs in St. Mary's Hall, property in Shakespeare's boyhood of the local guilds.

Not all bannerets and pennons, his version of history makes room for "poor servitors," common soldiers "Constrained to watch in darkness, rain, and cold." Shakespeare's eye, inspecting these common folk, doesn't idealize them, however. Unflattering similitudes say what they are: a hive of angry bees careless in stinging, feathers or summer flies commanded only by "the greater gust." As Shakespeare's story ends, two of his fickle commoners, seizing the unhappy king, hand him over to new masters. The great wheel running down hill, they know when to let go their hold.

Beginning with the funeral of Henry V, patriotic Shakespeare mourns the loss of France in the reign of his son and namesake. An English champion, Talbot, tries to make the loss good but is foiled by craven English, vultures of sedition. Losing in life, the hero wins in art, happy, said one theater-goer, to "have his bones new embalmed with the tears of ten thousand spectators at least." Not flesh and blood but "imaginary puissance," Talbot is only a "shadow of himself." Others, declaring his identity, equip him with "substance, sinews, arms, and strength." These others are his soldiers, persons of the play, also the playgoers "who in the tragedian that represents his person imagine they behold him fresh bleeding." Making them do this is Shakespeare's achievement in *Harry the Sixth,* formalized art depending on language and gesture.

Early Shakespeare has a metronome on the piano and his lines, not spontaneous-seeming, are often no livelier than "the clock that tells the time." Speech is mostly native English, jagged with thingness. (Jonson was wrong about the foot-and-half-foot words.) No "multitudinous seas incarnadine," not yet, and the words fall like stones in the water. But scraps of latinity bedizen the verse, this educated playwright showing off his Virgil to the discomfit of anti-Stratfordians. A decorative poet, he adorns his tale with figures of speech, sometimes off the point. Rhyme, calling attention to itself, suits the tale, a long way from naturalistic theater. Blank verse, freed-up poetry pretending to real life, makes early Shakespeare nervous, so he brings it to heel with rhetorical guidons:

> So many hours must I tend my flock,
> So many hours must I take my rest,
> So many hours must I contemplate,
> So many hours must I sport myself.

Stylized, not inept, this is art imitating nature, where nature is the "brief abstract and recòrd of tedious days."

With the victory of the House of Tudor, Shakespeare's tetralogy reaches its term, sixty some years of violent altercation resonant with poetry, much of it declaimed. Dramatic give-and-take isn't part of his equipment, and his speeches are like arias where the hero comes to the "footlights" and sings. "Suspiration of forced breath," Hamlet calls these big speeches, but they don't lack for power. A "Nuntius" or Messenger—Shakespeare reaching back to Roman Seneca and his medieval forebears—prefers telling to showing. "Sad tidings bring I to you out of France," etc. Shakespeare's heroes want to hear more—"Be copious in exclaims," is how they put it—and mostly the playwright obliges. A more practiced Shakespeare, clapping on his Ancient Pistol mask, poked fun at this "silly stately style." It has its decorum in the Henry plays, though, Shakespeare hearing in history only "a clamor in a vault."

Marching back and forth across the platform stage, his captains and kings, struggling to escape from history, contend irresolutely like the tide-driven sea against the wind. Spastic heroes, they pledge faith and break it, kill or pray to God, erupt into poetry, all in a breath. Rhetoric is impartial, handed round to hero and villain. Transcending point of view, Shakespeare is his magnanimous self. Always ready with an apothegm, this sententious playwright is endlessly quotable but his philosophic sayings dance in air. He has his surrogates, First and Second Citizen, absorbed like himself in homiletic wisdom. Shaking their heads, they think that disaster is when clouds appear. Then "wise men put on their cloaks."

> When great leaves fall, the winter is at hand.
> When the sun sets, who doth not look for night?
> Untimely storms make men expect a dearth.

Later Shakespeare is more eloquent, but as guides to conduct his familiar quotations don't take us much farther than this.

Linear, not focused, Shakespeare's first English histories are less dramatic compositions than a "direful pageant." The medieval cycles, still played at Coventry in his younger time, offered a congenial pattern, corroborating his sense of things. (At the end of his career he reaffirmed this sense in another pageant play, *Henry VIII*, and you can say that in his end is his beginning.) Form in the cycle plays, Shakespeare's chronicles too, is imposed from above, these playwrights not detecting a shape beneath the skin. On stage right King Henry and his "power" sit down, on stage left the emulous King Edward. Action, metonymic, oscillates between them. Crossing the Channel, we are in France where Lewis, the French king, lends an ear to rival suitors, "*angeli boni* and *mali.*" One, on his left side, asks support for the lawful king, another, on his right, for the pretender. "She weeps and says. . . . He smiles and says," giving us our moiety of sorrow and joy.

Fortune, a muffled goddess, arbitrates the proceedings. The wheel turning, Talbot dies, insulted over by Joan of Arc. "Pucelle or puzzel" the whore, a far cry from the romantic heroine of Michelet or Bernard Shaw, she gets her just deserts in the following act. This fishwife is theatrically effective. Margaret, coming after Joan (as Nature abhors a vacuum), works Duke Humphrey's ruin, falling victim herself on the next revolution of the wheel. Then come Richard of York, Warwick the Kingmaker, in the sequel play Richard of Gloucester. Successive apparitions like the show of kings in *Macbeth,* they have their fierce energy in common. A gargoyle, not a man, grotesquely comic and very engaging, Richard, wading through blood, takes the throne for himself. But Fortune "in her shift and change of mood" rejects him. Shakespeare has another metaphor, describing the up and down. For the hero-villain and the rest of them, prosperity, mellowing, drops sooner or later in the rotten mouth of death. This rhythm is physiological.

Subject to a greater power than they can contradict, Shakespeare's characters are thorns in the way, or weeds, shallow-rooted, or like the "stock" of a flourishing tree. In youth they put forth leaves (but caterpillars eat the leaves or the knife is set to the root), in age (as entropy governs) the withered vine droops sapless to the ground. High point of Shakespeare's first work for the theater, the famous scene in Temple Garden where the soon-to-be-embattled nobles pluck the white rose and red, says that "growing time . . . ripened" is decisive. Knowing no better truth, late Shakespeare still goes on like this. E.g., his Posthumus to Imogen:

> Hang there like fruit, my soul,
> Till the tree die!

For some of Shakespeare's characters and some of his critics, the stormy up and down of history makes a moral fable, showing how "sin will pluck on sin." But greatness of spirit, anyway amplitude, covers and effaces a multitude of sins. In the last act of his tetralogy, Shakespeare, reversing the order he finds in the chroniclers, appoints battle speeches for his hero and villain. The villain gets the last word, also the better lines. This has consequence and Richard, more gravid than the lack-blooded hero, stands out against the sky. A skeptical Englishman's version of the curse on the House of Atreus, Shakespeare's retelling of "York and Lancaster's long jars," devoid of moral point or purpose, has no issue but itself. None of this says it is bad.

Not primarily a lyric poet, Shakespeare needs the theater, and dramatic art gives him his voice. You see this in the sonnets, impersonal poetry where thesis meets antithesis, begetting a third term. (It isn't synthesis exactly, perhaps an emulsion, but the collision of energies sparks him into life.) Never saying much in so many words, Shakespeare intimates meanings through complementary action, the hallmark of all his art and a way to "hear" him.

In his first play, successive stage directions introduce the Duke of York "fighting hand to hand" with England's enemy, La Pucelle, then amorous Suffolk with another enemy, Queen Margaret, "in his hand." One Englishman does his duty, another evades it. Characteristically mute, Shakespeare directs attention to his speaking tableaux. The juxtaposing of scenes is meant for implicative, the playwright bidding us mind true things "by what their mockeries be." Sometimes, though, the counterpointing seems tautologous, an embarrassment of riches, or the point it enforces is only ad hoc, holding for this time and place, not tomorrow. If ad hoc, then maybe accidental? In Shakespeare's theater, true things and their mockeries shade into each other. This world of his is tenebrous, hard to negotiate.

In the roughneck comedy of Jack Cade's rebellion, his great triumph in the Henry plays, comedy dogs history, sponsoring definitions. Already Shakespeare, dramatic historian, is feeling his way to the comic analogies of *Henry IV,* Part One, where low Falstaff at the Boar's Head stands in for King Henry. Cade does this, resuming the makers and shakers. "My mouth shall be the Parliament of England," says the vulgar anarch. But that is what King Edward says: "my will shall stand for law." These voices that echo and scenes that mirror each other perplex as much as they enlighten. Is the ruffian a counterfeit copy of the king? a faithful replication? Which is the true man and which is the thief? Crosscutting from Cheapside to the king's palace, Shakespeare, raising questions, leaves them unresolved. That is how he teaches, and on this side his first history plays sketch the future of his art.

5

Wild-Goose Chase

LIKE CERTAIN CHARACTERS of his coming into their happiness, Shakespeare appeared on stage when time was "mellow" or ripe. This ripened time is the Shakespearean moment. Only a few decades between the fag end of medieval drama and the asperities of the modern world, it accommodated his hybrid art, soon to fall in disfavor. (He was hardly in his grave before plays learned a tidy decorum, no more "hot ice and wondrous strange snow.") A generation earlier Shakespeare would have found no theaters in London, a generation later no audience worth his steel. In his lifetime, Stratford Council prohibited plays, anathema in "well-governed cities and boroughs." Before the seventeenth century had reached its halfway point, London theaters were dark, closed by edict of the Saints (1642), and the audience he knew had vanished, not to return. He was lucky, coming up in the nick of time.

Meaning to write plays, Shakespeare found an audience that welcomed this, and Londoners turned out in great numbers to hear him. When he began to write, four theaters in or near the City were vying for custom. Puritans thought them damnably convenient. Entertainment for mass man, plays offered the best bargain in town. Men with an afternoon to kill had their choice of "gaming, following of harlots, drinking, or seeing a play." Harlots charged sixpence, a minimum rate, and moralists spoke bitterly of a "six-penny whoredom" or "six-penny damnation." Books diverted the well-to-do, a small octavo selling for a shilling, i.e. twelve pence. Where a quart of ale went for four pence and a quart of sack for eight pence, general admission to the public theaters cost a penny. Another amenity competing with plays, tobacco by the pipeload cost three pence. Playgoers got their money's worth, open-air entertainment at a fast clip. "Two-hours' traffic," the Chorus to *Romeo and Juliet* called it.

Shakespeare's audience, not exclusively the upper crust, mixed shop-keepers, students, and "handicraft men"—artisans, highly skilled—with their families and apprentices. "Foists" or pickpockets went to the theater too, for business, not pleasure, also prostitutes, "Winchester geese." They worked out of brothels near the Bishop of Winchester's palace on the south bank of the Thames. Philip Henslowe, theater manager, collected the brothel rents for the bishop.

Cultural conditioning affects views of Shakespeare's audience, also his playhouse, not least his plays. Victorians thought theater-goers in his time a vulgar rabble. Robert Bridges, an eminent Victorian, warned lovers of Shakespeare against degrading themselves "to the level of his audience . . . wretched beings who can never be forgiven their shame in preventing the greatest poet and dramatist of the world from being the best artist." I.e. Shakespeare wrote down. Reacting to this, later scholars, riding a liberal tide, proposed a democratic Shakespeare. He addressed the whole of society, plebians included. Unwilling to settle for a make-believe theater, they made this entertainer write up.

Scholarship, not pure, has its fashions like other things, and in recent times the wheel has turned again. Some, banishing the hoi polloi from the playhouse, say how Shakespeare's audience, no cross section, rep-resented the upper levels of the social order. But the plays and the testimony of Shakespeare's contemporaries suggest that the people who went to hear him were more heterogeneous than they are today, also more perceptive. Some in this audience, gentrified, paid an extra penny and sat in boxes that ran around the edges of the playhouse. Nobles wanting to be seen rented cushions and sat on the stage. Most, however, were groundlings. Reviled by the better sort, they stood in the pit, unroofed and exposed to the weather. Shakespeare, biting the hand that fed him, has a hundred jokes at their expense. In his *Henry VIII*, a fastidious gentleman finds himself stifled with the "rankness" or stink of their joy.

Groundlings fed on garlic, onions, and herring, staples of a poor man's diet. Cleanliness, not yet next to godliness, wasn't among their virtues. Well-born patrons kept the wind between them and these ham-handed men. Disrespectful of "culture," they munched apples and cracked nuts while Orsino, exotic on the platform stage, said how music was the food of love, etc. Shakespeare, fascinated, watched them "thunder at a playhouse and fight for bitten apples," thrown down from the galleries like cigarette butts. "Great noises that fill the ear" delighted the groundlings. Catering to this, Shakespeare has his actors beat on drums, fire off cannon, or ring the "dreadful bell" that frights the isle of Cyprus in *Othello*. Getting "a glass in their heads," they made their own noise, turning the playhouse into a bloody scene of "affrays, assaults, tumults, and quasi-insurrections." In February 1580, "near a thousand" of them rioted at the Theater in Shoreditch. Loyal to their class and not too poor to resent an insult, they stuck together like hogs, a disdainful chronicler said, "whereof, when one grunts, all the herd comes to help him."

But mass man in this time wasn't an unleavened lump, and the groundlings had the right tools for estimating Shakespeare. Still in touch with the medieval habit of mind where light invaded darkness and the other way round, they understood that Hamlet, Horatio's "sweet prince," was both hero and brutal revenger. Ambitious, he wanted the throne and said so. At the same time, he said he could be bounded in a nutshell. Scurrile but tender, an athlete in training but fat and short of breath, much put upon by others but a scourge to them too, this Hamlet mingled contradictions like the web of our life. Otherwise, the groundlings wouldn't have believed him.

Brought up in the university and partly a snob, Hamlet gave them low marks for their taste. They made little of coterie plays like *Gorboduc*, the first English tragedy, unrelievedly sober, i.e. dull. This was Hamlet's kind of play, "caviar to the general." Groundlings liked their plays enlivened with a jig or a tale of bawdy. (Shakespeare, different from Hamlet, took respectful note.) They weren't short on pia mater, though, whatever detractors said, and plays holding their attention had to be "pregnant" with thought. "Grave men," a Puritan writer called them, wishing they wouldn't go to the playhouse. Looking over the house, a traveler observed "many honorable women." Refined or well-to-do ones sat in the galleries, others stood in the pit, side by side with their men. A modern historian thought they must have been "light," not so. The year after Shakespeare died, another Puritan wrote bitterly of "swarms of wives" thronging the theaters.

Courtiers, out for a lark, made fun of the men and tried to seduce the women. But the groundlings, much maligned, knew a good thing when they saw it. Co-begetters of Shakespeare's art, they instructed him in what he was and might be. This was important, "for the eye sees not itself/But by reflection, by some other things." In the next generation, many, dejected by price inflation, hysterical preachers, or a new kind of play, abandoned the theater. For the present, however, Shakespeare banked on their support. They were his best patrons and he couldn't have got on without them.

HE OWED A greater debt, not payable unless by art, to James Burbage, woodworker or joiner. "A stubborn fellow to his enemies," not least when they tried to take the bread from his table, Burbage had a low boiling point and a nose for money. This temperamental mix begot a single idea and it made him immortal. He created Shakespeare's playhouse.

"Reaping but a small living" by his humble occupation, the joiner left it and became a common player. By 1572 he was heading his own company, the Earl of Leicester's Men. Shakespeare, aged nine, saw this company when it played Stratford. Itinerant players, Leicester's Men set up their show in guild halls or the great halls of gentlemen's houses. In London at Revels' times, red-letter days like Christmas, Candlemas, or All Saints, they played the Inns of Court. A paneled screen or reredos, cut with two doors and rising to a musicians' gallery, gave them their temporary stage. In 1594, again in 1602, Shakespeare got a boisterous welcome from the benchers of Gray's Inn and the Middle Temple.

Revels were bacchanalian, "most used by night when otherwise men commonly sleep and be at rest." Taking dictation from a Lord of Misrule, the benchers, normally staid, threw themselves into masking, dancing, and theater. This meant different things. Once at "Grand Christmas" in the Inner Temple, a cat and fox, brought on stage tied to a staff, were "by the hounds set upon and killed beneath the fire."

Mostly, London companies played in public inns like the Boar's Head in Whitechapel Street outside Aldgate. Some regard the innyard as the progenitor of all playhouse design, others point to the banquet hall, still others to the bear gardens. The rule for each is simplicity, and this holds for Shakespeare's plays in performance. A ready-made theater, the Elizabethan inn lacked only a wooden "scaffold" or stage, easily supplied by boards laid on trestles. Rooms for lodging, grouped around an interior court, opened on a gallery, girdling the inn. From this roofed-over "penthouse," spectators looked down on the play in the yard and the groundlings, glued together. Carriers or ostlers, leading their horses into the street, passed under an arch where the ticket-taker collected his penny. He split the proceeds with the landlord. Burbage, when he built his playhouse, adapted this model, enemies said. He had a secret key to the "gatherer's" box and took the lion's share of the proceeds.

For Shakespeare and his clientele, "scaffold" and "stage" were one and the same. "This world is but a scaffold for us to play our tragedies and comedies upon," one theater-goer said, suggesting the theater's kinship to the block and the gallows. Tower Hill, south and east, had its gorier stage. Planks littered with straw made a rough platform, encircled with a railing draped in black. Half filled with sawdust, a basket sat beside the block, awaiting the head of the victim. On this scaffold Shakespeare's Buckingham felt the long divorce of steel. An actor, he showed his mettle in the final exigent.

Wooden stairs, a little shaky, ascended the scaffold. "See me safely up," said Thomas More to the headsman, "for my coming down I can shift for myself." In the next century the stage moved to Whitehall. A "royal actor," Charles I, heir to the throne in Shakespeare's later time, adorned the "tragic scaffold,"

> While round the armèd bands
> Did clap their bloody hands.

This theatrical figure offers a clue to Shakespeare, playwright and headsman. Contemplating his victims, he said eloquent things but his eyes dropped millstones.

Elevated so all could see, the stage functioned as an altar for transacting high business, sometimes as a shambles like the floor of the bear pit. This was when it accommodated Shakespeare's quarry of the slain. Calf's blood or sheep's blood stained the wooden planking, "but in no wise" blood of an ox or cow. "That will be too thick," said an expert in these matters. Faithful to its setting, Elizabethan tragedy, an august rite but adulterated, drew vitality from darkness. Not inevitably moral, it had its sordid side, and plays of the time often verge on absurdist theater. This is true for Shakespeare's tragedy from *Titus Andronicus* to *King Lear*. Its only competitor, Aeschylean tragedy, is like that. Strong for rational behavior, embodied in the law courts on the Hill of Mars, it takes truce with the Eumenides, implacably other. They lived in darkness under the hill.

Shakespeare, ignorant of Aeschylus, salutes the Furies too, and Sackerson the bear prowls his world of theater. Torn by dogs on Bankside, the "head-lugged" bear—or stag or hart—resembles the tragic hero, brought to bay and dragged down by the hounds. Sometimes Shakespeare's heroes, tied to the stake, must fight the course, "bearlike." Macbeth, having no option, differs from the hero of the old Psychomachia, a fair fight between good and evil. Shakespeare adjusts this hopeful pattern for tragedy, and his heroes and heroines, choosing for themselves, are also determined. In Shakespeare's comedy too: "Have you not set mine honor at the stake," Olivia asks "Cesario,"

> And baited it with all the unmuzzled thoughts
> That tyrannous heart can think?

Players in the 1560s, at home in the innyards, noticed a fly in their ointment. London inns lay within the Lord Mayor's jurisdiction. An important functionary, chosen each year from one of London's twelve principal guilds, he needed deferring to. In *Henry VIII*, Shakespeare gives him a place up front for Queen Elizabeth's christening, and the king, deferential, says he is much beholden to the Mayor and his good brethren. The brethren were aldermen, twenty-six in number, one for each ward of the city. Most, like Stratford's Sanhedrin, detested the stage, "Satan's shop or schoolhouse" where apprentices and school-boys learned "the art and mystery of whoredom and adultery."

At eight on Sunday mornings, the Lord Mayor and Aldermen came to Paul's Cross, an open-air pulpit, to learn what they thought. In the world Shakespeare lived in, a theater of God's judgments, untoward events had their meaning but seeing it needed sharp eyes. When an earthquake shook London, April 6, 1580, preachers told them this meant God's displeasure with plays. (The earthquake, long remem-bered, claimed two victims, churchgoers attending a sermon.) Some-times Shakespeare's characters go on in this vein, Gloucester in *King Lear,* for instance. An old man and superstitious, he relates our mun-dane troubles to eclipses in the sun and moon. But where prodigies and portents function for Shakespeare as a kind of shorthand, sug-gesting that men at no time are masters of their fate, preachers at Paul's Cross, inspecting the heavens, wrested the world to their purpose. Plague visiting London in 1577, they discovered the cause in sin. However, one said, "the cause of sin are plays: therefore the cause of plagues are plays."

Before Shakespeare came up, the Mayor and Aldermen set out to get rid of the theaters. They pointed to "evil practices of incontinency," soiling the "chambers and secret places of great inns." Maids, especially orphans, were "inveigled" there, money went down the drain, and the Queen's Majesty's subjects, gravitating to the innyards, skipped divine service on Sundays and holy days. Also speeches in plays were 'un-comely and unshamefaced," i.e. playwrights said what they felt, "not what we ought to say." This critique has its kernel of truth. All art being subversive of official sanctions, Shakespeare inspired uneasiness in many.

Most of the London inns he knew are long gone but the George in Southwark survives, and once a year workingmen actors, honoring Shakespeare's birthday, put on scenes from his plays in the courtyard. Shakespeare knew the George, of old the George and Dragon until Protestantism got rid of the dragon, also the Bull in Bishopsgate Street. Hobson, the Cambridge carrier, had his London stables at the Bull. Customers wanting to hire a horse got the one nearest the stable door, "Hobson's choice." Plays performed in this inn gave young Shakespeare food for thought, among them an early version of *The Merchant of Venice*. Scholars identify a small colony of Jews in Shakespeare's London, but ten to one he got his Jew from this play.

The greatest clown of the age, Dick Tarlton, mainstay of the Queen's Men, acted at the Bell in Gracechurch Street. "Gracious" Street as Shakespeare called it housed another inn, the Cross Keys, favored by Banks the showman and his dancing horse, Morocco. In the mid 1590s, Shakespeare, at Burbage's playhouse in the summer months, shifted to the Cross Keys Inn for winter. On Ludgate Hill not far from St. Paul's stood the Bel Savage. An Indian princess, Pocahontas, stayed in this inn the year Shakespeare died. When *Dr. Faustus* was played there, the Devil himself, said a Puritan writer, took part in the play.

True or false, the whiff of brimstone hung about London's innyards, City Fathers thought. Petitioning to pull down the wooden scaffolds, they were stopped from doing this by Privy Council, and almost until the end of Elizabeth's reign innyards still hosted the players. It was always nip and tuck, though, hard on truculent James Burbage. Later, summoned to appear by the London Corporation, he told them defiantly that he wouldn't be bound. But he saw how the wind was blowing. In the 1570s, the old religious drama was finally suppressed. This drama was Catholic, and some Protestants who liked stage plays wanted to replace it with a new drama on Protestant lines. Easygoing meliorists in a radical age, their day in the sun wasn't long. To root-and-branch reformers, all plays were sinful. Burbage, estimating these draconian men, considered the "continual great profit" that might be got from a permanent playhouse, located in the suburbs out of harm's way. This needed capital and his income—as a joiner, maybe £15 a year, a bit more than this as a player—didn't begin to meet the need.

Well-to-do John Brayne, grocer of London, was his brother-in-law. A speculator, already backing plays at the sign of the Red Lion in Stepney, the grocer listened to his kinsman, then sold all he had, first the store, then his house. It wasn't enough and he pawned his wife's clothing. By the fall of 1576, Burbage had sufficient. Translating idea to fact, he built the first public theater in England. He called it the Theater, there being no other. This "invention" of his changed the way men and women read the world.

The change, not one of degree but kind, is from medieval to modern. In the medieval time, playgoers assembled in open fields outside town. Banner-bearers, going before the play, appointed the time of performance. *The Castle of Perseverance,* promised in the banns, began at 9 A.M. Actors dug a ditch around the "platea," and this improvised space made a stage. A manuscript drawing approximates the "castle," not much more than a hayrick, beneath it the bed of Mankind. At the foot of the bed was the cupboard of Covetousness. When men got old, this sin gripped them most. After the performance the actors packed up, the people went away, and the theater no longer existed.

Burbage's playhouse, still there when the play was over, shows how function follows form, a proposition familiar to Shakespeare the poet. Satisfying a need, no doubt latent in the nature of man, "homo ludens," it had its own needs. It needed actors on call and/or the actors, a liveried fellowship, needed a fixed habitation. These pressures, mingling their spurs in the soil of Shakespeare's boyhood, shaped things to come. Alfresco theater went the way of the pageant wagon, and the strolling player, domiciled, became the Lord Chamberlain's Man.

This development waited on other days. Burbage in the meantime had a living to make. Canny, he built in Middlesex north of the city, near the highway that ran through Bishopsgate. Outside the gate lay the Liberty of Holywell, part of the parish of St. Leonard's, Shoreditch. Coming down from the Middle Ages, "liberties" guaranteed the freedom of religious establishments. Careless of Caesar, monks and nuns in their priories stood above the law. Once monastic land, Blackfriars, like Whitefriars, was a London liberty, i.e. segregated ground. In Shakespeare's time, each furnished the site of a playhouse. Holywell liberty harbored "rogues and beggars," later actors and playwrights, rejoicing in a disreputable freedom. (Sometime in the 1580s, Shakespeare swelled their number.) The Benedictine convent was gone, a casualty of the Dissolution, and the holy well choked with rubbish. But this Crown land, off limits to the London sheriffs, still preserved its ancient freedom. For Burbage and his fellowship, that was decisive.

THE THEATER, west of Shoreditch High Street, stood a few feet east of modern-day Curtain Road. Street and road, roughly parallel, run north and south, joined by a dogleg, Holywell Lane. Hereabouts was the Moorditch, flowing south to the city sewer outside the wall and marking the eastern limit of Finsbury Fields. This vast open tract, narrowing like a funnel, merged with Moorfields on the south. In the City's possession for going on two hundred years, it served Londoners as a public playground. Militiamen drilled there, archers let fly, and families came out from the City for picnics. Having eaten, young men "breathed" themselves, shooting, wrestling, or "casting the stone." Shakespeare's entertainments competed with these pastimes.

Playgoers bound for the Theater on horseback left the City at Bishopsgate and rode out along Shoreditch High Street. Some put up their horses at the Lion in Shoreditch, others, carrying on past the orchards and garden plots, turned west on Holywell Lane. At the playhouse door, if old stories are true, "Shakespeare's Boys" awaited them, eager for custom. Most playgoers came by foot. From the postern at Moorgate, a footpath across the fields led to the Theater but a brick wall barred access. Burbage, a man with a sense of humor, opened a gate through the wall, so made City land the thoroughfare to his playhouse. When Shakespeare played and acted there, the "concourse of people through the fields" was a sight to see.

Giles Allen, country gentleman and brother of a former Lord Mayor, held the land the Theater stood on. Living in Essex and not coming up often, Allen, in the idiom of a later time, clipped coupons. Burbage leased from this rentier for twenty-one years, with an option to renew for ten more. (Later, the option gave trouble.) The Theater was big, making room at a guess for 1,500 people. Admiring contemporaries knew it as "the great house." Preachers called it "the chapel of Satan."

A polygon or wooden O rising on a brick foundation, the Theater looks in old maps like the Bankside "gardens," long famous or notorious for baiting bears and bulls. Puritans promoted another resemblance, to the bawdy houses, whited sepulchers, nearby. Plaster, interspersed with boards, herringbone style, covered the exterior. Paint brightened the inside, decidedly ornate. Around the pit, open to the sky, were the galleries, provided with benches. Playgoers, the same who flocked to public hangings, clambered over the benches, forcing their way to the front. They wanted to be "an object to all men's eyes," said a local Pecksniff, counseling "retreat from plays and theaters." Also they wanted uplift, heroics, sentiment, often lachrymose, bloody business, and piety. This was entertainment.

Theater, Globe, and the rest of them no longer stand. But specifications still exist for Henslowe's Fortune (1600), based on the Globe, and they suggest what Shakespeare's playhouse was like. A sketch of the Swan, made in 1596 by a Dutch visitor, Johannes de Witt, shows this playhouse as it looked (or looked to him) from inside. De Witt has the "heavens," a stage canopy or "shadow" extending outwards from the third gallery and overhanging the rear of the stage. Two on-stage pillars hold up the canopy. Behind them is the tiring-house (dressing rooms), pierced by two doors. The pillars, a necessary evil, broke the view. But Shakespeare made everything serve, and in plays of the later 1590s and after they double as trees. "This is the Forest of Arden," says Rosalind.

Evidently a novelty in the early 1590s, the heavens appealed to Henslowe when he redid the Rose (1592). Later, at the Hope (1613), he made his heavens cantilevered, so got rid of the pillars. The Boar's Head, a hostelry, did without the heavens in 1598, but turning into a playhouse, added them the following year. Likely the Theater patterned itself on provincial inns or guildhalls, unfurnished with pillars and heavens. Alterations undertaken early in the 1590s indicate, though, that Burbage, his eye on Henslowe, was getting in step with the times. These details, more than matter-of-fact, tell of imperious fashion, exerting its claims on Shakespeare's plays.

New fashion meant spectacle. Scornful Jonson in a prologue of 1598 says that in catchpenny plays, not his plays, "creaking throne comes down, the boys to please." Interested in pleasing, Henslowe laid out money for a throne in the heavens. Where most plays before Shakespeare make do with stage directions like "enter" and "exit," his contemporary Robert Greene requires that Venus be "let down from the top of the stage." Taking her departure, she doesn't exit but ascends. "If you can conveniently," this circus-master tells them, "let a chair come down from the top of the stage and draw her up." Shakespeare missed none of this. Challenged by the stage canopy, necessary for sheltering actors from the rain, he made a virtue of necessity, including the canopy in his bag of tricks. In his later plays, supernatural beings inhabit the heavens, descending when he needs them. (The claims of fashion notwithstanding, he doesn't need them often, and mostly his attention goes to our "middle earth.")

The third gallery, thatch covered, served Shakespeare too. Prospero has a stunning entrance "on the top," meditating vengeance on his enemies below. Like Jupiter in *Cymbeline,* he readies the thunderbolt, an all-powerful hero, most un-Shakespearean. (Later, however, abdicating his godlike role, he comes back to the rest of us.) In Shakespeare's first play Joan of Arc appears "on the top," like Shakespeare's white magician, "thrusting out a torch burning." She practices "arts inhibited" but they aren't enough to save her, and the flaring torch she carries is an image for Shakespeare's art, efficient in limited ways.

From the hut on the roof, Burbage, affronting the godly, shook out his flag on playdays. Each day he changed the bill, hard on the actors who had to con their lines. Comedy today, tragedy tomorrow. Performances, heralded by a triple flourish on the trumpet, began at 2 P.M. The brassy notes, at least, carried far. A disgruntled preacher at Paul's Cross said how the trumpet called a thousand to the Theater when only a hundred came to the sermon, summoned by "an hour's tolling of the bell."

Heart of the Theater was its platform stage, jutting into the middle of the yard. Rushes, freshly strewn, carpeted part of the platform. Shakespeare, exploiting this, bid his audience imagine a grassy dance floor in the fields of Navarre, a "green plot" for Bottom and the mechanicals, a garden for Antony to walk in. High in anger, the hero spurns "the rush that lies before him." Bottom, type of the literalistic man, speaks his low opinion of this theater in the mind, but in Shakespeare's comedy the joke is on him.

Illusion and reality ran together in the theater, sometimes a problem. Shakespeare, who asks his auditors to suspend their disbelief, didn't have to do this. Meaning to batter the villain or give the hero a hand, groundlings climbed up from the pit to the stage. A minor poet of the time, one of Ben Jonson's "Sons," remembered how a butcher came to Hector's assistance in his fight with the Myrmidons. The struggle wasn't equal, this unwelcome second protested, and "for a long time Hector could not obtain leave of him to be killed."

Coping with the problem, restorers of Shakespeare's theater suppose a low balustrade, enclosing the stage on three sides. De Witt's sketch doesn't show this but actors needed protection, not least from themselves. Some, tearing a passion to tatters, were in danger of pitching into the crowd. Lapsed in madness or crazy like a fox, Richard Burbage, James's son, tore off his doublet, stripping down to his shirt sleeves. The "vulgar," not buffered by a proscenium, thrust up against the platform, gaping at his antic behavior. They were in their element, said an enthusiastic spectator of "friendly Shakespeare's tragedies," when the tragedian stood "on tiptoe."

Except for mad scenes, wrestling matches, and such, actors dressed to the nines. Discarded noblemen's attire, a servant's perquisite, furnished some of the costumes. In Marlowe's *Edward II*, Gaveston, a foppish villain, "wears a lord's revenue on his back." Pretentious Dame Eleanor, sweeping on stage in *Henry VI*, Part Two, rivaled the Queen in contemporary portraits. The embroidered "stomacher," covering her chest, pinched in at the waist to make a triangle's point, and her "trunk" sleeves or "down" sleeves, slashed like an apple tart, were big around as the bore of a cannon. Uncivil Petruchio ridiculed this "masquing stuff" but most delighted in it, recognizing in the actors a heightened version of themselves. Costumes, reflecting somebody's wardrobe, paid no heed to history, and all time on this stage was insistently present. Titus Andronicus, hero of a "Roman" play, looks more or less Roman in a drawing of the 1590s, but the soldiers attending him, halberdiers, one wearing pantaloons, come straight from Shakespeare's England. The sense of the past is a modern phenomenon, and perhaps, for "naive" entertainment like theater, disabling.

THE GLOBE, when they rebuilt it from the Theater's dismantled timbers, showed the same structure on a grander scale. It had room for more people—3,000 at the Swan, said de Witt—and its huge platform approximated the stage of a metropolitan opera house. Otherwise, the builders left well enough alone. Backing the stage, as before, was the tiring-house, faced with doors. The prompter or "book-holder" followed the action behind a wicket in one of the doors. Shakespeare put this to account in his *Comedy of Errors* where the two Dromios, he of Syracuse within the house, he of Ephesus "in the street" outside, trade insults, perhaps a poke in the eye, through the wicket (3.1).

Older Shakespeareans imagined an enclosed "study" at the rear of the stage. In the mind's eye they saw two playing areas, the outer stage in front of the twin pillars, behind the pillars an inner stage closed off by a curtain or "traverse." Action, they thought, moved between these two areas. More recent historians take a skeptical view of the "inner stage," not visible in de Witt's reconstruction. "A historical curiosity," one modern scholar calls it.

But the on-stage pillars, really there in some theaters, suggest a metaphysical division, bisecting the platform fore and aft. Shakespeare's epiphanies, recorded in the plays, demand a "discovery-space," and perhaps a curtain provided this, not hung between the pillars but concealing an open door in the tiring-house facade. Early mountebank stages, where the tiring-house stood at the rear, had their curtain, so, very likely, did the temporary stages of banquet halls and innyards. When the regisseur pulled the curtain, the open door framed a vivid apparition. Or curtained "booths" were carried on stage through this door, eliminating the need for a recess or alcove. One way or another, the great platform, a promiscuous common like the open fields, gave Shakespeare a private enclave to work with.

In this felt interior, Portia displayed her caskets, Bassanio's choice. Lodovico, as *Othello* ends, bids them close the curtains that hung from the booth or the balcony above. This concealed the "tragic loading" of the bed, an object poisoning sight. Snorting like a horse, Falstaff slept behind the arras standing out from the wall, and Hamlet's sword, snaking through the hanging, found Polonius all ears. An epiphany is a discovery, as when the blind see, and *The Tempest* has a good one. Drawing aside the curtains, Prospero, in his role of "presenter," discovered Ferdinand and Miranda, playing at chess. Supposedly dead, there they were reincarnate, the second chance redeeming all sorrows. On the platform the sour elders, casualties of time, took it in.

Front stage and rear stage, not demarcated except by the pillars, made a continuum, like the past and future. "What's past is prologue," says a villain in *The Tempest*. This is point of view—a reading of how things are with us—and consequential for dramatic structure. Shakespeare, illustrating either, is like those old typologists who put the risen Christ side by side with Jonah, freed from the belly of the whale. In his *Richard III* he has two different settings occupy the same physical space. On one side of his stage he rigs a tent for the villainous Richard, on the other for the virtuous Richmond. Ghosts, boding good or evil, come to the hero and villain in dreams. The ghosts stand for past time, still quick. Much later in *King Lear,* Kent in the stocks and Edgar in the wild appear on stage together. They stand for goodness at the lowest and most dejected point of fortune. This mute tableau, unlikely but transcending realism, is an emblem, presenting the play.

A poet in the next age said that nature, hating emptiness, allowed of "penetration" less. (I.e. two bodies can't occupy a single space.) The pronouncement speaks for physics and a realistic theater. Simultaneous action is offensive to this theater, and later editors, rejecting Shakespeare's two-in-one settings, discriminate between them, creating separate scenes. The second scene is often headed: "Another part of the forest." Shakespeare's action is symbolic, though, of the essence of his stage, and more effective for its setting, not barren exactly but a tissue of words. In time to come, verisimilar settings made words gratuitous. Door knobs turned and teacups rattled in their saucers. This gain in realism meant a loss in possibility, and the theater after Shakespeare is cabined, cribbed, and confined.

Shakespeare's play, not confined to the stage, spilled over to the balcony behind it. From this second level, transformed by the playwright's all-creating word to a castle in Wales or a house in fair Verona, Richard II, like glistering Phaeton, descended to the "base court." Juliet, soliloquizing, spoke her love for Romeo. Hidden by night (candles intimating darkness), he stood behind one of the pillars, Capulet's orchard. From stage windows on the second level, Palamon and Arcite, two noble kinsmen imprisoned for life, looked down on the woman each of them covets. She was Queen Emilia,

> Fresher than May, sweeter
> Than her gold buttons on the boughs or all
> Th' enameled knacks o' the mead or garden.

Stone walls don't make a prison nor a coronet a queen, but language fortified by gesture is efficient for either. That is Shakespeare's idea and how he creates his illusion of reality.

First of all exigent, Burbage's structure offered hints to Shakespeare. Seizing them, he came to terms with his given. Constraints were few enough to let him do this. In the theater, Burbage thought, enough is as good as a feast. (Or perhaps he thought nothing and the money ran out.) Not an "unworthy scaffold," whatever Shakespeare told them, the Theater helped the playwright evoke his cloud-capped towers, etc., partly by taking second place to the play. Technical resources, pride of the regisseur like famous Inigo Jones, growing to a surfeit are also constraints. The history of theater from the Greeks to the present supports this.

Burbage's stage rested on a "cellarage," dead space concealed by wooden palings. Shakespeare located "Hell," a medieval reminiscence, in the cellar. Or it stood for the sea or our "dungy earth," place of skulls. The Grave Digger in *Hamlet,* mining this underworld, throws up a skull, and Fishermen in *Pericles,* drawing up their nets, find a suit of rusty armor in the meshes. Somebody in the cellar, like Cleopatra's diver who hangs a fish on Antony's hook, supplied this.

In the darkness beneath the stage, props owned by the company waited for the playwright to dispose them. *Item,* 1 Hell Mouth, 1 tomb of Dido, the City of Rome, Tamburlaine's bridle, Cerberus's 3 heads, 2 moss banks and 1 snake, 1 great horse with his legs, 1 black dog, 1 cauldron for the Jew. Taking a hint from this cauldron, the last resting place of Marlowe's Barabas, Shakespeare dug a pit for the sons of Titus Adronicus. Technicians, alerted when Aaron stamped on the floor, sprung a trap and they fell to their deaths.

Floor traps were mostly for spectral apparitions, like the Ghost of old Hamlet, coming up to revisit the glimpses of the moon. In *Dr. Faustus,* the Devil, seizing his prey, came up through the sulphurous jaws of the Hell Mouth. By and large, Hell and Heaven were states of mind, though, as for Marlowe's Mephistopheles, and place was where they said it was. Yesterday the place was France, King Lewis's palace, today, as language governed, the city of York. "Well have we passed and now repassed the seas," Shakespeare's King Edward assures them.

Stage props, metonymic or suggestive, were what they had to be: a chair for the dying Bedford in *Henry VI, Part One*, a coffin for King Henry, the cage Marlowe's Bajazeth is trundled in, a tree with golden apples for Greene's *Friar Bacon and Friar Bungay*. (This last, together with two coffins, was ready on call in the cellar.) Critics like Bottom, sensing the imposition, murmured against it. If you meant to show the sea, they wanted artificial waves, as in the realistic theater of Serlio and Sabbatini. Shakespeare couldn't manage this. "Do you hear the sea?" his character inquires hopefully. Describing it, though, he is very circumstantial.

Commenting on action, music underlined the words or called them in question. It wasn't yet an "intermezzo," vapid fun between the acts. Music of hautboys sounding "under the earth" predicted the death of Antony, or it sounded "i' the air," from the hut atop the "heavens." Through a trap door in the hut, Ariel descended on stage "like a harpy." Jupiter in *Cymbeline* disappeared through this trap, hauled up to his crystalline palace by stage hands. Not difficult to manage, it made a great coup of theater, like Donizetti's balloon going off at the end of *The Elixir of Love*.

Later the regisseur, challenged by difficulties, augmented them, pleasing himself. He gave the eye priority, good for movies but death on plays, and Shakespeare's deity and spirit flew through the air, attached to invisible wires. *Son et lumière* took over the playhouse, and the play turned into the masque. Painting and carpentry were the soul of masque, Jonson said.

Historians of Shakespeare's time report a War of the Theaters, Jonson pitted against his contemporaries, Marston, Dekker, etc. But the Theater War that mattered was between the new realism and old mimetic art, the approximation of reality. Dating from the years when these competitors were fighting it out, Shakespeare's *Winter's Tale* has a famous stage direction: "Exit, pursued by a bear." For this, they brought on a man in a bear suit. Nobody was fooled, except as he wished to be. Inigo Jones, had they asked his opinion, would have sent them for their bear to Henslowe's Garden, just over the way. Shakespeare, however, preferred the mimetic thing. He kept reality at art's length.

At Burbage's playhouse, people got things out, the sense of "catharsis." Supplying metaphors for life and death, plays gave shape to chaos, the mystery on the bestial floor. What was our life, one playgoer asked, but "a play of passion" accompanied by music, variations on a theme.

> Our mothers' wombs the tiring-houses be
> Where we are dressed for this short comedy.

Heaven the judicious sharp spectator is,
That sits and marks still who doth act amiss;
Our graves that hide us from the searching sun
Are like drawn curtains when the play is done.

Inept or transcendent, plays went in for big subjects, the battle with the Centaurs, the riot of the Bacchanals who tear the Thracian singer, Orpheus, to pieces, the death of Pyramus and Thisbe, showing how the course of true love never ran smooth. Philostrate, Master of the Revels in *A Midsummer Night's Dream,* hands a list of these "abridgements," entertainments, to Duke Theseus. Meant to "ease the anguish of a torturing hour," they brought the concourse of people across the fields.

WHERE BURBAGE LED, competitors followed, one in Middlesex, another in Surrey. Below Holywell Lane the Curtain, smaller than the Theater and catering to fencing matches, went up in less than a year. Fencing didn't mean debasement. Dick Tarlton, the time's great comic, was a Master of Fence and Shakespeare studied this discipline, part of the play. Bringing on stage his duelling Tybalt and Mercutio, Laertes and Hamlet, he saw to it that they persuaded. Henry Lanman, not a theater man, an absentee landlord out to make money, called his new building for the non-load-bearing wall that fronted London's Wall and kept off the weather. In the next decade, acquisitive Burbage got control of the Curtain, and Shakespeare, commuting from one theater to another, played it in the late 1590s.

"There goes the neighborhood!" irate locals said, when Jerome Savage opened Newington Butts. (It took them a while but they got rid of him, "a very lewd fellow" who "liveth by no other trade then playing of stage plays.") Leading actor of the Earl of Warwick's Men, Savage crossed the Thames for his new venture, building a mile south of London Bridge. Elephant and Castle, an underground stop on London's Northern Line, marks the spot, remote from the City on the other side of St. George's Fields. "In the south suburbs, at the Elephant,/ Is best to lodge," says a traveled man in Shakespeare. He says nothing of plays, however. Even *Titus Andronicus,* gory as they like it, failed to bring out the crowd, and Newington Butts languished "by reason of the tediousness of the way."

But it signaled the rise of Bankside as the new venue for London's theaters. The Rose came first, "upon the bank called Stews." Next came the Swan, close by in the Liberty of Paris Garden, south of modern

Blackfriars Bridge. Toward the end of the century Shakespeare played the Swan, Francis Langley's theater. Draper and goldsmith, i.e. usurer, Langley made money breed. Not less than genius, this crass activity fertilized Shakespeare's drama. The famous Globe, "glory of the Bank," opening its doors in 1599, was built for profit's sake, incidentally to give him a forum.

The skirts of Shakespeare's city were notorious for crime, "dark dens for adulterers, thieves, murderers," said Henry Chettle, printer and playwright. Whores congregated in St. George's Fields. Shakespeare's Pompey, a bawd, tells how city burghers meant to pluck down the "houses," but in Clink Liberty, outside the pale, riffraff made the law a scarecrow, their perch, not their terror. Knowing how "we are all frail," Elizabethans connived at this, turning a negligent eye on the Bankside. In this "bubbling stew of corruption," bear-baiting pandered to blood lust. Wednesdays and Sundays were the appointed days. Variations, like "the whipping of the blind bear," enlivened this entertainment. Philip Henslowe, crying up his bear garden, advertized the "pleasant sport" of the pony and the ape on its back. "To see the animal kicking against the dogs, with the screams of the ape, beholding the curs hanging from the ears and neck of the pony, is very laughable," a spectator said.

Henslowe, dyer by profession, also slum landlord, pawn broker, and brothel keeper, had a skin like a rhino's. Down-at-heels playwrights approached him for loans, offering their plays as collateral. His diary records the transactions. "Lent unto Benjamin Jonson . . . upon his writing of additions in *Jeronimo*" (i.e. *The Spanish Tragedy*). Site of Shakespeare's first great triumph, the Rose was Henslowe's theater, located like the Globe in the parish of St. Savior's, just west of Southwark. The square tower of the medieval church, pointed with four spires, looked down on what used to be a rose garden.

Public theaters in Shakespeare's London, competing with blood sports, faced a different challenge in the private theaters. Blackfriars was the famous one, near modern Playhouse Yard and Queen Victoria Street. Until the Dissolution a community of black-robed friars, Dominicans, lived within the precinct walls. Sometimes Parliament assembled in the great hall of the friary. Katherine of Aragon submitted to a trumpery trial in this hall, Henry VIII wanting legal color for his divorce. In the next century Shakespeare's company, making the friary their playhouse, reenacted the proceedings in the same room she was tried in. Art rectifying nature, this time the result was different, not in law but in essence, and Shakespeare's Katherine is vindicated where King Henry stands condemned.

Blackfriars, the forerunner of all modern indoor commercial theaters, was the second playhouse to occupy the site. Credit for the first Blackfriars goes to Nicholas Farrant, master of the boy-players at the Chapel Royal, Windsor. Just after Burbage opened in Shoreditch, he leased the old friary for plays. His actors sponsored a genteel theater, appropriate to this "eyrie of children." (Hamlet's schoolfellow is disparaging the boys a generation later.) Their tongues were tart enough, though, and more than once the Crown shut them down. A new lease on life, beginning in 1600, ended for good eight years after this. Elizabeth and James liked going to plays but not as they held the mirror up to nature.

The boys having worn out their welcome, Shakespeare's fellows, King's Men, moved into Blackfriars. From August 1608 until he retired, he divided his time between this private theater and the Globe, a public theater, just a wherry's ride away across the Thames. Public or private made no difference, his company performing *Othello* at Blackfriars, *Macbeth* at the Globe. The play was the thing.

For the health of theater, some other things make a difference, however, first the mere fact of a playhouse, not fly-by-night but standing four square. Fraught with possibility, a universe opens between the old platea and Burbage's wooden O. In subsequent decades, this theater underwent a thousand permutations, none of them so important, though, as its first realization. Put against the Globe, Blackfriars was cosier, more comfortable in winter. It had a smaller stage, lit by artificial light. Some annalists of theater understand late Shakespeare in terms of these differences. Step by step, they say his early histrionics—

A horse, a horse, my kingdom for a horse!

reflect the big stage and the unroofed auditorium where leather-lunged actors cried to be heard. As explanation, all this is suspect.

Explanations there are, though, e.g. the cultural mindset, dictating what kind of plays could be written. Tragedy died in England soon after Shakespeare, and serious comedy, living longer, flickered out at the century's end. A less catholic view of things, perceptible in Shakespeare's lifetime, worked the death of both. As the theater's arteries hardened and narrowed, public came to mean brutalized and private jejune. At the private theater, its standoffish patrons said, you weren't "pasted to the barmy jacket of a beer-brewer." This middle-class man couldn't pay for a ticket and anyway didn't like the bill of fare. He went to the public theater, some such vulgar cockpit as the Red Bull (1605), where he could see a play for two pence "with a jig to boot." The Blackfriars' boys preview this dichotomy. Scorning the rough-

and-tumble at the Theater and Curtain, they delighted exquisites like the Earl of Oxford, John Lyly's patron. (Some, nonplussed at the thought of an untitled Bard, insist that this Oxford wrote Shakespeare.) Accomplished in mimicry, the boys gave the adult companies a run for their money. Ben Jonson, in a tender-whimsical epitaph, remembered one of them, Salathiel Pavy. He specialized in old men, playing them "so duly,/As, sooth, the Parcae thought him one." Deluded, these Fatal Sisters took him off at thirteen.

Lyly was the boys' playwright. Lessee of the first Blackfriars theater, he lasted only a year. His neighbors in the 1580s, London's feather-makers, most of them Puritans, jibbed at a theater on the doorstep. Jonson, who liked to tilt at Puritans, made a joke of this. With their wigs and headdresses, were they not "as much pages of pride and waiters upon vanity" as any actor or playwright? For Lyly and the boys it wasn't a joke, however, and in 1584 the landlord took back his lease. Burbage in the end didn't fare any better. He wanted a roofed-over theater, winter quarters for his Shoreditch houses, so acquired Blackfriars in 1596. But "diverse honorable persons," making sure they were heard, said "what inconveniences were likely to fall upon them by a common playhouse." That was that for Burbage, his "great charge and trouble" notwithstanding. Still outside looking in, he died a year later.

Lyly, démodé, necessitous, and bitter, lived into the early years of the new century, dying ten years before Shakespeare. An anxious place hunter, he hoped to be Master of the Revels. This member of the Royal Household, the Lord Chamberlain's underling, looked after plays given at Court. Not getting his benefice, Lyly addressed a begging petition to the Queen. He asked for a plank "to waft me into the country where, in my sad and settled devotion, I may in every corner of a thatched cottage write prayers instead of plays—prayers for your long and prosperous life and a repentance that I have played the fool for so long, and yet live."

Grandson of William Lily the grammarian, a thorn in young Shake-speare's side, Lyly is Shakespeare's first master. At Blackfriars in the 1580s, later at the singing school attached to St. Paul's, he made his courtly comedies, eight all told, "junkets," dainty sweetmeats. "When you can eat no more," Lyly said to the ladies, "tie some in your napkin for children." Art, not life, engaged him, not a bad thing. But his art, unlike Shakespeare's, had only one dimension, and society and its problems took a back seat to amour. Alexander the Great in love was one of his subjects, the theme of *Campaspe*, Racine without the Jan-senist toughness. In his *Gallathea*, a sea monster, papier-mâché, craves virgin tribute. Wearing men's clothes, the young heroines escape this fate but fall in love with each other. They look ahead to Shakespeare's comedy where young women, played by boys, pretend to be men. But Shakespeare, oddly attracted to this hothouse situation, is harping on his old string, appearance and reality and the gulf between them. "Fortune forbid my outside have not charmed her!" his Viola says in *Twelfth Night*.

Readers and playgoers were in Lyly's debt, an admirer said, "for a new English which he first taught them." This English was "Euphuistic" after his famous novel, *Euphues: The Anatomy of Wit* (1578). Englishmen, Lyly noted, wanted to "hear finer speech than the language will allow, to eat finer bread than is made of wheat, to wear finer cloth than is wrought of wool." The right man for his time, he fine-tuned the language, balancing clauses or phrases equal in length and identical in structure, sometimes in sound. Sententious proverbs and exemplary stories drawn from history and Pliny's fake science tricked out his prose-poetry. Young Shakespeare doted on it, "sweet smoke of rhetoric!"

Real-life people didn't speak like Lyly's characters. Better for them, he might have risked saying, if they did. His Euphuistic style, a travesty, died before him "of its own too much." Shakespeare, remorseless in parody, assisted at the obsequies. Falstaff to Hal is Lyly to his readers: "For though the camomile, the more it is trodden on the faster it grows, yet youth, the more it is wasted, the sooner it wears." They laughed at this easily when the drama had got out of its nonage.

But the palace of wisdom, linguistic competence too, is gained via the road of excess. The "nest of singing birds," Shakespeare's England, didn't get that way all at once, and in the beginning the music sounds shrill, sometimes disordered. In a hit-or-miss time for music, before they learned to "govern the ventages," stops on a musician's pipe, Lyly taught precision. Shakespeare, trying on styles, learned his finicking art from this costermonger of language.

The costermonger's art has an unexpected yield, Shakespeare's first comedies, *Love's Labor's Lost, The Taming of the Shrew, The Two Gentlemen of Verona*, and *The Comedy of Errors*. Plays of the late 1580s and early 1590s, bursting with energy, they give you the sense that a cork has been drawn from the bottle. *Love's Labor's Lost*, sometimes verging on greatness, is the best of them, *The Two Gentlemen of Verona*, more like life than art, is the least. All four are impure or variegated, "wild laughter in the throat of death." This is Shakespeare's comic mode and peculiar to him, not tragicomedy, a disingenuous art, first tears, then laughter, but tears and laughter together, "the yolk and white of the one shell."

In two of his comedies Shakespeare works "the liver vein," seat of passion. The other two are farce, a diminishing word that does them less than justice. Going back to grammar school, he renews acquaintance with Plautus and Terence. Educated contemporaries, smelling the lamp and liking it, thought he was their acolyte. For *The Taming of the Shrew* and *The Comedy of Errors,* the connection is partly misleading, however. Taking a cue from these Roman masters of farce, Shakespeare outstrips them, being farcical and other things too.

Shakespeare's genius is primarily for comedy, and where his early histories are sometimes imperfect essays on the way to better things, his first comedies are already there. Deft at crowd pleasing, he is better, straight off, than Plautus and Terence, or polished Noel Coward in our time. This is surprising. A young man of genius can rivet you with night thoughts, appropriate to youth—Tourneur and Marston, Shakespeare's contemporaries, are like that. But comedy, the vision and prerogative of a mature sensibility, argues greater sophistication than tragedy. Shakespeare, to the manner born, possessed this.

Not a realistic playwright and never in comedy, he woos you "by a figure," the plot, absurd to sense. E.g. four young men, starving the body to banquet the mind, burn the midnight oil, a three years' commitment *(Love's Labor's Lost).* Two young men, pursuing one woman, are followed by another woman, disguised as a man *(The Two Gentlemen of Verona).* Two sets of twins, known to others but not to themselves, seek each other in fairy land *(The Comedy of Errors).* In the world of everyday, fathers beget their children, but in Shakespeare's a child begets his sire *(The Taming of the Shrew).* This comic subplot, telling of the "old pantaloon" and his son who spends all, draws from the commedia dell' arte, essentially a puppet play, lavish of means, not ends. But already in the womb of time a deep theme is stirring, and in Shakespeare's future is the better child who "repairs" the parent's youth.

For his major story in *The Taming of the Shrew,* Shakespeare revamps the old tale of "Florentius' love." (Chaucer's Wife of Bath tells a version of this, and perhaps that is where Shakespeare found it.) On pain of death the hero must answer the riddle "What do women most desire?" An old hag knows the answer but to get it he has to take her for wife. He doesn't want to do this, asking leave in such business "to use the help of mine own eyes." Shakespeare's heroes, cocksure but myopic, are like that. This one, closing his eyes, weds his tormentor and she turns into a beauty. The transformation means something but Shakespeare keeps tight on meaning and won't give up his secret except "by a parable." For sentimental readers, deploring or excusing *The Taming of the Shrew,* his meaning is still "folded" or covert.

Like some others in the guild of professional funny men, Shakespeare has his silences, offputting. But he isn't dour and his inveterate skepticism doesn't preclude an exhilarated sense of things. Probably these two sides of him have a contingent relation. Much of his humor is of the dig-in-the-ribs variety. Earlier critics, embarrassed for him, used to say he had to pander to the groundlings. How does the matter stand with the master and mistress, his interlocutor wants to know. Pat comes the answer: "When it stands well with him, it stands well with her." Shakespeare has a taste for this, good clean dirt.

His smutty jokes, a lot of them, are implicative, however, suggesting that the body is more than a clog. Young Platonists in *Love's Labor's Lost* deny this, and the body brings in its revenges. Lapsing from chastity or wanting to, one of them adores his mistress' slipper. He loves her by the foot, they say, where "He may not by the yard" (i.e. penis).

The slapstick comedian gives no trouble to moderns but at Shakespeare the wordsmith most draw the line. His characters talk until Doomsday, their to-and-fro jokes making a "set of wit" like tennis, popular in his time. Bandying words, he certifies his agility but has to honor conventions, in his case linguistic. This is where moderns leave him in droves. Frightened off by the preciosity, they haven't acclaimed his first comedies much and probably never will, or not unless time, revolving, brings his odd proclivities around again.

"Wit's peddlar," Shakespeare pecks up wit like a pigeon, then, chewing it deliberately, gives it back on demand. The wit, often perverse, shows most in his fascination with the latencies of words. Threads gathered in his hand, they have no integrity. Or else, in a world where solid things, "dislimning," look indistinct to him like water in water, words alone have integrity. "Vermicular" or wormy, scornful Bacon called them, but Shakespeare, challenged by words on their slippery side, thinks this is all to the good. His vocation, the competence and pleasure of civilized man, is to "bottom" the words, tying the end of the thread to the spool. Failing close attention, the skein, as he unwinds it, will foul or ravel "and be good to none."

"Let's part the word," i.e. divide it, his young men and women bid each other. Manipulating language, they have tongues like a razor's edge,

> Cutting a smaller hair than may be seen,
> Above the sense of sense.

More than the honied prose, this meticulous dividing, work for a razor or a pair of calipers, attracted Shakespeare to the Euphuistic style. Both learner and teacher, he taught himself, posterity too, how the pedantic practice of form begets freedom. This is his tribute to Lyly.

Sifting words in his "bolting hutch," a bin or strainer where flour is sifted from bran, Shakespeare has his kinship to the benchers of the Inns of Court. At these London law schools, says Stow in his *Survey*, they grew "ripe in the knowledge of the law" by the practice of "bolting" or arguing moot cases. The patient sifting was how they found out truth, instrumental for good. Shakespeare differs from the benchers, though, the difference setting him apart from most in his age, almost all in the age to come. His particular truth doesn't go anywhere, and "gnosis" or knowing, not "praxis" or doing, is all he has to offer. Sidney, his contemporary, dusts off these old Greek words in his "Defense of Poetry," intending a distinction between mere knowledge and getting things done. Anticipating the future, he puts his money on "praxis."

"Scholastic" Shakespeare, not hastening on to the City of God, treats a sentence as a formal occasion. What was a sentence? Only "a cheveril glove," kidskin, very supple, "to a good wit." A medieval excruciator born out of his time, Shakespeare is keen to know how many angels can dance on the head of a pin. He gets much innocent fun, profit too, from posing his far-fetched questions. The profit, involved with handsomeness, is partly in making the terms square or tally. Partly, though, it consists in establishing relations the dictionary gives no inkling of. This is a way of defining "oxymoron," the yoking together of discrete particulars, fire and powder, for instance. Romeo, says Juliet, hating and loving, is a "dove-feathered raven," and the union of fire and powder, "which, as they kiss, consume," declares the play.

Pulling the glove on or off or turning the wrong side out, this writer is notably exact. "There's a time for all things," says Antipholus S. in *The Comedy of Errors*. That is the "proposition," controverted by the servant in his role of "respondent." (Oxford entrance examinations, "Responsions," still remember the old back and forth.)

DROMIO S. I durst have denied that. . . .
ANTIPHOLUS S. By what rule, sir?
DROMIO S. Marry, sir, by a rule as plain as the plain bald pate of Father Time himself.
ANTIPHOLUS S. Let's hear it.

The proof being in the pudding, Shakespeare lets us in for forty lines of "Sic" and "Non," one disputant attempting to nail down his ad hoc truth, the other to pick it to pieces. "Anatomizing" the word, Shakespeare doesn't lose sight of his story. His lexical bantering complicates the story, though, and you have to sit up straight to catch his drift.

Some schoolboys in this age still had the old proneness for Shakespeare's dialectics. Stow recalls how one of them, ascending a makeshift stage, was by another opposed and answered and finally put down. "Then the overcomer taking the place, did like as the first, and in the end the best opposers and answerers had rewards." This being a formal age, young scholars, meeting in the street, hailed each other in Latin. *Salve tu quoque, placet tibi mecum disputare?* Hail to you too, says First Scholar, does it please you to dispute with me? *Placet,* says the other. Yes, it pleases. "And so proceeding from this to questions in grammar, they usually fell from words to blows with their satchels full of books."

A quarrel worth having, it fed the sinews needed for grammar, law, and theology, poetry too. Down the road, Shakespeare meant to lay bare the roots of behavior. For example, in *King Lear:*

Now, gods that we adore, whereof comes this?

The close pursuit of language, a formal enterprise, was how he readied himself for the task.

Putting it this way makes him more purposeful than he was in fact, and mostly comic Shakespeare is indulging himself. But if you look at the future through the lens of the past, you can see how the indulgence pays off. Case in point, *The Two Gentlemen of Verona,* where Proteus, an equivocal hero, tells Speed, a clownish servant, that his master has taken ship before him. Words on their aural side breeding for quick-eared Shakespeare, the ship becomes its homonym:

SPEED. And I have played the sheep in losing him. ["Ship" and "sheep" for Elizabethans have the same pronunciation.]
PROTEUS. Indeed, a sheep doth very often stray,
    An if the shepherd be awhile away.
SPEED. You conclude that my master is a shepherd, then, and I a sheep?

But this conclusion, the clown thinks, isn't supportable. He evades it with a bawdy quibble, endlessly absorbing to Shakespeare.

SPEED. Why then, my horns are his horns.

They bat this one back and forth, stretching their "cheveril" wit "from an inch narrow to an ell broad." Romeo has a phrase for their polite activity, "the wild-goose chase." A good rubric for early Shakespeare, in comedy, tragedy too, it means that wherever first horseman goes, second horseman has to follow. Switching and spurring, first horseman

Proteus changes direction: "Gavest thou my letter to Julia?" But Speed, skillful in manage, is on his heels:

SPEED. Aye, sir. I, a lost mutton, gave your letter to her, a laced mutton [i.e., prostitute]. . . .
PROTEUS. Here's too small a pasture for such store of muttons.
SPEED. If the ground be overcharged [too crowded], you were best stick her.

Still chuckling to himself an act later, Shakespeare returns to the scene of the crime. Launce, a second comic, owner of a vile cur, ought to be on shipboard too, says the straight man, Panthino. Delaying, he'll lose the tide.

LAUNCE. It is no matter if the tied were lost, for it is the unkindest tied that ever any man tied.
PANTHINO. What's the unkindest tide?
LAUNCE. Why, he that's tied here—Crab, my dog.
PANTHINO. Tut, man, I mean thou'lt lose the flood. . . . [Copious in meaning, he embroiders on this until Launce calls a halt.] Why dost thou stop my mouth?
LAUNCE. For fear thou shouldst lose thy tongue.
PANTHINO. Where should I lose my tongue?
LAUNCE. In thy tale.
PANTHINO. In thy tail!

Shakespeare and his audience, peas in a pod, crack up at this. A scandal to moderns, men and women in a hurry, he milks the same joke again in *The Taming of the Shrew*.

Handed on by the age, a rough-and-ready sociology is part of his baggage, onerous for the time to come. People in his time took a dim view of women, saying how good ones were better off "unknown to other folks." What was a wife? Petruchio tells them:

> She is my goods, my chattels; she is my house,
> My household stuff, my fields, my barn,
> My horse, my ox, my ass, my anything.

Shakespeare's wife, unlike Shakespeare, didn't need to go to school, and when he went up to London, following his star, she stayed home in Stratford. Mostly, a woman's place was in the home.

Making rueful allowances for the *Zeitgeist*, moderns have Shakespeare falling in with this, for instance in his *Comedy of Errors*.

> The beasts, the fishes, and the wingèd fowls
> Are their males' subjects and at their controls.
> Men more divine, the masters of all these,

Lords of the wide world and wild watery seas,
Indued with intellectual sense and souls,
Of more pre-eminence than fish and fowls,
Are masters to their females, and their lords.

Point counterpoint is the rule for Shakespeare, though, par excellence
the writer without opinions, and this timeserving homily requires its
complement. A woman speaks the homily and a man controverts it.
Berowne in *Love's Labor's Lost* finds his learning "in ladies' eyes":

They sparkle still the right Promethean fire;
They are the books, the arts, the academes,
That show, contain, and nourish all the world.

But this hero, who speaks a piece of the truth, is innocent of "Padua"
and what they are doing there. He lives in "another part of the forest."

Faithful to context, Shakespeare's comedies have their own rules,
prescribed by the playwright. Not history or pop psychology, they
don't mirror the time but honor the given, a decorous commitment.
Instructing us in the nature of some women, they say nothing of
"Woman," an abstraction not congenial to Shakespeare. Kate, his
termagant woman, like Goneril in *King Lear* wants to change arms at
home and give the distaff to her husband. This seems a bad idea.
Elsewhere it works out for the best, as in the *Two Gentlemen* where
an aggressive heroine, putting on man's clothes, shows how this rever-
sal is happy. Always for Shakespeare, nothing is good without "respect" or context. But "always" isn't one of his words.

The Taming of the Shrew studies right relations in an arbitrary
context, Tudor marriage. "Inside," the wife stands to her husband as
the subject to his prince. Disobedient, "what is she but a foul contending rebel"? This heroine, rebelling, presents a problem, canvassed by
Shakespeare. (A good way to read him is as the problem solver, in-
trigued by technical questions.) Giddy, she thinks the world turns
round, or her eyes are bleared by "counterfeit supposes." Confusion
clears, however, as she disputes herself, and the happy ending follows.

In a different context, perhaps a different state of mind, Shakespeare
inspected his problem again. Turning the tables in *The Merry Wives
of Windsor*, he has a foolish husband submit to his wife. This submission is the high point to which the play climbs. "Pardon me, wife,"
says the penitent, properly submissive, "Henceforth do what thou
wilt." This is happiness too.

Obedient to its rules, *The Taming of the Shrew* gives dispassionate
pleasure. Kate, as Shakespeare deploys her, is a counter in the game or

a "haggard," female hawk, whose wild state needs taming. If you prick her, she doesn't bleed. But this punctilious comedy is more ferocious than it has to be, inclining you to ask what drew Shakespeare to his fable. (Prudent biographers will leave such questions alone; however, faint heart never yet won fair lady.) When people are insane, Shakespeare calls them "informal" (a nice riposte on modern times where formality is a term of reproach). This equivalence offers a point of access for his play, perhaps his pestered marriage.

Readers glimpse Shakespeare's Anne in his earlier work, not a roman à clef but life corrected by art or art revenging itself on the life. Did Shakespeare marry an easy mark like that other Anne, willing consort of Richard III, a shrew like Katherine, a wanton like Rosaline, Dark Lady of Navarre, a Rubenesque harpy? That would be Venus in his *Venus and Adonis,* reeking and smoking as she feeds on her prey.

Katherine, repentant shrew, flatters the ears of uxorious husbands—

> Thy husband is thy lord, thy life, thy keeper,
> Thy head, thy sovereign. . . .

Boding peace and love, best of all "quiet life," this domestic comedy vindicates the playwright, and that is where its amazing energy comes from. In the end the termagant gets just deserts, "Love, fair looks, and true obedience" are paid, and put-upon husbands go away happy.

Pleasing himself in *The Taming of the Shrew,* was Shakespeare doing the other thing in *The Two Gentlemen of Verona?* Too complaisant by half, his Valentine evokes the dejected poet of the sonnets, down in the dust before a faithless friend, the fair young man. "All that was mine in Silvia I give thee," says the hero as the outraged audience heads for the doors. (Under his breath he mutters obscenely: "but yet thou mightst my seat forbear.")

But Shakespeare's erotic triangle, though felt as personal, even morbidly, is also an eternal triangle, familiar from *Euphues* (two men plus one woman) and anyway as old as the hills. Starting out in the theater, this father of twins dramatizes the misadventures of a pair of twins. However, he found twins in his source. "Black is the badge of Hell," fashionable persons said. They thought blonde was beautiful, like Petrarch's mistress Laura, too good to be true. Shakespeare didn't think so, and Rosaline, the Dark Lady who throws her "sun-expelling mask away," is first of all a manifesto. Rejoining on those romantic poets in his time who make "flesh a deity, /A green goose a goddess," unromantic Shakespeare proposes a real woman, i.e. fictitious. This one when she walks treads on the ground.

A type or antitype, Rosaline is an unlikely heroine, however. Her brow is velvet, the eyes two pitch balls, but this "whitely wanton" is light in the dark, "one that will do the deed" even if Argus with his hundred eyes were watching. Much about betrayal, horns, and wittols in Shakespeare. Sometimes "all the argument is a cuckold and a whore."

Heading straight for the altar, Shakespeare's young men and women take a left turn. At war between "will and will not," he sees to it that Jack doesn't get Jill. In the bittersweet ending he declares himself, though, and all his comedies have this reversionary sting. "Sweet and happy" is the word as his characters go off in *The Taming of the Shrew.* But Sly participates in the ending, sowing seeds of future discord. Perhaps in an uncut version, different from the Folio's, the ending resumes the beginning.

Like Bottom's dream that has no bottom, the vision of the drunken tinker intimates reality, mysterious.

> Am I a lord? And have I such a lady?
> Or do I dream? Or have I dreamed till now?

Dreaming entoils them in *The Comedy of Errors,* a function of their mortality, "feeble, shallow, weak." Wandering in illusions, Shakespeare's heroes, bemused or "mated," need a helping hand. Without this, the happy ending is "past thought of human reason," certainly for them, perhaps for us too.

So Shakespeare has a problem, how to get his little people out of their *selva oscura.* Dropped letters and overheard conversations, staple of the *pièce bien faite,* are one way. Teasing his audience, he glances at this briefly, setting up expectations of a happy (specious) ending. His Dromio S. has "privy marks" about him, the mole on his cheek, wart on his left arm, etc. So, providentially, has Dromio E. This version of *Cox and Box,* archetypal farce, dramatizes the peril that besets us as we have to fend for ourselves.

Another way or "remedy" presents itself, however, and Berowne, an equable pessimist, suggests it:

> For every man with his affects is born,
> Not by might mastered, but by special grace.

In the end, dowered with the special thing, comic characters in Shakespeare put off the "old Adam" and emerge new-appareled. Their metamorphosis, involuntary, comes "by miracle," though. Driving on the rocks, old Aegeon and his family find out safe harbor. Or rather Fortune chalks forth the way, bringing in "some boats that are not steered."

A great line, proleptic, winds up Shakespeare's play: "After so long grief, such nativity!" This intimates the world of *Pericles, Cymbeline, The Winter's Tale,* and *The Tempest.* In his first comedy, Shakespeare feels the future in an instant. But in his beginning and ending too, the appeal to grace or fortune begs all questions.

6

A Motley to the View

ADVANCE MEN, like those banner bearers who advertized the older drama, swept Shakespeare's way in London. People knew them as University Wits, Marlowe and Kyd, Peele, Lodge, Nashe, and Greene. Scholar playwrights in their own "conceit" or estimation, they condescended to the theater, ruled by the likes of Henslowe, who couldn't spell their names. Lyly, senior to the Wits, was part of their fraternity, "nursed upon the self-same hill," Oxbridge. A common player, member of the "basest trade," Shakespeare didn't belong.

The Wits jeered at players, "antics garnished in our colors," elsewhere puppets "proud with Aesop's crow." I.e. some "cobbler" put the words in their mouth. Edward Alleyn, creator of Marlowe's supermen, resembled this crow, "pranked with the glory of others' feathers." Greene, not meaning praise, likened him to Roscius, the famous Roman actor. Roman or English, an actor was a "daily counterfeit," butt of a gentleman's scorn.

Shakespeare, taking evasive action, condescended to "Roscius" too. "What scene of death" had this vulgar *histrio* now to act? etc. But public means bred public manners, and Shakespeare's lowly station dogged and perhaps betrayed him. "No outrageous thing," says his Lucrece feelingly, "From vassal actors can be wiped away." Worse than actors were actor playwrights, upstarts not credentialed by the academy. Nashe drew their picture, "excrementory dishlickers of learning." He said they set themselves up like "Turks" or targets to be spat at for silver in Finsbury Fields. This put Shakespeare in his place, one he didn't covet.

Shakespeare the nobody owes his first incarnation to the Wits, and the anti-Stratford cult enters history on their coattails. Obnoxiously present to Greene and his friends, the real-life playwright looks like a hoax to anti-Stratfordians. But the snobbery that dismisses him, familiar to readers of the Sunday supplement, is the same, yesterday and today. Shakespeare, notoriously "the butcher boy," answers also to "lying rascal," "poacher," "illiterate clown," and "drunken Warwickshire rustic." For some, even his name, a talisman in reverse, inspires revulsion, and they call him "the huckster Shagsper of Stratford." The idiom, though modern, approximates Nashe's blunderbuss style.

Shakespeare's modern detractors confront a problem the Wits were spared, his dramatic repertory, spanning more than two decades. Pleasing many and pleasing long, the plays stand beyond reproach, a monument without a tomb. But the man who was Shakespeare didn't write them. Anti-Stratfordians, alleging this, take their cue from the Wits. No men of royal "siege" or seat showing up in his family tree, no learned men either, he wasn't worth a gentleman's or scholar's perusal.

Unlike the Wits, anti-Stratfordians have a stand-in. Bacon is the famous one, dignified in later life as Viscount St. Albans. Other claimants include the Earls of Oxford, Rutland, Salisbury, Southampton, and Derby. Marlowe, not ennobled and dead before most of the plays were conceived, is a claimant by virtue of his Cambridge degree. Anti-Stratfordians who measure the extent of Shakespeare's achievement distribute his plays among a committee, like the syndicate of translators that prepared the King James Bible. Some committeemen are Bishop Lancelot Andrewes, Dr. Donne, Ben Jonson (with a pair of honorary degrees to his credit), Sir Walter Ralegh, and Sir Francis Drake. Queen Elizabeth heads the list of women claimants (Shakespeare being her illegitimate son). Joining the Queen is the Countess of Pembroke, a celebrated bluestocking and sister of Sir Philip Sidney, also Mary Queen of Scots, executed in 1587. A ghost from Shakespeare's past, Anne Whateley, retired to a nunnery, makes an unusual claimant. Mostly, for the man or woman who was Shakespeare, either noble lineage or academic honors constitutes a sine qua non.

Beginning in Shakespeare's lifetime, the attempt to get him out of the pantheon comments less on him than on the icon-smashers. Jibes at his expense appear most envenomed in down-and-outers like Greene who studied desert and didn't find it, or in the rational-minded like Dr. Freud, Mark Twain, or the American demagogue Ignatius Donnelly. Men of good hope, they want an orderly universe where every effect announces its cause, no innocent dreams, no surplus value, etc. Shakespeare's genius, not abiding their questions, meets them like a personal affront.

Loving a lord, anti-Stratfordians love personality too, vivid in the toper Jonson, Mad Jack Donne, or Marlowe the Overreacher. An impersonal maker, Shakespeare doesn't give them enough to take hold of. Like the Cantor of Leipsig, he made his plays and poems for the greater glory of God and the innocent pleasure of man, at the same time for personal profit. Quintessentially the artist, Flaubert before Flaubert without the pretension, he had nothing left over. Readers who don't estimate his austere commitment find it easy to deny his existence.

He walked the streets four hundred years ago but did this unobtrusively, and the legends, collecting since, seem born of a need to make him apprehensible, such a man as might have lived next door. What did he really think, look like, most relish or detest? His contemporary Donne, a querulous place-seeker, incidentally a great poet, wrote many letters, contaminating his art. He anticipates modern times where the artist, like the movie star, sits enthroned in the market place, energizing gossip.

A fertile source of gossip, the Wits were professionals on their best side (i.e. what was best about them went into the work). They might have seen in Shakespeare a less hectic version of themselves. But jealousy inflamed them and they sought to make the swan of Avon fly an ordinary pitch. This occasioned the snobbish talk, a way to bring him down to their level. Much of the talk was window dressing. Proud of their sheepskin and calfskin, they wore "the livery of learning," not its substance. Greene, writing himself M.A. of Cambridge and Oxford, promises more than he pays. When he ventures on a Greek phrase, says his scandalized biographer, "he lays himself open to the suspicion of having mistaken the future middle for the infinitive mood."

Writers first, the Wits were scholars when it suited them. Like Marlowe in his *Tamburlaine*, they riffled pages in Ortelius the geographer, not searching out a reference but looking for high-sounding names. Opportunist to the core, they had their eye on the box office, the one barometer worth consulting. Highminded men like Sidney, their eye on timeless values, wanted to know if plays honored the rules, codified by earnest Italians. Cynical or more perceptive, the Wits, creatures of their own time, asked what worked and gave pleasure. Like it or not, this allied them with Shakespeare, pragmatic to the tips of his fingers.

. . .

THE WITS were scapegraces, forecasting Romantic poets "in their misery dead." George Peele, "the English Ovid," died at forty, some said of the pox. His one surviving letter, written in his last illness, cadged support from thick-skinned Lord Burghley. This First Secretary didn't reply. Alliterative contemporaries had a field day with Peele, "product of London streets and gutters," otherwise "frivolous, shiftless, sensual, drunken, dissipated, depraved." His physical person went with this: squint-eyed, short of leg, swart of complexion, his voice high-pitched like a woman's. Peele left five plays, pastoral and martial, none of them lifelike, stuffed with poetry, though. "A most noted poet in the university," he was M.A. of Oxford, a credential that did him no good.

Peele took his M.A. in 1579. This year Shakespeare turned fifteen, Spenser published *The Shepherd's Calendar*, heralding a new poetry, and Sir Thomas North a translation of Plutarch. Shakespeare, short on Greek and Latin, quarried it later. Also in 1579 Stephen Gosson, a running dog for the London Corporation, launched his major attack on the stage, *The School of Abuse*. Gosson, who once wrote plays, called playwrights "unprofitable members" of society. "Privy" or secret moths, they nourished idleness, "the mother of vice." This gives Peele more and less than his due. He didn't make or lose a lot of money but his blank verse, not simple tick-tock, tells of "duration." In 1584 he brought them to their feet in his *Arraignment of Paris*. England, he said, predicting Shakespeare's *Richard II*, was an ancient seat of kings, second Troy. Then comes the canorous thing, latinate and golden: "Y-compassed round with a commodious sea." His Queen Elizabeth, robed in purple, veiled in white, who "giveth arms of happy victory," is anybody's queen. But the "long" line, ensuing, burns a hole in the page: "And flowers to deck her lions crowned with gold." No one else could do this when he did.

Late in the 1590s, wise heads said to Lodge: "And give up verse, my boy, there's nothing in it." He took this advice and became a physician, outlasting his fellow Wits, Shakespeare too. But that isn't why Lodge is remembered. Son of a wealthy Lord Mayor of London, scholar of the Merchant Tailors' School and Trinity College, Oxford, he went on to read law at Lincoln's Inn, surprising no one. Life pulled him two ways, though. Dropping his studies, he sailed on a freebooting expedition to the New World and broke a lance with Gosson and the "Misomousoi." Here, like the other Wits when they put on their thinking caps, he disappoints us. Rehashing old pieties, his defense of the stage (1580) meets the poet-haters on their own ground. A commonplace sensibility except that he aspired, he wants them to know that plays and poetry are useful.

In the years of Shakespeare's apprenticeship, Lodge, pranking himself in other men's feathers, tried his hand at the drama, lyric poetry, verse satire, and Euphuistic romance. But he had his one success, *Rosalind,* a prose novella, and it still earns him a place in literary gazetteers. Shakespeare found this romantic narrative soon after its publication (1590). He pulped it for *As You Like It,* a bucolic fantasy enacting old conventions, at the same time exposing them. Death and the Devil, Shakespeare's familiars, walk up and down in Arcadia. Lodge, a camp follower, not a critic, didn't know this. However, he got Shakespeare thinking.

Thomas Nashe, the minister's son, lived from hand to mouth and died in straits, still in his thirties. No one knows where or when he died, before 1601. At Cambridge, town and gown called him "distracted." Thumbing his nose at both, he made his name a byword for "every untoward scholar." Nashe watchers, Argus-eyed, chalked up his misdemeanors. Greene warned him about this, the pot calling the kettle black. An angry revenant in Shakespeare's England, he mocked from the fringes, looking backward to a world where people knew their place. This newfangled censor, Cato in a doublet, has a lot to say about the Sumptuary Laws, bare-breasted women, men who drink too much, foppish men, etc.

Much of his work is piecework, keeping the wolf from the door. He scribbled anti-Puritan tracts for the bishops, wrote a helter-skelter novel, patched a tragic play with Marlowe, a "seditious" play with Jonson. Not distinguished by intellect, only by talent, one type of the artist, he craved gentleman's status, dismissing a play of his as the "imperfect embryo" of idle hours. It was that kind of age. Thomas Kyd's hero, in the most popular play of the age, gave his mind to poetry when he was young—

> fruitless poetry,
> Which though it profit the professor naught,
> Yet is it passing pleasing to the world.

Shakespeare, dedicating his narrative poems, stoops to this otiose talk.

The time's self-anointed conscience, Nashe was Pasquil the lampooner, maker of "pasquinades," or Pierce Penniless, an up-to-date version of the medieval truth-teller, Piers Plowman. Greene called him "young Juvenal," and Lodge the "English Aretine," after that Italian satirist nicknamed the Scourge of Princes. Shakespeare, with a score to settle, rapped his knuckles, "half-penny purse of wit." Smiting too many offenders, the scourge pays none of them home, and Nashe's invective lands him on despair. His best song, a stunning threnody made in plague time, is the product of this, unexpectedly wholesome:

Beauty is but a flower
Which wrinkles will devour.
Brightness falls from the air;
Queens have died young and fair;
Dust hath closed Helen's eye;
I am sick, I must die;
    Lord have mercy on us.

The gift of poetry, charismatic, not earned, sets him apart from most in his time. Otherwise, like most he wanted the good life, denied him by "dry-fisted patrons." (He was in debtors' prison and they wouldn't go bail.) A contemporary makes him say that "if they had given his Muse that cherishment which she most worthily deserved, he had fed to his dying day on fat capons, burnt sack and sugar."

In the late summer of 1592, Nashe and Robert Greene, two gentle-men of Cambridge, banqueted together on pickled herring and Rhenish wine. Greene, surfeited, died a month later. A legend at thirty-four, six years older than Shakespeare, he was the Vagabond King. In Euphuistic prose, he embroidered on this: "As early pricks the tree that will prove a thorn, so even in my first years I began to follow the frettings of mine own desires." The desires, indulged, got him in trouble and he milked it in tracts for the time. "Never too late" to repent, said moral Greene to young gentlemen, intriguingly wicked "in the springtime of their youth."

In his own early time he traveled in Latin countries, an Italianate Englishman, "devil incarnate." Taking a wife, he cast her off, their son too, "having first spent up the marriage money." Apologies followed, fulsome but meant for real. Greene, alert to pathos, made capital of the long-suffering Dorothea, an interesting presence in his romances, "Niobe, all tears." His life copies the romances, melodrama titivated with moral asides.

Even his enemies allowed him bravado. At the end, mindful of the legend, he put up a good front, hiding poverty beneath a cloak decked with "sleeves of a grave goose-turd green." He thought clothes made the man, an imperfect truth but better than nothing. Henry Chettle, his executor, said he affected "the habit of a scholar-like gentleman, only his hair was somewhat long." Nashe remembered the hair, uncut and coming down to a jolly red beard, peaked "like the spire of a steeple." A man could hang a jewel on the tip of this beard. Men who detested Greene compared him to Judas, the red-bearded villain of the mysteries.

Middle class and provincial like Shakespeare the glover's son, he was a saddler's son of Norwich. Facile like Shakespeare, he flowed in numbers, mostly conventional. "Yarking up some pamphlet" took him, said Nashe, "a day or a night." Sometimes he discovered the ardors of convention, e.g. in the song from his *Farewell to Folly* (1591): "A mind content both crown and kingdom is." The type of the literary professional, he knew nothing of contentment, needing only a "topos" or point of departure. This is a reason to praise him, Shakespeare too. Both could write the life of a broomstick.

Skillful in mimicry, not so different from Aesop's crow, Greene got the trick of Lyly's honey-sweet language, also Marlowe's "huffe-snuffe bombast." Doing *Tamburlaine* in one play, he did *Faustus* in another. This other, *Friar Bacon and Friar Bungay,* more a play than Marlowe's, makes a better "composition" than anything on the English stage before Shakespeare. Where Shakespeare is one of a kind, Greene is emblematic, first among many. With him begins the merging of the artist and pariah. He looks forward to Beddoes, Poe, and John Davidson, anguished sensibilities, "one part genius, two parts fudge." A chasm separates him, though, from near contemporaries like Stephen Hawes, groom of the chamber to the first Tudor king. This court functionary, poet plus official wise man and magister ludi, filled a place and knew it. Not Robert Greene.

Shakespeare filled a place, and of course Greene despised him. More resilient than most (but not endlessly resilient: worn out at fifty-two), Shakespeare made his plays as he liked them, at the same time paying tribute to Caesar. This exacted a toll. He "could turn with all tides, tack about and take advantage of all winds, by the quickness of his wit and invention." Greene, rebuked by this address, compared him to the provident ant in Aesop's fable, a "waspish little worm." This reminiscence of his schoolboy reading, Shakespeare's too, surfaces without preamble in the posthumously published *Groatsworth of Wit.* Greene adjusts the fable, and the ant, esteemed for husbandry, turns into a niggard, meanly avaricious. Shakespeare is "the greedy miser" always thirsting for gain. "His thrift is theft, his weal works others' woe." That was how it looked to the grasshopper, a sufficient figure for improvident Greene. But Shakespeare presents the grasshopper too. Prosecuting fortune, no man more adroitly, he is also "fortune's fool," the prodigal who didn't take thought for tomorrow. Greene missed this other side, writ large in the plays and poems.

In the Age of Shakespeare, Greene, not Shakespeare, typifies the professional writer. Like a fiddler or "wait," he stood below stairs, expectant. Society having no use for his minor music, his hand is raised against it. The con man or "cony-catcher" par excellence, he stole from one novel to piece out another. In both he mixed moral bromides with prurient teasing. His most famous novel, *Pandosto*, shows this mix. (Shakespeare, getting his own back, turned it into a silk purse, *The Winter's Tale*.) The Cony-Catching pamphlets, an account of London's underworld, disingenuous like a modern exposé of pornography, were written, Greene said, to "discover the secret villainies of alluring strumpets." It wasn't all faking and one side of him believed this.

His sentimental side, not the blackguardly side, betrayed him. Lodged above the Dowgate, courtesy of his shoemaker landlord, he pegged away at a final potboiler. With him was his mistress, sister of a notorious hoodlum, also his bastard son Fortunatus. The hoodlum was "Cutting Ball," hanged on the gibbet at Tyburn. Dramatizing these last days, Greene called himself the swan who "sings medodiously before death." This sounds cheerful, and perhaps he didn't know he was dying.

His *Groatsworth of Wit* recites "the folly of youth, the falsehood of . . . makeshift flatterers . . . mischiefs of deceiving courtesans," etc. It has a loose plot telling of Roberto, "arch-playmaking poet." Come down in the world, he still preserves a single groat, enough to buy him a "million of repentance." This is patented Greene, scandalmonger and preacher, the man who has it both ways.

But sincerity, breaking in, ruined the swan song, and the racy prose turns captious, shrill with self-pity. Greene, dropping the mask, proclaims himself "the said Roberto." Too late for him, it isn't too late for former friends to profit by his example. Everybody recognized the friends, "fellow scholars about this city," Marlowe, Nashe, and Peele. "Base-minded men," they spent their wits making plays. Marlowe, up to his neck in trouble, could have done without this.

Greene, offering Marlowe a cloak, leaves him naked. He is the atheist who turned from God, worse, the pederast who said all were fools who didn't love boys or tobacco. This canard, abstracted from Marlowe's table talk, is repeated by Greene but tactfully dropped from the published *Groatsworth of Wit*. "Had it been true," says the editor, smirking, "yet to publish it was intolerable." Readers, alerted, read between the lines, and the evil Greene did lived after him.

Down on their luck, Nashe and Peele get off easier, but on Shakespeare, the rising man, Greene empties the vials of his spleen. His attack opens with a caveat inspired by the players, burrs who used to stick to him, now fallen away. "Trust them not," he tells the Wits, for there is an upstart crow, beautified with our feathers, that with his *tiger's heart wrapped in a player's hide* supposes he is as well able to bombast out a blank verse as the best of you; and being an absolute *Johannes Factotum,* is in his own conceit the only Shake-scene in a country.

This cut deep. Years later, Polonious says how " 'Beautified' is a vile phrase."

The upstart crow, an actor turned playwright, is perhaps a plagiarist, thief of other men's plumes. He isn't new to the theater, too popular for that. Already on the boards by 1592, his *Henry VI, Part Three,* made a cento of rousing quotations. Men declaimed the apostrophe addressed to Queen Margaret, triumphant at the battle of Wakefield:

O tiger's heart, wrapped in a woman's hide!

(The Duke of York, a fallen hero, shockingly misused, is this bad woman's reporter.) In Greene's reformulation, Shakespeare stands in for the villainous Queen. Daubing vice with a show of virtue, he conceals his ferocity under a player's hide. The rankling hatred, evidently long building, says that Greene and Shakespeare were friends.

Turning from Shakespeare, Greene addressed his long-abandoned Dorothea. A last letter prayed that she discharge his debt to Isam, the shoemaker: "I owe him ten pound, and but for him I had perished in the streets." Then he died, 3 September 1592, and the shoemaker's wife crowned him with laurel. They buried Greene in Moorfields near Bethlehem Hospital, "Bedlam," London's hospital for the insane. The Industrial Age dug up and ploughed under this quarter of the city, and the grave is lost, hidden beneath the trains in Liverpool Street Station.

Posthumous revenge, the *Groatsworth* raised a tempest in a teapot. Hearing that Greene's "letter written to divers playmakers is offensively by one or two of them taken," Chettle, the editor, published an apology. He said he hadn't been acquainted with either of the injured parties, "and with one of them I care not if I never be." About the other one, though, he had second thoughts, having since seen his demeanor, "no less civil than he excellent in the quality he professes," i.e. the player's trade. A little Heep-ish, he gave the character of the civil man. "Divers of worship have reported his uprightness of dealing, which argues his honesty, and his facetious [urbane] grace in writing that approves his art."

Chettle doesn't name names. Undeterred, Shakespeare's biographers fit Marlowe with the devil's horns. Shakespeare gets the halo. The upright, graceful man bears no resemblance to Greene's waspish little worm. But Shakespeare, mingling contradictions, resembles his Hamlet, a hybrid hero drawn from life. Or he had an unknown bottom, like the Bay of Portugal. Rosalind in *As You Like It* says how it couldn't be sounded.

BIOGRAPHERS ARE grateful to Greene for certifying Shakespeare's presence in London. By 1592 he was someone to reckon with, author of a successful trilogy, likely other plays too. "Likely" needs stressing. Shakespeare's First Folio, bringing together most of the plays, leads off with *The Tempest,* almost his last one, and his first editors are silent on the order he wrote in. Editors since have tried to pin this down. Speculative work, it makes a difference, not for the text, for the kind of man he was.

His first biographer thought him a prodigy who came into the world fully armed. "Perhaps we are not to look for his beginnings, like those of other authors, among their least perfect writings" (said Nicholas Rowe). "Art had so little, and nature so large a share in what he did, that, for aught I know, the performances of his youth, as they were the most vigorous, and had the most fire and strength of imagination in 'em, were the best." A whimsical essay is potential on the basis of "for aught I know," not biography. But more can be said than this.

A few rough rules of thumb for dating: Shakespeare's early plays favor rhyme, the later ones blank verse. (But in some early plays, notably *King John,* blank verse is favored, and rhyme makes a comeback in some later plays like *All's Well That Ends Well.*) Mature Shakespeare enjambs his lines more than the early poet, and his diction is more Latinate (but also more spare). As he gets older he turns more readily to prose (but hardly stints on poetry, more fluent than it used to be, at the same time vexed or "tortive"). Many of his plays fall together in groups, and even if no other evidence offered most readers would tend to aggregate the early comedies, the "problem" plays, late romances, and so forth. Similarities in plot or genre, if only skin-deep, prove nothing, however. In the *Henry IV* plays and *The Merry Wives of Windsor,* the same characters come on stage or they have the same names. But the history plays and Shakespeare's farce comedy are different in their bones, and for once, at least, there's nothing in a name. Making rules for Shakespeare isn't easy.

He was always news, even from the beginning, and sometimes contemporaries quote or echo him in print. Jonson, doing this in a play of 1599, gives a terminal date for *Julius Caesar.* Fifteen years later, introducing *Bartholomew Fair* to theater-goers at the Hope, he thought of

Shakespeare again, the cross he carried. This time the play was *Titus Andronicus*, first published in 1594. The judgment that praised it, Kyd's *Jeronimo* too, "hath stood still," Jonson considered, "these five and twenty, or thirty years." Not meant for precise but rounded off contemptuously, the numbers suggest an old play. For this, 1594 seems too recent. Lumping *Titus Andronicus* with *The Spanish Tragedy*, Jonson wants us to think of both as work of the 1580s, antediluvian. His Shakespeare, for better or worse, was already hard at it in the Lost Years.

Sometimes Shakespeare dates himself, as when, in a Chorus to *Henry V*, he salutes the Earl of Essex, campaigning in Ireland. This topical reference zeroes in on the time, between 27 March and 28 September 1599. Shakespeare isn't often that helpful. Bad weather, an occasion for poetry, dismays his principals in *A Midsummer Night's Dream*, and the weather was very bad in 1594. It often is in England. Mostly, Shakespeare's allusions, beguiling or gratuitous (like grace), hitch on to too much or too little.

An apparent exception is *Romeo and Juliet*, first published in 1597 but written several years before. As this play begins its inexorable progress, two old Capulets, both past their dancing days, recall "the nuptial of Lucentio," thirty years ago, and the Nurse thinks of Juliet's weaning: " 'Tis since the earthquake now eleven years." Some, invoking the London earthquake of 1580, want to date Shakespeare's play in 1591, a literalistic response. Time in *Romeo and Juliet* operates on two levels, though, slow-chapped for the elders, for the young lovers like "the lightning in the collied night." In the world "outside" the play, years have gone by, "heavy, slow, and pale as lead." But Shakespeare, toting them up, isn't fixing the date of composition.

Sensibility or literary tact will instruct readers that *Romeo and Juliet*, not coeval with the writing of the *Henry VI* plays, is a star of a different magnitude. This subjective approach to the problem of dating seems in a hard-headed age like throwing in the towel. Credentialed Shakespeareans do what they can to banish taste or intuition in favor of principles, hopefully scientific. But in the last resort, grappling with Shakespeare needs intuitive responses and tact must be the arbiter of judgment.

Only in the last resort, however. Much matter of fact invests Shakespeare's plays, bearing on the time they were written. In 1598 a literary clergyman, Francis Meres, listed six comedies, four histories, and two tragedies by Shakespeare, assigning a last-possible date for these plays. Title pages of the quartos sometimes carry a date, and sometimes Shakespeare gets credit as author. The Register of the Company of

SHAKESPEARE'S BIRTHPLACE. Shakespeare's father was living in the house on Henley Street as early as 1552, and in the west wing Shakespeare was born twelve years later. The property, carefully restored, now looks very much as it did two hundred years ago when the first surviving sketch was made.
Courtesy of Jarrold Colour Publications.

TRINITY CHURCH, STRATFORD. Shakespeare was baptized in this ancient church beside the Avon, and fifty-two years later was buried in the chancel.
Photo by Edwin Smith, courtesy of Olive Smith.

CLOPTON BRIDGE. A famous local son of Stratford built this stone bridge over the Avon the century before Shakespeare's birth. The road to and from London still leads across the bridge. In the 1580s when Shakespeare walked to London to begin his career in the theater, this was his starting-out point.
Photo by Edwin Smith, courtesy of Olive Smith.

MARY ARDEN'S HOUSE. Robert Arden, a well-to-do yeoman, sired a large brood in this Wilmcote farmstead but Mary, Shakespeare's mother, was his favorite. When John Shakespeare came courting in the 1550s, he walked across the fields from Stratford, three miles away.
Courtesy of Jarrold Colour Publications.

THE LAST JUDGMENT, GILD CHAPEL, STRATFORD. Shakespeare's father, John, during his tour of duty as Stratford Borough's Chamberlain, paid two shillings to have these "Popish" images defaced and whitewashed. For more than two hundred years, no one saw them again.

From Thomas Sharp, A Dissertation on the Pageants or Dramatic Mysteries, *1825*.

WILD MAN, CARVED ON A CHOIR STALL IN HOLY TRINITY CHURCH, COVENTRY, NEAR STRATFORD. This bestial creature, a type of Shakespeare's "unaccommodated man," haunted the imagination of his contemporaries.
Courtesy of the Royal Commission on the Historical Monuments of England.

ST. GEORGE AND THE DRAGON, GILD CHAPEL, STRATFORD. St. George skewered the dragon in Stratford's annual pageant until Reformers put a stop to this. An appropriate conjunction honoring England's best poet and her patron saint, the Feast of St. George falls on Shakespeare's birthday.
Courtesy of the Shakespeare Birthplace Trust, Stratford-upon-Avon.

SHAKESPEARE'S SCHOOLHOUSE. Bullied by the "abcedarius," a domineering pedant, Shakespeare learned his ABCs and much else in this Stratford "grammar school." Erected long before his time, it still functions today.
Courtesy of Jarrold Colour Publications.

THE GILD CHAPEL FROM THE GRAMMAR SCHOOL QUADRANGLE. Water-color by F. W. Whitehead, about 1900. Much of Stratford's prosperity in earlier days depended on the pious guildsmen-and-women who built this chapel and the grammar school beside it. Shakespeare in later days lived across the road.
Courtesy of Jarrold Colour Publications.

ANNE HATHAWAY'S COTTAGE. This twelve-room Tudor farmhouse, picture-perfect with its thatched roof, timber-framed walls, and latticed windows, glorifies the hamlet of Shottery, a mile west of Stratford. When Anne Hathaway was born here in 1552, her family dwelling stood on the edge of the Forest of Arden. Some say Shakespeare in *As You Like It* gave its likeness.
Courtesy of Jarrold Colour Publications.

ANNE HATHAWAY, an ink drawing dated 1708 and supposedly a copy of an earlier picture. The costume details of cap and ruff fit the Elizabethan period, and handwritten verses describe this formidable-looking woman as "Shakespeare's Consort." Most of their married life, these two lived apart.
Courtesy of the Everett Needham Case Library of Colgate University, Hamilton, N.Y.

CHARLECOTE MANOR WITH THE GATEHOUSE, a nineteenth-century engraving. An old tradition that won't die has young Shakespeare poaching venison and rabbits on the grounds of Charlecote, not far from Stratford. Whipped for his transgressions, he lampooned the manor lord, then fled to London, a scandalous beginning to an illustrious career.
Courtesy of Jarrold Colour Publications.

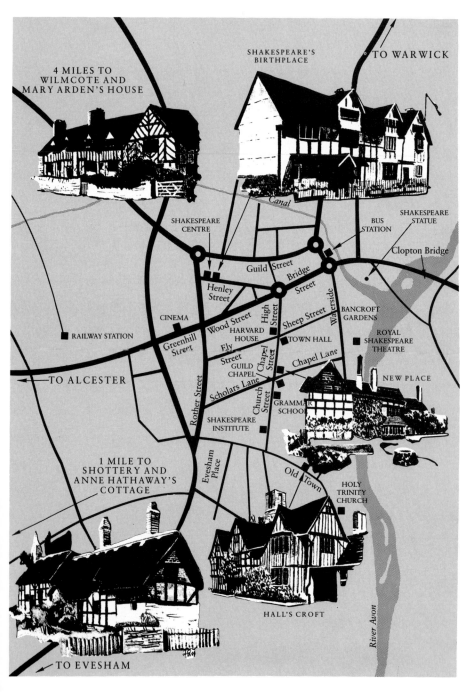

SHAKESPEARE'S
BIRTHPLACE

TO WARWICK

4 MILES TO
WILMCOTE AND
MARY ARDEN'S HOUSE

Canal

SHAKESPEARE STATUE

SHAKESPEARE
CENTRE

BUS
STATION

Clopton Bridge

Guild Street

Bridge

Henley
Street

Street

Waterside

CINEMA

Wood Street

High Street

Sheep Street

BANCROFT
GARDENS

RAILWAY STATION

Greenhill
Street

HARVARD
HOUSE

TOWN HALL

ROYAL
SHAKESPEARE
THEATRE

Ely
Street

GUILD
CHAPEL

Chapel Street

Chapel Lane

TO ALCESTER

Rother Street

Scholars Lane

Church Street

NEW PLACE

SHAKESPEARE
INSTITUTE

GRAMMAR
SCHOOL

1 MILE TO
SHOTTERY AND
ANNE HATHAWAY'S
COTTAGE

Evesham Place

Old Town

HOLY
TRINITY
CHURCH

River Avon

HALL'S CROFT

TO EVESHAM

STRATFORD. "A proper little market town" when Shakespeare lived there, it housed fewer than 2,000 people. To walk round its boundaries took about twenty minutes.

From The Shakespearian Properties *by Dr. Levi Fox, Jarrold Colour Publications.*

QUEEN ELIZABETH I IN 1585, attributed to Nicholas Hilliard, the most gifted English painter in Shakespeare's England. Elizabeth reigned for forty-five years and like Shakespeare combined the qualities of lion and fox. She liked going to plays and Shakespeare's were often performed in her presence.
From the collection of the Marquess of Salisbury, Hertford House, Hertfordshire.

HENRY WRIOTHESLEY, THIRD EARL OF SOUTHAMPTON. This prominent nobleman was Shakespeare's patron and the narrative poems are both dedicated to him. Later in life, he played a part in colonizing the New World.
From the collection of the Duke of Portland, Welbeck Abbey.

Inside the engraving, the following labels appear:

THAMESIS

Three Cranes

The Gally fuste

The Eell Schipes

The Bear Gardne

The Globe

J. C. VISSCHER'S ENGRAVING OF LONDON FROM THE BANKSIDE, ABOUT 1616. In the foreground are Shakespeare's Globe and the Bear Garden, a theater of cruelty, across the Thames old St. Paul's. Shakespeare at different times in his career lived on both sides of the river.

GEORGE INN, SOUTHWARK. The last survivor of London's galleried inns, this one and others gave hints for Shakespeare's playhouse, the Globe. Pressed together in the innyard, the "groundlings," Shakespeare's best patrons, surrounded the stage on three sides, while the better sort looked down from above.
Courtesy of the National Trust Photographic Library, London.

HELL MOUTH. Detail from the Last Judgment in Gloucester Cathedral. In plays of Shakespeare's period, evil doers like Marlowe's Faustus were hustled into the Hell Mouth by demons. Shakespeare's theater located Hell in the "cellarage" under the stage.

TITUS ANDRONICUS. This drawing from the 1590s illustrates a scene from Shakespeare's goriest play. Tamora, queen of the Goths, pleads with the hero for the lives of her sons, pointed to by Aaron the Moor, a monster of iniquity. Modern playgoers are generally revolted by this early tragedy, but Shakespeare's contemporaries loved it.

Courtesy of the Marquess of Bath, Longleat House, Warminster, Wiltshire.

Stationers, London booksellers, supplies many dates, here and there flagging error. Entries in the Register functioned as a kind of copywright, often ignored in Shakespeare's time but useful to editors in time to come. *Troilus and Cressida,* not published until 1609, first appears in the Register six years before. A "blocking entry," this dates the play. The Revels Accounts record performances at Court, and sketchier records exist for the public theaters and law schools. Henslowe in his Diary cites a number of the early plays (though it isn't always clear what his citations mean). Later plays get mention in other diarists and letter writers. When fire destroyed the Globe, June 29, 1613, Sir Henry Wotton wrote about this, telling how cannon, fired off in the course of "a new play," set the house ablaze. He writes about the play too, authorizing a date for *Henry VIII.*

But the evidence for chronology, fragmentary or abundant, sponsors different conclusions. The orthodox view concludes that Shakespeare began to write for the theater in 1590–91. Set in concrete a half century ago, this view derives from E. K. Chambers, building on the labors of Edmund Malone. Late-blooming Shakespeare is substantially the creation of these two great scholars. At first, they thought, he tinkered anonymous hack work, old chronicles of York and Lancaster or early versions of *King John* and *The Taming of the Shrew.* Necessarily, his own versions postdate these source plays. By the time Greene attacked him, dilatory Shakespeare had only a few plays in his scrip.

This laggard in theater, copious and facile for most of his career, doesn't meet our expectation. What was he doing in his early time, and if not very much, what put Greene out of temper? His biographer takes the view that what he was doing was making plays, as many as ten by 1592, the first histories and comedies, *King John,* and *Titus Andonicus.* These plays comprehend the three kinds of drama, comedy, tragedy, and history, and Shakespeare in the Lost Years, honing his skills, tried them all. Work of his nonage and full of prosperous things, it isn't uniformly successful. Already he has his "poetics" by heart, the patterns or conventions that declare him in future. But he hasn't fleshed them out or estimated what they mean, and like steely bones wanting "paste and cover," sometimes they look bleak in the wind. This is especially true of his first essays in tragedy.

As always, he built on other men's work. He caught the accent of Peele and Marlowe, singing masters, useful for sonority. Kyd gave him a high-colored sketch for his *Hamlet.* That famous Elizabethan "Anon," author of a picaresque *Henry V* and a maudlin *King Lear* preferred by Tolstoy to Shakespeare's, came in handy too. A little later in the 1590s, when he wanted guidelines for pastoral or the new erotic "epyllion," just coming into vogue, he read up Thomas Lodge. Absorbing what these writers had to teach him, Shakespeare, a version of King Claudius, kept them in a corner of his jaw like a sponge. Having squeezed them he spat them out, then made his own kind of play, coining silver in Finsbury Fields.

Indulgent critics in this century, not so different from Greene, assimilate Shakespeare to his Autolycus, his eye taken by the linen hanging on the line at the new playhouses north and south of the Thames. But he wasn't an old-clothes man or "botcher" and didn't dress himself in borrowed garments. Some of his so-called source plays, not sources at all, were progeny of his, abducted and deformed by lesser lights and pirate printers. This piratical activity says that early Shakespeare pleased. No longer a tyro in 1592, he stood near the top of his profession. Had he died in his twenties, Shakespeare would have been missed. Chettle, apologizing, had reason to defer to this established playwright, and emulous Greene to detest him.

IN THE YEARS just before Shakespeare came to public notice, acting companies flourished briefly, then sank from view, disrupted by plague, a patron's death, or quarrels among the principal actors. A brawl in the playhouse finished off Leicester's Men, James Burbage's old troupe, and a riot of London's prentices in June 1592 led Privy Council to shut down the theaters. Before they could reopen, plague, an evil planet, loomed over the "high-viced" city. This kept the theaters shut for nearly two years. Companies like Pembroke's Men, forced to sell their costumes and playbooks, went under. Shakespeare practiced survival. His biographers, hopeful but mostly disappointed, look for traces of him on the wild and violent sea.

Out of the wreckage new alliances formed, Edward Alleyn making the focal point for one. A giant of a man, he was England's first great tragic actor. In 1591, at the wooden O in Shoreditch, Alleyn headed a combined company named for the Lord High Admiral and the Lord Strange. But Burbage, up to his old tricks, siphoned off money from the gatherer's box, and Alleyn threatened to hale him before "their lord and master." Headstrong temperament inflamed this quarrel over lucre. Burbage swore "that he cared not for three of the best lords of them all," and Alleyn, leaving the Theater, threw in with Henslowe at the Rose. Solidifying the connection, he married Henslowe's stepdaughter. Big roles were his forte and the company poet, a "famous gracer of tragedians," supplied them. The poet was Christopher Marlowe.

In 1594, when the Lord Strange, Earl of Derby, died, his company split two ways. Some, following Alleyn, went over to father-in-law Henslowe on the Bankside. Others, led by young Richard Burbage, stayed with father Burbage at the Theater. They formed the Lord Chamberlain's Men. At this point, Shakespeare comes into focus.

First glimpsed, he is dancing attendance at Court. For two comedies or "interludes" played before the Queen in December 1594, the Treasurer of the Chamber lists payment to "William Kempe, William Shakespeare, and Richard Burbage, servants to the Lord Chamberlain." Henry Carey, Lord Hunsdon, was Lord Chamberlain this year. An important officer of the Royal Household, he sat with Privy Council, so backed up the players in their tug-of-war with the London Corporation. Where the Master of the Horse looked after the Queen's Stables and the Lord Steward her Kitchen, the Chamberlain saw to the Household "upstairs," including the Queen's entertainment. Shakespeare, Groom in Ordinary of the Chamber, helped provide this, keeping a drowsy emperor awake.

The Chamberlain's Men, first in the annals of the stage in his time, were only one among many in their formative years, and competitors strove with them for popular favor. Some suppose that young Shakespeare broke in with the competition, an actor or hireling attached to the Queen's Men or Pembroke's. More than one of these companies put on his plays—like "Titus & ondronicus," played by Sussex's Men—and the repertories of other companies gave him brummagem stuff he turned golden. Not a "dresser" of plays but an alchemist who had the "stone," he transmuted whatever he found in his workshop. It is in character that he was a mercenary, loyal only to his daemon. But the word is too expensive for this hard-working playwright. Romantic poets have a daemon. He had a living to make, and whatever company would take him was the one for him.

The company of players Hunsdon lent his name to became the King's Men in the reign of James I. Joining this fellowship early in his career, Shakespeare never left it. The connection, partly servile, wasn't always to his taste. King James, "the wisest fool in Christendom," had his fetishes, and Hunsdon, choleric and tactless, was known for a "custom of swearing." Shakespeare and fellows, low down on the totem pole, bore the brunt of this. If he turned Turk in his fortunes (fell on hard times), Hamlet told Horatio, he might get himself a fellowship in a "cry" or pack of players. But the noble patron facilitated the play. Already in the 1580s, James Burbage, sheltering from the wrath of London's City Recorder, called himself Lord Hunsdon's man. Shakespeare, wearing Hunsdon's colors, later the King's, walked with impunity in a world that set snares for his feet.

Gentry in his age, glorifying the idle life, heard attacks on the theater as personal to themselves. Between this upper crust and the common player, an unlikely alliance came into being. (On a small scale, it predicts the Civil War, already making noises off-stage.) Licensing the players, a hundred peers and knights took them under their protection. When the Lord Mayor and Aldermen banned plays from the City, Crown lands gave them houseroom. Puritans railed but Shakespeare's plays got a hearing.

The affinity of high and low against the rest of society, "fat, sleek-headed men," is one of Shakespeare's subjects, and often in the plays his mind is seized by an old ballad, "The King and the Beggar," sometimes the Beggar Maid. He is the beggar or servingman, "a motley to the view." In the sonnets he tells bitterly of putting on this fool's garment, another of his disguises. It kept him in pocket but envenomed a proud man, like the shirt of Nessus the centaur, dipped in poison. "Generous ... in mind and mood," a fellow-poet called him, i.e. *generosus,* a gentleman by nature. But "the stage doth stain pure gentle blood," said this poet ruefully, and Shakespeare lived in disgrace "with Fortune and men's eyes." He said his name received a brand from the entertainer's role, an infection strong as plague. What was a player? Jonson, insolent like the Wits, answered in his *Poetaster:* a "lousy slave ... rascal ... two-penny tearmouth ... stinkard ... presumptuous varlet." Making money on plays, Shakespeare bought a coat of arms but that was merest whitewash, and the old invidious statute of Henry VIII, reenacted a few years before Elizabeth died, still classed him with rogues, vagabonds, and beggars. Men who hated his profession reminded him of this.

ALLEYN, self-styled "the fustian king," bestrode Shakespeare's early theater like a colossus. An anecdotist remembered him "so acting to the life that he made any part (especially a majestic one) to become him." His company, the Admiral's, challenged Shakespeare's for preeminence. In 1598 a decree of Privy Council limited the number of acting companies in London to the Admiral's Men and the Chamberlain's Men. The fewer the companies, the easier to keep them in line. Careful of its authority, the Crown looked with a jealous eye on departures from the line, laid down by the Master of the Revels.

For the next forty years, the Admiral's Men and the Chamberlain's Men ruled the roost between them. (The boys at Blackfriars and Worcester's new troupe disputed this, but they were pretenders.) Starting off with an advantage, the Admiral's Men lost it when Marlowe died, stabbed by an assassin in a low tavern brawl. This left the field clear for Shakespeare.

Marlowe's obit might read: born in Canterbury 1564, son of a shoemaker. Educated at the King's School and Corpus Christi College, Cambridge. Taken up early by powerful patrons, including the Walsinghams, Thomas and Francis. (See under Francis Walsingham, spymaster to the Queen.) In a half-dozen spectacular plays, beginning with *Tamburlaine*, about 1587, boosted London's theater out of the Middle Ages into the modern world. Translated Latin poetry and left unfinished a witty paraphrase of the old romantic tale of Hero and Leander. Died at twenty-nine, May 30, 1593. This factual account leaves out almost all that matters, Marlowe's "mighty line" and "brave translunary things." Among great makers cut off before their prime, he ranks first, and only the loss of Keats bears comparison.

A revolutionary in the theater, more decisive for its subsequent fortunes than Shakespeare, he inherited an older theater peopled by shadows, e.g. the Vices and Virtues of *The Castle of Perseverance* who fight for the soul of man, a personified abstraction. Scanting body for soul, older playwrights had an end in view, salvation. Marlowe's end is entertainment.

Not capable himself of flesh-and-blood character—mysterious, he must have thought it, possibly boring—he has no characters, only gigantic cartoons. This is the link with his medieval forebears. All the while, though, he meant to explode them. Agreeing with the makers of the morality play that character is nothing, he scouted their moral intention. Fiercely polemical, unlike laconic Shakespeare, he thought that to build things you had to tear them down. (Sorel and Artaud are distant cousins of his.) Creating a vacuum at the heart of the play, he filled it with "scenes" and heart-stopping music. The scenes don't connect, "Democritean" Marlowe being innocent of cause. But he delivered the theater from its ancient obligation to justify or falsify the ways of God to men. Just here, Shakespeare's story begins.

Shakespeare's plays, rising from character, are replete with intention. But they have no didactic intention and are satisfied to render the moment as it actually consists. This is thanks to Marlowe. Neutral in first and last things, he is like that Ovid he translated, light years removed from the pious humbug they tried to foist on Shakespeare the schoolboy. Sensation is the meat he feeds on, relished for its own sake. Shakespeare's war of wit and will doesn't much engage him. Even in *Faustus*, a temptation play, it seems mostly facade. But he knows about horror, grotesque comedy too, and his Jew of Malta, going into the cauldron at the end of the play, is very diverting.

Iniquitous business is the stuff of Marlowe's plays, bassed by appreciative chuckling. The important question is whether the business is well carried. Form, Shakespeare's province, eluded Marlowe to the end, and his dramatic structure, panoramic, is that of a picaresque novel. He wrote a single play, unified or rather galvanized by the presence of an amoral hero. *Edward II*, his masterpiece, is more dramatic than *Tamburlaine*, having twice as many speeches (Marlowe, for once, curbing his instinct for grand opera). But his plays and poems, more or less "mature," are more alike than different, and the hero in all of them is a version of the shoemaker's son. An upstart like Shakespeare but defiant about this, he thinks the career belongs to the talents. The suffrage he gets from us, independent of moral judgment, depends on the cunning exercise of his mother wit.

Unlike many lesser men, Marlowe wants decorum, and the mighty lines, not especially appropriate to the surrogates who utter them, make a tissue of elegant extracts. The elegance amazes, though.

> Base fortune, now I see, that in thy wheel
> There is a point, to which when men aspire
> They tumble headlong down. That point I touched,
> And seeing there was no point to mount up higher,
> Why should I grieve at my declining fall?

Caesar is Brutus' evil spirit and Marlowe is Shakespeare's. They were of an age, came up together, and learned and borrowed from one another's plays. But Marlowe is the master, Shakespeare the acolyte, and his special "luster" thickens when the other shines by. It wasn't so much that Marlowe's brilliance cast him in the shade as that the nature of the brilliance, all primary colors, no chiaroscuro in it, baffled his genius. When he tries the Marlovian thing, as in *Richard III*, he makes vivid melodrama, cold, however, and this kind of success left him bored or fretful. His cardboard cutout lacked humanity, right for the genre, not right for him, and opening up the play in the middle of things, he gave Richard a guilty conscience, bad dreams, etc. This bespeaks moral Shakespeare, the man who thinks causally, but mollifying his hard surface, he spoiled what he had made.

Marlowe, altogether colder, wasn't prone to this mistake. On the limited ground he marked off for himself, he is the better playwright. The limitation is key, much too cabined for Shakespeare. His *Richard III*, first-rate farce and other things, is more theatrical than his panoramic plays. But readers and playgoers who like their Shakespeare indigenous will prefer the warmer climate of *Henry VI*, Part Two.

Still hankering after Marlowe's kind of success, Shakespeare tried again in *King John*, a play with all the ingredients, horror, pathos, and comedy. In a patriotic time, not long after the Armada, he worked the patriotic pedal, knowing what would please. Propriety doesn't detain

him, and he puts a rousing tribute to England, "that white-faced shore
. . . water-wallèd bulwark," in the mouth of the Duke of Austria, no
Englishman he. This speech warms the cockles, though, and no doubt
Shakespeare's audience applauded.

Cashing in on the popularity of Shakespeare's play, a dishonest
scribbler brought out a plagiarized version in 1591, *The Troublesome
Reign of King John*. Shakespeare's source, older scholarship called it,
assigning Shakespeare's *King John* to 1596–97. The standard view of
the relation between them, it hasn't gone unchallenged, and some recent
scholarship wants to turn the relation around. Dating the play depends
partly on the eye and ear, "traded" (experienced) pilots or impression-
istic reporters. For one reader, at least, *King John* looks and sounds
like early Shakespeare.

That isn't true on every page. Distinguished rhetoric, signaling mature Shakespeare, patches the play:

> the hearts
> Of all his people shall revolt from him
> And kiss the lips of unacquainted change,
> And pick strong matter of revolt and wrath
> Out of the bloody fingers' ends of John.

That is how Shakespeare sounds when he comes into his kingdom.
More often, though, this play's verse is "spavined," i.e. actors reciting
it draw breath in the middle of the line. (Generally at the end, a full
stop awaits them.) One-syllable words turn up frequently, an index of
early Shakespeare, but speeches, unless impeded with these little words,
don't brook interference from the playwright. Tamburlaine is at his
elbow. Not much occupied with dialog, he likes the sweep of a formal
oration. Two orations, posed and complementary, seem better than
one.

Self-regarding and pleased with itself, evidently young man's work,
King John indulges much "beautiful" writing. A silver tear having
fallen in a grieving woman's hair,

> Even to that drop ten thousand wiry friends
> Do glue themselves in sociable grief,
> Like true, inseparable, faithful loves,
> Sticking together in calamity.

The grief has its occasion, little Prince Arthur, a pathetic victim in this
troublesome reign. Behind the histrionics, some imagine a stricken
Shakespeare, lamenting his own son, dead at age eleven. Bathos and
indecorum mar Shakespeare's writing after *King John*, for example in

Romeo and Juliet. But by 1596, the year Hamnet died, Shakespeare, more scrupulous and not so patient of himself, no longer tugs at our heart-strings.

Like many in his time and the time before him, he peoples his play with stereotypes, puppets in a mumming or pageant. As in the theater, "they gape and point" at his "industrious scenes and acts of death." This theatrical image is controlling for *King John,* a bloody arena where action is rotelike and purport mysterious. Old-fashioned theater, it begins with a question, addressed to the pit. (Or perhaps hopeful Shakespeare is catechizing himself.) "Now say, Chatillion, what would France with us?" But the question goes unanswered except by reasons-of-state. Pandulph the legate gives the "scheme" of Shakespeare's play, a contradiction in terms: "All form is formless, order orderless." Not what Shakespeare had in mind, *King John* looks like history as history.

Invisible "sticklers" with their batons marshal the flow of things, otherwise chaotic. Blocking out Shakespeare's stage, they set a Herald of France with Trumpets against an English Herald, accompanied by same, bring on "Two kings, with their powers" from stage left and right, or juxtapose two petitioners, soliciting the king. One goes down "upon my knee," matched by the other, her knee "hard with kneeling." The king, between and above them, makes the apex of a triangle. Finally, he declares himself: "England, I will fall from thee." This emblematic scene, a high point in *King John,* is visually striking but frozen.

For early Shakespeare, aggressively symmetrical in his dramatic practice, that is its virtue. *King John* is all carapace, and you look in vain for interior logic. Disguising its absence, symmetry confers the favor of unity (but not the unity of theme, "thriftless ambition," etc.). Asymmetry loosens, and early Shakespeare doesn't often risk it. In his first comedies, Dromio S. meets Dromio E. and four young women of France pair off with four men of Navarre. In early tragedy too, for instance *Titus Andronicus.* This play opens with a crowd scene, possibly confusing, but Shakespeare sorts it out. Four sons of Titus enter first, two by two, then the hero and antihero, Tamora, Queen of Goths. Her three sons follow, trailed by Aaron the Moor. Number makes coherence, four virtuous Romans against four wicked Goths. Filing in behind them come other Goths in fetters and Romans with halberds. The logic of the play demands that these supers complement each other, just so many in either camp.

Having no center, the play wants to fly apart. Here was a way to prevent this. Later Shakespeare takes his chances, finding form in the material. His plots go their own way and characters are given their head. Marlowe, more timorous in his stagecraft than Shakespeare, persists in the reliance on number or "magic." Nihilistic, so a prey to chaos, he had something to fear.

In *King John* a restive Shakespeare seeks to exorcize Marlowe's spell, part of this play's fascination. Wheeling up his battery of familiar conventions (microcosm = macrocosm), he trains it on "history," not sensational incident, deponent sayeth, but cause and effect. Exhalations, whizzing in the heavens, portend no good to us. The land is like the body, infected by disease. Sin is a disease, a boil ripe for breaking,

> And when it breaks, I fear will issue thence
> The foul corruption of a sweet child's death.

This organic imagery, insistent in Shakespeare's play, attests the moral maker in spite of himself.

Ransacking his sources, Hall and Holinshed, Latin chronicles and old romances of Coeur-de-lion, he looked for a positive cathode. But his "eponymous" hero, not only villainous, was supine. History foiling him, he put it aside. From a single hint in Holinshed, he created the Bastard Faulconbridge, comic, irrepressible, above all energetic. This Philip gets the play's best speeches, and everyone remembers him on "tickling Commodity." His patriotic hymn, sounding like a trumpet at the last curtain, still makes the hairs rise. (Answering no questions, it absorbs them in rhetoric.) A made-up character, better than anything history had to show, he brings Shakespeare's play alive.

But he isn't a hero, only incarnate ego. Nothing amiss in that, Marlowe considered. In *Edward II,* a play without a hero, energized particles stream in an airless container. Triumphant theater, it isn't Shakespeare's kind of theater, and ignoring the lesson of *Richard III* he lays hands on his buxom cartoon. Pinched by remorse, the provincial Machiavel of the first scene aspires to humanity. Where he was "himself alone," a comic grotesque, he professes respect for the powers above, love for "dear Mother England," etc. This change is for the better but comes as a surprise. Unluckily for Shakespeare, the audience feels itself imposed on, and *King John* has never ranked among his successes. The chance was always there to salvage his play: only titillate the crowd and let meaning and all that alone. Marlowe might have made a great success of *King John.*

AS THE LAST DECADE of the century opened, Marlowe and Shakespeare dominated London's theater, twin stars, one ascending, the other at the apogee of his powers. They shared the firmament with other playwrights, among them Thomas Kyd. A classic manqué, like the author of *Dracula,* he wrote *The Spanish Tragedy.* This great shocker of the 1580s still reverberated in the next century, distant thunder.

In his tribute to Shakespeare, Jonson, mustering contemporaries, made room for "sporting Kyd." This engaging pleasantry calls up the wrong image, "Sporting with Amaryllis in the shade." Unmatched for vulgar ferocity in the history of English drama, *The Spanish Tragedy* inaugurated the vogue of the revenge play, more like truth than fiction. Of its numerous progeny, Shakespeare's *Hamlet* is only the most famous.

It is possible to see Kyd as a nice man with a living to make, the shopkeeper type alert enough to estimate the cash value of trading in horror. Or perhaps his great success was fortuitous, and hitting a nerve in *The Spanish Tragedy* he didn't know he had done this. An opportunist like Shakespeare but without a fixed point, he lacked the discriminating power. Also he lacked artistic conscience and his raison d'être is visceral tickling. That is deplorable but lucky for the future. Toward the end of his life, turning up a dead end, he wrote classical tragedy where all is told and nothing happens. His last play, a sterile exercise, pleased the cognoscenti.

He wrote a Hamlet play too, earlier than Shakespeare's. Years later his fellow Wit Thomas Lodge recalled "the ghost which cried so miserably at the theater like an oyster wife, 'Hamlet, revenge.' " Kyd lives in the similitude. Handing on a plot to Shakespeare, he stuck close to his source, a medieval horror story, and though his *Hamlet* is lost *The Spanish Tragedy* gives its quality and kind. Chorus to the tragedy, a Ghost from the Underworld "and with him Revenge" enters like Lazarus, "come back to tell you all." This triggers ensuing action, the Dumb Show presenting murder most foul, the sinister mumming of the play-within-the-play, the hero's madness, real or pretended. Shakespeare's hero is mad as he falters beneath the burden of the mystery, Kyd's hero Hieronimo because the plot demands this. Plot for Shakespeare enacts the theme, where in Kyd it stands alone, hurly burly without implication. His governing question is "How."

Like Marlowe, only never so superb, Kyd appeals to energy, and character for him reduces to caloric quotient. His onstage butcheries, not pertinent but splotches of color, are meant to delight. He has designs on our person, by no means to his credit. Stage directions, culled at random, suggest where he is going and where he hopes to take us: "They hang him in the arbor. . . . They stab him. . . . They bind him to the stake. . . . He turns him off. . . . She runs lunatic. . . .

He draweth out a bloody napkin [dyed in his son's blood]. . . . He bites out his tongue." In *Titus Andronicus*, Shakespeare puts this last to use when he brings on stage his heroine Lavinia, "her hands cut off and her tongue cut out, and ravished." Shakespeare's play is more perverted than Kyd's, being the product of a greater talent. But the Ghost, concluding *The Spanish Tragedy*, gives the rubric for both: "these were spectacles to please my soul."

Kyd and Shakespeare have a model in Roman Seneca, first-century moralist who burned while Nero fiddled. From this closet playwright, each learned how not to write plays. Seneca's plots are exceptionally nasty but no blood flows on stage. Compunctious, he keeps his action to the wings or the green room, and a Chorus or Nuntius does duty for ocular proof. Telling, Seneca thinks, is better than seeing. A considerable poet, like Racine in the age after Shakespeare, he makes it worth your while to read him.

This can't be said for Kyd. His rhetoric, a schoolmaster's, is inert on the page.

> O eyes, no eyes, but fountains fraught with tears;
> O life, no life, but lively form of death.
> O world, no world, but mass of public wrongs,
> Confused and filled with murder and misdeeds.

Metered, this isn't poetry, and the lively (i.e. lifelike) form of death, muffled by the sclerotic style, goes unnoticed. But Kyd understood that living theater isn't language alone. This is his special virtue, maybe faute de mieux. In an age when the drama, balanced on a tickle point, was in danger of being coopted by bookmen, he denied their major, good taste. Dispensing with taste, he made the crowd bear witness.

Ratified by Shakespeare, Kyd's impure amalgam carried the day. This victory was hardly foreordained. Fastidious Sidney, a great poet but bad critic, thought dreary *Gorboduc* was the way to go. He had his learned followers, Bacon, dabbling in drama at Gray's Inn, Samuel Daniel who wrote a Cleopatra play that begins after Antony is dead, nostalgic Fulke Greville, the same who called himself Shakespeare's master. His "Turkish" plays, very talky, gather dust in the stacks.

Sidney's best scholar is Jonson. In two Roman plays invoking "the reader extraordinary," he sought to redraw tragedy on purely Senecan lines. A great man of theater, Jonson went off the rails owing partly to envy of Shakespeare, an ignis fatuus, he told himself. Improving on *Julius Caesar*, Jonson in *Catiline* gave them classical tragedy, the real thing with all its longueurs on. Caesar, fallen at the base of Pompey's statue, red with blood, seemed to him a breach of decorum. Wanting to hide this, he opened a chasm between life and art.

In his art of Grand Guignol, Kyd soldered it up. A public executioner, he spared nobody's feelings, and his tragic hero, plunging the scarabs in his eyes, did this in full view of the crowd. Captivated by Seneca's bloodthirsty stories, Kyd saved the gore but threw out the static form. We don't gather his shifty truth from hearsay. Like Thomas called Didymus, he lives by "the sensible and true avouch of eyes." Shakespeare, instructed, stands on Kyd's shoulders.

Out, vile jelly!
Where is thy luster now?

This bodying forth, savage when it had to be, is Kyd's great contribution, and without him there would have been no *King Lear*.

Before *King Lear*, however, came *Titus Andronicus*, a witches' brew mixing Kyd and Seneca's *Thyestes*. Older critics, revolted, struck it from the canon. Already in the Restoration, one playwright, "improving" Shakespeare to suit the taste of a new Augustan Age, has heard that a few master touches were his, nothing more. But Meres includes *Titus Andronicus* on his list, the Folio reprints it, and to our consternation (for we are all Bardolaters) this bad play is certainly Shakespeare's.

"Even Homer nods" won't do to explain it. Better for our friendly sense of Shakespeare the man if it were more inept than it is. Some suppose a disingenuous playwright, out to beat Kyd and Marlowe at their own game. E.g. the villain Aaron, a virtuoso in depravity, "better" than Marlowe's Ithamore, relishing his crimes, or the heroine Lavinia pleading with a stony-hearted foe for her honor. This is like the tremulous and famous scene in *King John* where little Arthur begs his life. Listening, we wonder that grief should bear such an emphasis. But Shakespeare is practicing scales.

Badness is relative, as for Scribe and Sardou, makers of the well-made play. Destitute of soul and reflecting the Machine Age, their plays are only better mousetraps. The machine still runs, however, and this is true of Shakespeare's play. Technically proficient, it puts him further on than Peele and Marlowe, loose-limbed and episodic, or the panoramic playwright who opened with *Henry VI*. *Titus Andronicus* teems with incident, possibly surprising but never confused. "Rather a heap of rubbish than a structure," said Shakespeare's Restoration critic. As dramatic criticism, this misses the mark.

Some of Shakespeare's blank verse is uncommonly suave, here and there ringing like an apothegm:

What fool hath added water to the sea,
Or brought a fagot to bright-burning Troy?

The birds chant melody on every bush,
The snake lies rollèd in the cheerful sun,
The green leaves quiver with the cooling wind
And make a checkered shadow on the ground.

Later in the century, many writers got the knack of meter-making argument. But in the context of the 1580s *Titus Andronicus* shows to advantage, and only Shakespeare in this time had the skill to bring it off.

The debit side of the account is the most of it, though. On stage they sup full of horrors (but the horrors, stuff of a waxworks, are only generalized frisson). Shakespeare's music, winsome or stirring, ignores this. Like his mythological allusions, more than fifty of them stuck about the play, the poetry is like fake pilasters. Pointing no moral, it adorns the tale. Shakespeare's undoubted competence, so far from acquitting him, calls attention to the trifling thing it serves, "a clown in regal purple dressed."

Capable of this in his young man's time, Shakespeare repudiates it later. Form, suiting content, dictates it too. "Post hoc" goes by the boards and things happen for cause. Oddly, though, his bare-bones play is the same in youth and age. Reading backwards from late Shakespeare to his first tragedy, more than one modern critic comes upon *King Lear,* an Ur-version. Each play has a protagonist both noble and flawed, closes with a dead march and the binding up of wounds. "Order well the state," Shakespeare's character says, "That like events may ne'er it ruinate." And so on.

Tact, a reader's obligation, will see that the resemblance, as it builds on the outwall, is only generic. In the catalog both plays go for tragedies, and "Shoughs, water rugs, and demiwolves" are all called by the name of dogs. Not, however, in "the valued file" or list where quality governs. Unredeemed, as jurists like to say, by social value, *Titus Andronicus* is the simulacrum of *King Lear.* Costume drama without provenance or felt context, it plays in a vacuum. Society, elsewhere Shakespeare's preoccupation, is only a painted cloth at stage rear.

But young Shakespeare has got his conventions in place, and even some of his patented phrasing. Often his plays, rising for half the action, find a watershed in the mathematical center, then fall away to the end. Macbeth's fate is sealed when, in 3.3, Fleance, Banquo's son, escapes the "reach of hell." Already it is like this (only without import) in *Titus*

Andronicus. "Hie thee to the Goths," says the hero to his son (3.1), predicting the denouement, auspicious by design. Signaling the future, almost in reminiscent ways, *Titus Andronicus* has its uncanny side, as if Shakespeare's later plays were in his head before he wrote them.

One of Shakespeare's indulged prattlers, not much loved by posterity, the froward son Lucius is little Macduff in the egg. Speaking this play's epilogue, he presents Friar Laurence in *Romeo and Juliet,* or Horatio, making sense of *Hamlet's* "quarry of the slain." Titus himself (in 3.1 and 3.2) is Richard II, rehearsing sad stories of the deaths of kings. The wretched Clown with his pigeons, a stand-up comic in the midst of woe, evokes the Clown who brings the asps to Cleopatra. Two stars don't keep the firmament in *Henry IV,* Part One, and they don't do this either in *Titus Andronicus.* The end of *Cymbeline* resumes a passage in the first scene of Shakespeare's play, and as his last scene prepares the talk is of Coriolanus. These clues are false, however, and suggest that we want to mind "true things by what their mockeries be."

It isn't the later tragedies Shakespeare is pointing toward, rather the Heroic Drama of the Age of Dryden and its fustian heroes, Aurengzebe and Montezuma. The echoes reverberate eerily, though, and Shakespeare's first tragedy suggests a mature playwright, standing outside himself and framing a sardonic comment on the nature of his art. This Shakespeare reads like Max Beerbohm on Shakespeare.

But *Titus Andronicus,* neither parody nor a potboiler made in cold blood, defines apprentice Shakespeare, letting us see the great distance he traveled. From the first the mold or form was available to him, not yet the means to fill it. Or, turning this around, you can say of young Shakespeare that his means are more abundant than his ends. References to negritude, frequent and disparaging in *Titus Andronicus,* illustrate this. His barbarous Moor is known for a villain, being thick-lipped, wall-eyed, and swart. "Is black so base a hue?" Yes, it is, Shakespeare thinks. So far, he is like his naive suitor in *The Merchant of Venice,* whose golden mind stoops not to shows of dross.

But this easy response isn't felt as sufficient, and more than a decade later Shakespeare looks again. How is it Desdemona could fly to the "sooty bosom" of such a thing as the Moor? She has her interesting answer, or Shakespeare, in the years between, has hammered it out: "I saw Othello's visage in his mind."

Discoveries like this, often hard won, occupied Shakespeare's nonage. Empirical as much as ethical, they speak of the artificer, a type of the assaying man. This is what Jonson saw in his First Folio tribute:

Who casts to write a living line, must sweat,
. . . and strike the second heat
Upon the Muses' anvil: turn the same,
        (And himself with it) that he thinks to frame;
Or for the laurel he may gain a scorn,
        For a good poet's made, as well as born.

"Art had so little . . . a share in what he did"? No judgment wider of the truth than this one. Shakespeare's oeuvre, flawed but open to correction, gives it the lie, and Rowe to the contrary, we are to look for his beginnings among his least perfect writings.

As an artificer, what was he like? Not a prodigy like Mozart and not the late-bloomer imagined by Chambers-Malone. The towering genius apart, he seems like other men cumbered with insufficiencies, things to learn, unlearn, and query. Napoleon on Elba said he had fought fifty battles and learned nothing he hadn't known from the beginning. Shakespeare couldn't say this.

Venturing on tragedy, he saw the resemblance to the scaffold, bear-pit, and cockpit. At first, however, discrimination eluded him. Rome and the whole world was "a wilderness of tigers," their altercation signifying nothing. In *Titus Andronicus,* a callow Shakespeare threw up his hands.

SHAKESPEARE AND KYD knew each other as professionals but Kyd and Marlowe were friends. In 1591 they shared a chamber to-gether. Later, in Bridewell prison, pulled in by the thought police for a "lewd and mutinous" libel he had nothing to do with, Kyd remem-bered old times, saying what he hoped was wanted. This included abusing his former chambermate, "intemperate and of a cruel heart." How could they suppose that he "should love or be familiar friend with one so irreligious"? But the evidence told against him, three incriminating sheets "denying the deity of Jesus Christ our Savior." One of his inquisitors annotated this: "Found amongst the papers of Thos. Kyd, prisoner." Kyd was son of a London scrivener, and perhaps had the bad luck to indite this damning table talk himself.

On the rack he blabbed, discovering "Marlowe's monstrous opin-ions." Item, Marlowe reported St. John to be Christ's Alexis, "that is, that Christ did love him with an extraordinary love." Others, like Richard Baines, a government spy, amplified these "heretical conceits." They had Marlowe saying that all Protestants were hypocritical asses, that the woman of Samaria and her sister were whores, Christ knowing them carnally, also that the angel Gabriel, bringing the salutation to Mary, was bawd to the Holy Ghost. This is impudent fun, and any bright schoolboy, looking nervously over his shoulder, might have talked it. Not the sequel, however: "That all the Apostles were fishermen and base fellows, neither of wit nor worth." Supercilious Marlowe stands before us in this judgment, inspecting the world through a lorgnette.

He was dead before they could take him. Himself a government agent, perhaps he knew too much and the order went out to seal his lips. Quarreling over the bill at the tavern in Deptford, he took a dagger through the eye. "A great reckoning in a little room," enigmatic Shakespeare called this. Hearing the news, a scribe of the Privy Council wrote on Baines' report: "A note delivered on Whitsun Eve last of the most horrible blasphemies uttered by Christopher Marley who within three days after came to a sudden and fearful end of his life."

Moralists derived a lesson from the death of Marlowe, "a poet and a filthy playmaker," struck down by "the thunderbolt of God's wrath." His violent end, not sensational, causal, admonished "players that live by making fools laugh at sin and wickedness." Partly this pharisees' talk is particular, reacting to the time's bête noir, a "profane wretch" infamous for crimes of mind and body. But the invective raining down on Marlowe isn't reserved to him, and Shakespeare, filling the triple role of poet, playmaker, and player, is comprehended in it. Hindsight honors the culture hero who showed his back above the element he lived in. Looked at from ground level, though, the point of view of the time, Shakespeare seems not so different from the rest of them in theater, "rhymers and stage-players, that is, plain rogues."

The Lord Mayor's commissioners let Kyd out of prison, a broken man and tarred fatally with Marlowe's atheistical brush. Doors closed in his face when he supplicated a patron. Within the year he died, aged thirty-five, rejected by his closest kin. (Shakespeare, in the month of Kyd's death, drew his first payment from the Treasurer of the Royal Chamber.) Kyd's mother, not his father, came before the Archdeacon's Court to witness the probating of his will. Shown an inventory of her son's possessions, she disclaimed interest "in the goods, rights, and credits of the said deceased person, now or in the future."

7

The Dyer's Hand

SHAKESPEARE, spared imprisonment, violence, and poverty, might have fallen victim to plague. The year he first appears in London it broke out in the city, "very hot," said a public notice, warning of "great mortality" to come. Between December 29, 1592 and December 20, 1593, the dead numbered 10,775. Body bearers with cart or barrow went through the streets, a bell ringing before them. "Cast out your dead," they cried. "Have you any dead bodies to bury?" Donne in his *Devotions* (XVII) recalled this grim procession: "Never send to know for whom the bell tolls; it tolls for thee."

Citizens, their pockets stuffed, fled London, a house on fire. But outside the walls none dared receive them, not "so much as into barns." So they perished, some "with more money about them than would have bought the village where they died." It did no good to run away. A letter of the time tells of one refugee, a complacent woman, who "in the way to Croydon, turned back, looked on the city, and said, 'Farewell, London, and farewell, plague'; but soon after was taken sick, had the tokens on her breast, and these words to be distinctly read: 'It is in vain to fly from God, for He is everywhere.'"

Shakespeare, living in London, survived four major visitations of plague. Portents, often cryptic, announced it. In 1593, a heron, "harbinger and prologue" to the rising death toll, sat all afternoon atop St. Peter's church, Cornhill. Doggerel verses in the burial register of this church record one survivor's thanksgiving:

> In a thousand five hundred and ninety three
> The Lord preserved my house and me,
> When of the pestilence there died
> Full many a thousand else beside.

London's graveyards couldn't hold the dead. Laid in the earth, they were thrown up again, making room for more "before they were resolved to dust." In their "everlasting lodgings" the gallant and beggar lay down together. Thomas Dekker, Shakespeare's fellow playwright, saw them in heaps of ten and twenty.

Plague menaced Stratford the year Shakespeare was born. In 1602–3 it came back to London, carrying away a sixth of the population. Thomas Lodge, once a Wit, wrote a *Treatise of the Plague*. (Later this good physician died at his post.) In 1603, when Lodge's treatise went to the press, nearly three thousand were dying each week. One was Ben Jonson's son. "My sin was too much hope of thee, loved boy," Jonson said. In these years Shakespeare, turning from tragedy, meditated comedy, *Measure for Measure* and *All's Well That Ends Well*, mordant but a celebration of life. Around him, death, mocking what man could accomplish, scoffed at his state and grinned at his pomp. By 1605, however, christenings in the ravaged city had about returned to normal. This statistic comments on Shakespeare's sangfroid.

Carried by the black house rat, plague came from the bite of the rat-flea but nobody knew this. Sucking blood from the infected rat until its stomach filled with a solid mass of bacterium, the "blocked" flea turned desperate for food. Any animal became its prey, man included. It dropped from the thatched cottage roof on a man's shoulder, and in one to four days he was dead. In the later seventeenth century the brown field or sewer rat, preying on the black rat, interrupted this fatal sequence. At about the same time, the old land routes from the east, "rodent pipe-lines," gave way to sea routes. Rats lived on shipboard too, but in the depths of the hold where blocked fleas found it harder to get at the crew. Fleas had only a brief infective life after the host died, decreasing the threat of disease even further. Environmental changes play into this story, not fully explaining it. Though no one knows exactly why, plague, after Shakespeare's time, petered out in England.

Londoners in the meantime made sense of their affliction. They studied "Providence." Plague, from the Latin, meant a blow or stroke, and they traced it to the hand of God. In mid-summer 1593, the Queen and her Council laid the plague to His Providence, retribution for sin. Preachers, invoking Psalm 38, called it God's arrow. Knowing no help but prayer, they sent parishioners to church, said to be proof against infection. But the rat-flea, carried in on clothing, went to church with the people.

Astrologically minded people, like Shakespeare's Ulysses, located the source of plague in the "ill aspects" of stars,

> when the planets
> In evil mixture to disorder wander.

The scientifically inclined, like Dr. Lodge, pointed to an imbalance of humors in the body. They recommended chewing lemon rind, smoking tobacco, or drinking beer, "pottle-deep." The best remedy, a costly one, was powdered unicorn's horn. Boiled in wine, it made a mouthwash.

Plague came on suddenly, the mortality rate in the first weeks of an epidemic approaching 90 percent of those infected. Symptoms included extreme prostration and coughing or spitting blood. The lymph glands, inflamed, produced hard buboes or swellings, "bubonic." Victims endured great pain from the suppurating buboes, especially in the armpit or groin. Some, frenzied, tore off their clothes and headed for the river, a merciful death. Others, restrained by force, were sent to pesthouses, "ravished," said Lodge, "out of the hands of their parents and friends." Nurses in these hospitals, improvised ghettos, hurried on their patients' deaths. Plays of the time remember the "woman-keeper," no murderer more cunning, "Though she had practiced seven years at the pesthouse." Shakespeare in later years lived near the site of the pesthouse in St. Giles-without-Cripplegate.

Most victims, living dead, were incarcerated in their own houses. The door, marked with a red cross, bore the inscription: "Lord Have Mercy Upon Us." Outside the door, warders watched by turns, a necessary precaution against "running abroad." Shakespeare got a joke from this in *Much Ado About Nothing*. His hero Benedick, says Beatrice, phlegmatic enough, "is sooner caught than the pestilence, and the taker runs presently mad."

Competing with the pestilence were dysentery, typhus, and smallpox. When warm weather came, Londoners put off their louse-infected garments. This checked typhus. But cold weather checked plague, and in springtime its fury redoubled. Either way, Shakespeare's people were losers. Smallpox left scars, pitted circles, on the face, and women feared its disfiguring. Shakespeare handles this lightly, a theme for badinage.

"O, that your face were not so full of O's!" says his Dark Lady Rosaline, disparaging a rival.

Shakespeare's London, emblematic of his tragedy, was an accident waiting to happen. "Very handsome and clean," said affluent travelers, inspecting the goldsmiths' quarter. This was in Cheapside, different from parishes like St. Savior's, Southwark, or the eight out-parishes, including St. Leonard's, Shoreditch, home to Shakespeare and London's poor. Death, said Dekker in his Plague Pamphlets, "hath pitched his tents" in these "sinfully polluted suburbs." But poverty, not sin, polluted the suburbs.

Making no distinction between age or sex, plague was class-conscious, attacking "few among the wealthy." In 1593 it wiped out the poor of Westminster. The black rat, ill at ease in manor houses built of brick and roofed with slate or tile, lived by preference with the poor in their hovels. Ignorance and poverty went hand in hand. Barber-surgeons, letting blood, threw it into the streets. Pudding-wives and tripe-wives threw paunches, guts, and entrails into the channels or gutters, meant for cleansing. The Corporation told them to load their refuse in tubs and carry it down to the Thames. This polluted the river, source of London's water. Falstaff, duped by the Merry Wives, went into the Thames at Windsor, "like a barrow of butcher's offal."

Food for rats, filth piled up in dunghills, perfuming the streets all summer long. Contributing to this were the shambles of St. Nicholas-within-Newgate. Trailed by his ferocious dog, the rat-catcher undertook to get rid of the rats. "Rats or mice!" sang the catcher, his familiar street-cries adding to London's din. "Ha' ye any rats, mice, polecats, or weasels? Or ha' ye any old sows sick of the measles? I can kill them, and I can kill moles, and I can kill vermin that creepeth up and creepeth down and peepeth into holes." But in plague-time, people killed dogs.

When deaths in London rose above fifty a week, playing came under ban within three miles of the city. This pleased the devout, averse to bear-baiting, dancing, bowling, and stage plays. London's Mayor and Aldermen complained that "assemblies of the people in throng and press" boosted the chance for plague, "God's visitation." This was true, also a handle they could turn. In 1583 the Court of Aldermen singled out the Theater and Curtain, frequented by "great multitudes of the basest sort . . . and many infected with sores running on them." It wanted Privy Council to shut the playhouses, "occasion of God's wrath and heavy striking with plagues." Grindal, London's bishop, wanted them shut for a year, "and if it were forever it were not amiss."

The closing of theaters in 1592 cost Shakespeare the rostrum he spoke from. Deaths fell with the new year and playing resumed. But the plague, only dormant, flared up again, and the theaters closed once more at the end of January, not reopening for good until June 1594. Players, "padding the hoof," went into the country. In 1592 they went to Gloucester and Coventry, a year later to Bath and Maidstone and north as far as York. Some imagine young Shakespeare pushing on further, to Duncan's castle in Scotland, where he made acquaintance with the temple-haunting martlet, guest of summer. Or, crossing the Alps, he rode the "tranect" or *traghetto,* "the common ferry/Which trades to Venice." One of Shakespeare's older scholars has a monograph about him and the waterways of Northern Italy.

Readers who set Shakespeare on the road in plague-time point to his "Italian" plays or the itinerary he spells out in the sonnets. E.g. packing up in London (48) he puts spurs to his horse (50), rides "large lengths of miles" (44), is "tanned" by the weather (62), and plays before the locals, a motley to the view (110). At night, worn out with travel, he goes to bed at his inn (27). But his friend's absence drives away sleep and, still weary, he gets up with the birds (27–28, 43, 61). In Bath he takes the waters, "healthful remedy/For men diseased" (154). Love is what ails him, however, and for that no remedy offers. This peripatetic Shakespeare is like his Sir Walter Blunt, a faithful reporter "stained with the variation of each soil" between north and south.

Reportage isn't Shakespeare's style, though, as Jonson liked to tell him. (No seacoast in Bohemia, etc.) He got his "seething" bath from the Greek Anthology, the weathered look from the makeup man, and his north Italian haunts from someone's novella. No doubt he traveled widely in 1592–94, not ceasing to do this long after the plague abated, but his mythic travels were mostly in the mind. That doesn't say they weren't real.

PLAGUE, an ill wind to some, drove Shakespeare on writing but not for the stage. In this tragic time, he should have written his "Dies Irae." Instead he made jeux d'ésprits. His long narrative poems, *Venus and Adonis* and *The Rape of Lucrece,* date from the plague years, also most of the sonnets and his *Lover's Complaint.* All this is vogue poetry, popular in the 1590s and turned out according to rule. The "epyllion" or love poem celebrated Eros, sonnets had fourteen lines, and if you meant to write tragedy, like Shakespeare in *Lucrece* and *A Lover's Complaint,* you used the rime royal stanza. Centrifugal in his tendency,

Gulliver among the Lilliputians, he found reining in to be a help, not a hindrance. For that, established forms do better than self expression, and he comes across as most himself when most in harness.

Catering to the new fashion for sex plus witty moralizing, *Venus and Adonis* occupied his idle hours in 1593. In the spring of the year, the Stationers' Register licensed this poem for publication. A year later came its sequel, *The Rape of Lucrece*. (Not published until 1609, *A Lover's Complaint*, only 329 lines, looks like a trial run at the genre.) Entries in the register were minatory, warning the author not to take his words lightly. "Words are no deeds," says Shakespeare's Henry VIII, but that was only true in the playhouse. In the real world, the censor took the word for the deed.

Shakespeare, prudent among other things, galls nobody's kibe in his love poems. One comic and lubricious, the other tragic but felt as ossified, like funerary sculpture, they make a pair of contrasting bookends fit for a gentleman's shelves. Shakespeare the genre painter, doing comedy today, turns to tragedy tomorrow. He thought that lustful Venus, woman on one side, needed her complement, chaste Lucrece. Many of his sonnets, paired performances that go in different directions, are like this. Singleminded readers, not estimating circumambient Shakespeare, suppose these "prolusions" insincere.

A prolusion, much cultivated in old-fashioned schools, is when you show off your skill, as by responding to the question: How would it be, if or on the other hand? Shakespeare's plays, artificial compositions, ask and answer such questions. In *A Lover's Complaint*, faithful to his dramatic practice, he casts himself in the role of a woman "betrayed." Given her predicament, what does she do? She sits on the "weeping margent" or bank of a river,

> Like usury, applying wet to wet,
> Or monarch's hands that lets not bounty fall
> Where want cries some, but where excess begs all.

It sounds like Shakespeare, and Edmund Malone saw his hand in every part of "this beautiful poem." Perhaps, Malone thought, he "meant to break a lance with Spenser." He hadn't much in common with a narrative poet like Spenser, however, and his *Lover's Complaint*, lacking the stage, is less dramatic than histrionic or stagey. Sad souls should have company but Shakespeare's heroine emotes in a vacuum.

Consummately the actor, Shakespeare, said Chettle, was excellent in this "quality," playing many parts in one person. That wasn't from dearth, betokening the man who is nothing in himself, rather from plenitude. Like his impetuous ocean, forever eating at the flats, he needed a "list" or border to confine him. He was lucky and the "player's hide," a tough integument, met the need. Without it he would have foundered "in his own too much." Jonson, he of the rocky face and mountain belly, spreads himself to the time in lyric poetry that takes off from the first-person pronoun. Bigger than most but dwarfed by Shakespeare, only the morn dew to his grand sea, Jonson could afford this. Shakespeare, trammeled with personality, struggled to disperse it, speaking through roles and voices not his own.

The life, not less than the art, shows this need in him to dramatize, putting on shapes like the God of the Creation. (They brought him down to size.) At one time or another he was local Dick Whittington, edifying poet, parvenu anxious for a patent of gentility, kingmaker in his closet, martyrologist and hagiographer, testy parent, young gadabout, speculator in land. Characters in his plays, true to themselves, look askance at the protean man with his "forest of feathers." Hamlet, no friend of theatrics, speaks slightingly of "actions that a man might play." This phrase comprehends the playwright.

Reading him, you have the sense that he recoiled at the shifts and expedients he was put to. Near the end of *Lucrece,* he allows himself a long aside on "perjured Sinon," who brought the wooden horse to Troy. It isn't much on the point but he couldn't let it alone, and glancing at this story early (in *Henry VI*, Part Three), he kept coming back to it. (Other versions of the story feature the chameleon or serpent under the flower or the far-reaching man who obscures himself beneath a veil of wildness.) In the play-actor Sinon, mild-seeming, just, the gait humble, "eyes wailing still," he looked at himself. "A piece of him," as Horatio tells the fellows of the Watch.

But the dissimulator yearned to speak heart's truth. Others did this, why not Shakespeare? One-dimensional men, they were "integer vitae" where he was myriad-minded, a mixed blessing and he knew it. The yearning, importunate, is written in the love poems, especially *The Rape of Lucrece.* He made a virtue of necessity when plague closed the theaters.

Intellectuals in Shakespeare's time, "fantastics" too, applauded *Venus and Adonis,* the "first heir" of his invention. "Let this duncified world esteem of Spenser and Chaucer," says a character in *The Return from Parnassus,* an amateur play performed by students at Cambridge. "I'll worship sweet Mr. Shakespeare, and to honor him will lay his *Venus and Adonis* under my pillow." Young lovers of poetry read his poem to pieces, and for most early editions only a single copy survives. *The Rape of Lucrece,* a "graver labor" (Shakespeare's phrase), won him his first *succès d'estime.* "The younger sort," said Gabriel Harvey, a notorious pedant, took much delight in *Venus and Adonis,* but his *Lucrece* had "something in it to please the wiser sort." This praise sends up danger signals.

Not ephemera like plays, the poems confirmed Shakespeare as a serious writer. This was his intention. Going down to the printing house, he proofread both for the press. On his plays, eighteen of them printed in his lifetime, he looked, if at all, with an indifferent eye. Prospective readers, Americans or Japanese in the distant future, left him unmoved. Some contemporary playwrights, solicitous of readers, help out with scene divisions and cast lists, not he. Notorious as a playwright for never blotting a line, he never proofed one either.

The publishing trade, his conduit to posterity, served him ill and he might have been outraged. Publication "staled" the plays, so he or his company sought to keep them from print. But pirate printers, scorning "the ungrateful hoarders-up of such treasures," got hold of his manuscripts by hook or crook, then (in the acid phrase of the Folio editors) "maimed and deformed" them. Careless of punctuation, they set up his prose as verse or dropped words from his text, often whole lines. Some plays they mangled beyond recognition, like the first quarto of *Hamlet.* His texts, cheaply bound, held together until the day of sale. They weren't literature, not much honored on Stationers' Row, only a product. Even at that, the product wasn't always Shakespeare's, but unscrupulous publishers traded on his name "whether the author be willing or no." Appearing on a title page, it helped "vent" the play. Once Shakespeare complained but mostly held his peace. If he had a gorge, it rose slowly.

All this changes when he turns poet. In *Venus and Adonis,* running to 1,194 lines, only two errors surface, only three in the 1,855 lines of *The Rape of Lucrece.* Plays, bread and butter work, didn't merit this painstaking. In *Henry IV,* Part One, a quarto of 1598 and as the quartos go more accurate than most, the rate of error is about one hundred sixty per 1,000 lines. The comparison suggests Shakespeare's judgment of his work. Posterity's judgment is different, and for every reader of *Venus and Adonis* and *The Rape of Lucrece* there will likely be a hundred of *Hamlet.* Offhanded critics, explaining this, call the poems "artificial," but that is only true when they succeed. *Hamlet,* lively but not real life, succeeds as it is "composed," unlike the source Shakespeare drew on, a version of things as they really happened down on the bestial floor.

Venus and Adonis has a "fire-hot" heroine, goddess of Love, and the matter of this poem is ostensibly sexy. But Shakespeare, unfolding it, mostly kept to books, not life. Ovid, of all the major poets the least at home in the brazen world, gave him his lead. (When he followed it he prospered, not when he struck out on his own.) He got much pleasure from sex, a messy activity not easily accommodated in the golden world of the love poem. But this artificial composition has its rules, bringing passion to heel. The more he honors them, the less he smells of the lamp. His epigrams persuade but aren't meant for thoughtful, and his hyperbolic conceits don't so much inform as bedizen. This effaces the natural world.

He read the *Metamorphoses,* his favorite Latin poem, in Arthur Golding's absurd translation (1567). Where Golding has Ovid reproving "vice in youth and age," Shakespeare sees how vice (or life) is insulated by art. "For shame," cries his hero, "leave me here alone,"

> "For all my mind, my thought, my busy care,
> Is how to get my palfrey from the mare."

Hard lines, the naked goddess thinks, and readers concur.

Some, proposing an artless Shakespeare, think he wrote his poem in the country and brought it with him up to town. That can hardly be. Vestiges of life in Stratford, personal to him and recollected in tranquillity, crop up in the poem but art is the most of it. The highbrow motto from Ovid, blazoned on the title page, proclaims this:

> Let the common people admire vile things;
> May golden-haired Apollo lead me to the Muses' springs.

A courtly sciolist or trifler, Shakespeare is offering credentials. He has been to Urbino where Castiglione and the rest of them looked down their nose at the vulgar.

Convention, always his useful springboard, not what he believed in but what he took off from, said that males were virile, females coy and submissive. His Amazonian female, like the Centaur at the marriage feast, slings "the tender boy" Adonis under one arm, her horse's rein over the other. Elsewhere this "bold-faced suitor," more Martial than Venereal, thrusts the lackwit hero to the ground. This was Shakespeare's chance for carnal rough-and-tumble but he let it go by. In *Venus and Adonis,* neither man nor woman is substantially there, and emblems or metonyms stand in for real persons. Lustrous but iconic, they don't make a felt whole. Shakespeare's Venus, coolly anatomized, isn't flesh and blood but an artificial landscape with mountains, dales, pleasant fountains, and sweet bottom grass. Adonis, a deer, shelters in this grass. The last thing the poet wants for his erotic "exhibition piece" is reality breaking in.

Thematic parallels, often noticed by Shakespeare's critics, link his poem and his first seventeen sonnets. Venus wants Adonis to propagate the species, and Shakespeare at sonnets wants his friend to do this too. But that is only paraphrase, a false clue for poetry. Venus has an ax to grind, and her rhyming couplets are heard as sophistic:

> Seeds spring from seeds, and beauty breedeth beauty;
> Thou wast begot, to get it is thy duty.

The "real" (i.e. ideal) epyllion, made in Heaven and remote from mundane business, requires that you fine-tune your ear. "She's Love, she loves, and yet she is not loved." Ringing changes on the word, Shakespeare leaves reality to those who can best support it. Rhetoricians have a term for his studied iteration.

The love poems represent a new departure for him, doubtless attractive. Like his dyer's hand, Shakespeare at plays is subdued to the element he works in. Or he is like that expert horseman he glances at in *Hamlet,* growing to the seat or saddle as if "incorpsed and deminatured" with the horse. Another way to describe him is in terms of the "Psychomachia," familiar from his schoolboy reading and dramatizing a spirit war between good and evil. "Rude will," embodied evil, mutinies with "wit's regard," and in the worst-case scenario the hero, his judgment darkened, is destroyed. This dramatic competition, enacted on a stage offlimits except to the actors, keeps Shakespeare in his place. Saluting both parties, he lets them go at it. Tampering breaks the rules.

In *Venus and Adonis* and *The Rape of Lucrece,* not enacted but told, constraints are fewer or you can say that Shakespeare wriggles free of harness. His six-line stanza, adapted from a "metamorphosis" poem by Lodge, suggests this. Ending with a couplet that rhymes twice when he wants it to, it gave him his comic effects. A cunning metrist, he understood that double rhyme is always comic (unless unselfconscious, as when "Cockney" poets take it in hand), and readers laughed with him, not at him. "Fie, fie," says Adonis:

> "you crush me; let me go.
> You have no reason to withhold me so."

The rumpty-tumpty is deliberate, part of the fun. But Shakespeare's comedy isn't always meditated. Beginning *Lucrece,* he made a first commitment to the sesta rima form, then dropped it for decorum's sake, rime royal with its extra line being approved for weighty matters. Sometimes attention wavered and he left the double rhyme unamended. When this happens, the laugh is on him.

Neither stanzaic form, whether six lines or seven, involved him in the fruitful trouble he got from blank verse or the sonnet. Not contending with the form, he wins his triumphs too easily. In *The Rape of Lucrece,* most are didactic, the poet putting his cards on the table. Tarquin, "trafficking" for gain, is deluded, Shakespeare thinks, like men for whom "the profit of excess"

> Is but to surfeit, and such griefs sustain
> That they prove bankrupt in this poor-rich gain.

Sententious Shakespeare is only getting started, though. A second stanza embroiders the thought, then a third applies it. "With this key Shakespeare unlocked his heart." Posterity, regretting the unwonted candor, has given its voice for the playwright.

Marlowe, much on Shakespeare's mind in the early 1590s, is the uncontested master of the love poem. His *Hero and Leander,* licensed for publication in 1593, has a grove

> Where Venus in her naked glory strove
> To please the careless and disdainful eyes
> Of proud Adonis that before her lies.

The light shines through Marlowe's abstract diction, very un-Shakespearean but right for what it wants to accomplish. Taking this immaculate exercise for a model, Shakespeare is working against his bent. Like Mozart writing for the harp and flute, instruments that didn't please him except that he made them please, perhaps he courted the challenge.

He doesn't always rise to it, and this tells about him and the nature of his genius. Life invades his poem where Marlowe, more ruthless, keeps it under glass. Leander, swimming the Hellespont, beats aside the waves

> Which mounted up, intending to have kissed him,
> And fell in drops like tears because they missed him.

Wicked and salacious, this gives romantic tragedy its quietus. But that says too little for Marlowe.

In the climax of the poem he works a miracle, indigenous to him. His Hero and Leander, though purged of gross mortality, are more than figurines, and not disrupting the artificial form they transcend it:

> She trembling strove, this strife of hers (like that
> Which made the world) another world begat
> Of unknown joy.

Shakespeare isn't up to this, and his poem, impure or spotted, not "translunary," falls back to earth.

Being what he is, acquisitive Shakespeare can't keep the real world out-at-doors or not forever. His alfresco analogies tell of a roving eye, the "As" clause counting more than the "So" clause:

> Or, as the snail, whose tender horns being hit,
> Shrinks backward in his shelly cave with pain . . .
> So, at his bloody view her eyes are fled.

Verity, indulged, makes the artful glitter of the poem seem tawdry, and natural description (like the recollected image of poor Wat the hare) is sensed as a wearied man's refreshment. Rejecting his donnée, "hammered gold and gold enamelling," Shakespeare isn't heartless enough, i.e. artistic. Art palls, life is clamorous, and this sympathetic poet, not tying himself to the mast, pays attention. For example, his "trampling courser":

> Round-hoofed, short-jointed, fetlocks shag and long,
> Broad breast, full eye, small head, and nostril wide,
> High crest, short ears, straight legs . . .
> Thin mane, thick tail, broad buttocks, tender hide.

Meanwhile, the filigree context recedes.

Shakespeare, failing, renews himself, and his poem, more circumstantial than Marlowe's, opens on a larger world. In *Venus and Adonis* the parts are more than the whole, and nobody wants to blue-pencil his vignettes. Interpolated, not organic, they spoil the poem as an integer, though. *The Rape of Lucrece,* his least formal composition, fails in different ways but for the same reason. Shakespeare, "growing to a pleurisy," menaces the form or evades it. Out of sight and out of mind he isn't. Like old Capulet on the eve of the wedding, he has his hands on all the ropes. We want "a wilderness where are no laws," quoting his distressed heroine, but he lands us up in the schoolroom.

Full of what he knew, he stuffed his poem with themes familiar from the tragedies to come. Grace fights with Desire, and Tarquin the ravisher holds disputation " 'Tween frozen conscience and hot-burning will." But interior monolog conveys the dispute, or rather this is Shakespeare speaking, satisfied to take the word for the deed. His war of wit and will, nakedly presented, lacks the adventitious blurring by which we recognize the plays. (In his poems he wants to get on with the business.) There was a dish of stewed prunes in the bawdy house, Pompey tells them (in *Measure for Measure*), "a dish of some threepence," not China but good. "No matter for the dish," the magistrate thinks. But the irrelevant "truth," qualifying the abstract theme (justice v. mercy), is indispensable for this "problem" play. Without it we have the Decalogue, "thus he said."

Starting out, Shakespeare looked to models, principally Livy's Roman history and a popular "Complaint" by "well-languaged" Daniel. Chunks of his reading are embedded in the poem, e.g. the formal blazon presenting Lucrece (her lily hand, rosy cheek, and so forth), or the extended apostrophes, set pieces, to Night, Opportunity, and her "copesmate," misshapen Time. Not surprisingly, this conventional baggage fatigued him. Getting going, he dropped it and spoke *in propria persona*. Electing to do this, he was true to himself but false to his genius, and personality drenches, so vitiates his poem.

Shakespeare, pointing the moral, is merged in Polonius laying precepts on Laertes. For this, the ingenuous rubric is Gertrude's: "More matter with less art." Not hiding among the stuff, like Saul son of Kish, he takes center stage, losing dimension for his protagonists, incidentally for himself. Betrayal is nagging at him, not for the last time. His own case seems reflected in that of the wretched husband (it might be Posthumous in *Cymbeline*) who sings his wife's praises, kindling a rival's lust. But the play is of magnitude because it has perimeters, and the poem, open-ended, leaks away.

Versions of Shakespeare, Iachimo and Imogen are distanced from him by the footlights, so felt as themselves. Tarquin and Lucrece, coming too close for comfort, pay the price for this. Lucrece, reflecting bitterly, is Hamlet denied his play, or Shakespeare at sonnets, were he to run the stop sign at the end of the poem. Essentially dramatic and circumscribed by their form, the sonnets are everybody's possession. Shakespeare's truth in *Lucrece,* more personal, so less consequential, suggests how things might have been with him had he not dramatized the old Psychomachia. Not a well-mannered poet like Spenser in *The Faerie Queene,* he needed the stage, a saving limitation.

RICHARD FIELD, Shakespeare's Stratford countryman, set up his poems for the press at Field's printing house in Blackfriars. Then they went for publication to Paul's Churchyard, "at the sign of the White Greyhound." The stationer John Harrison, whose shop this was, offered *Venus and Adonis* for sixpence. Some centuries later, canonized as literature, a copy of the fourth edition brought £15,000. Shops in the cathedral close, the center of London's book trade, bore colorful names like Harrison's, the Holy Ghost, the Angel, the Fox, the Green Dragon, the Flower de Luce and the Crown. From these shops more than 70 issues and editions of Shakespeare's work appeared in his lifetime. Some of the work went on sale in Fleet Street near St. Dunstan's church but most of it saw the light in Stationers' Row.

In all this vast output, only the two love poems carry an author's dedication. Each is addressed to Henry Wriothesley (pronounced "Rizley"), third earl of Southampton and Baron of Titchfield. Sailing his skiff adroitly, Shakespeare caught this patron's eye. Patronage meant money and a lot of it changed hands (Davenant told Nicholas Rowe), enough to purchase a house in Stratford, a share in the Chamberlain's Men, and then some. This is wishful thinking but Shakespeare's dedications, pregnant with flattery, deserved a fair return. "Right Honorable," he begins, commending *Venus and Adonis:*

> I know not how I shall offend in dedicating my unpolished lines to your Lordship, nor how the world will censure me for choosing so strong a prop to support so weak a burden. Only if your Honor seem but pleased, I account myself highly praised, and vow to take advantage of all idle hours, till I have honored you with some graver labor. But if the first heir of my invention prove deformed, I shall be sorry it had so noble a godfather, and never after ear so barren a land, for fear it yield me still so bad a harvest. I leave it to your honorable survey, and your Honor to your heart's content, which I wish may always answer your own wish, and the world's hopeful expectation.
>
> Your Honor's in all duty,
William Shakespeare.

Admirers of Shakespeare wonder at the tone of self-deprecation: "unpolished lines . . . so weak a burden . . . idle hours." Many think that familiarity fostered greater assurance. The dedication of *The Rape of Lucrece,* a year later, suggests that it didn't.

> The love I dedicate to your Lordship is without end, whereof this pamphlet, without beginning, is but a superfluous moiety. The warrant I have of your honorable disposition, not the worth of my untutored lines, makes it assured of acceptance. What I have done is yours; what I have to do is yours; being part in all I have, devoted yours. Were my worth greater, my duty would show greater; meantime, as it is, it is bound to your Lordship, to whom I wish long life still lengthened with all happiness.
>
> Your Lordship's in all duty,
William Shakespeare.

This second time round, tacitean Shakespeare has shortened up on his style but his "untutored lines" still beget apology. That was the convention. Maecenas didn't want a Romantic poet, puffed with divine afflatus. "Still scribbling, Master Shakespeare?" said Southampton, archly playful, and Shakespeare agreed it was so.

Among Southampton's credentials were a brace of M.A.s, one from Oxford, another from Cambridge. At St. John's College, Cambridge, he and Marlowe (enrolled at Corpus Christi) overlapped by two years. St. John's was Nashe's college too, before him Robert Greene's. Edward de Vere, Earl of Oxford, dissolute, probably homosexual, sometimes a poet, studied there in the 1580s, also Henry Constable, remembered for sonnets. This literary coloring rubbed off on Shakespeare's patron, celebrated in his time as "a dear lover and cherisher . . . of poets." Dedications poured in on him and he welcomed the applause. When he died, one eulogist, summoning the Virgilian context, instructed the tribe of poets to

> peruse
> His globe of worth and eke his virtues brave,
> Like learned Maros at Maecenas' grave.

But patronage had another face, often frigid, always fickle. Nashe, adulating this young nobleman too, came away empty-handed. "O peerless poesy, where is then thy place?" footloose Spenser inquired in his October eclogue. He wanted a corner in the prince's palace but they packed him off to "salvage" Ireland. Shakespeare got something from his dutiful epistles, not the thousand pounds Rowe assigned him and not as much as he was worth. But whatever he got, he paid for.

In 1593 or thereabouts, when Shakespeare wrote the love poems and Southampton was twenty, Nicholas Hilliard made his likeness in miniature. Hilliard, a rare artist in an England not notable for pictorial art, looked for the shape beneath the skin. His Southampton, a beautiful boy, self-smitten, is Narcissus. Under the arched eyebrows the eyes gaze downwards, the long nose is pointed, the curling love-locks, reddish- gold, fall below the shoulders in an artful disorder. Southampton has a petulant mouth. He liked having his picture done, and fifteen of these portraits survive. The familiar one in the White Tower, London, later than Hilliard's miniature, shows him with a wisp of beard and thin moustache. But the pouting lips and lowering eyes still say what he looked like when Shakespeare first knew him.

Ten years Shakespeare's junior, he was born October 6, 1573, a scion of the up-and-coming men deplored by Pope Pius. His grandfather Thomas, the first earl and Lord Chancellor under Henry VIII, rose to power as a client of grim Thomas Cromwell. This archetypal civil servant despoiled the Church for the Crown but the first Southampton feathered his own nest, building Titchfield in Hampshire from the plunder of Hyde Abbey, his share in the spoils. Riding on Fortune's Wheel he went up and down, down under the Protector Somerset, up again on his fall, down under the new Protector Warwick, soon to be Duke of Northumberland. Shakespeare's wary people in Snitterfield watched the revolution of the times.

Henry, the second earl, a Catholic and a malcontent, died in his thirties. Like Marlowe's Edward II, he has a whiff of the epicene about him. Thomas Dymock, a gentleman of the bedchamber, was his Piers Gaveston. "This house is not for them," said his estranged countess, "that will not honor Dymock as a god." Southampton's father left a will taking care of his favorite and adding this proviso: "that the said Thomas, for the good opinion and trust I have of him, should be specially one of those appointed after my decease to be attentive to, and daily about, the person of my son and heir."

Years later, Court gossip accused the son of homosexual leanings. An informer's letter describes him, on doubtful service in the Irish wars. Careless of men's opinion, he lolls on a pressed bed with his own favorite, Captain Piers Edmonds. This hanger-on of Essex's, a professional soldier, was Corporal-General of Southampton's Horse. The Earl (says Secretary Cecil's informant) "would cole and hug him in his arms and play wantonly with him." To "cole" or "cull" is to fondle, as in "cull-me-to-you," a rural name for the pansy.

Achilles and his "brooch" or pendant Patroclus reenact this dallying in *Troilus and Cressida,* Shakespeare's tale of sawdust soldiers in a war that never ends. Achilles, not Homer's hero or Chapman's, is a bully and "parcel" coward, self-indulgent, whatever else. Patroclus is Achilles' "male varlet." "What's that?" Patroclus asks them, setting up Thersites. "Why," says this baleful Chorus, "his masculine whore."

Southampton, a boy of eight when he came to the title, grew up a Crown ward in Burghley's mansion on the Strand. The Lord Treasurer, a begettor of the Protestant work ethic, pushed his young protégé hard. Oxbridge laurels weren't sufficient, and he read for the law at Gray's Inn. Bacon was a bencher there. Bacon, Oxford, Marlowe, Shakespeare, later Essex and the Queen, all were his acquaintance. "No young man more outstanding in learning," an admirer said, "although his mouth scarcely yet blooms with tender down."

But on his way up, the young man stumbled badly. At Court, a fox in the henhouse, he preyed on the maids-of-honor, alienating the Queen. His guardian arranged a splendid marriage-of-convenience but he didn't want to get married. (Essex by then was the god of his idolatry.) Rejecting the offer of Lady Elizabeth Vere, Burghley's granddaughter and daughter of the Earl of Oxford, he preferred, rumor said, to pay an enormous fine, £5,000. Almost bankrupt, he married anyway and might as well have kept his money. Elizabeth Vernon, round-faced and golden-haired, wasn't the simpering beauty who looks out of her portrait, and when Southampton got her pregnant she made him lawful prize.

His biographers compare the Earl to Shakespeare's disagreeable hero in *All's Well That Ends Well* or the plausible seducer of *A Lover's Complaint.* He had his plausible side but his young man's ardors, piquant in the beginning and too histrionic to be other than real, suggest a less complicated man, one of Shakespeare's child heroes. He wasn't to know how Shakespeare's eye assessed him, and however close they were he never looked in Shakespeare's heart. The sonnets were beyond him. If he read them, he took them for straightforward panegyric. "Shall I compare thee to a summer's day?" In his relation with Shakespeare, who was used by whom is a question.

His mistress adored him, like most women and some men. Two of the men were Charles and Henry Danvers, and in 1594, the year of *Lucrece,* he helped them escape the country after a fatal brawl. In 1601 Sir Charles Danvers died on Tower Hill, "rather like a bridegroom than a prisoner appointed for death." (Stow's characterization of him looks forward to Shakespeare's Claudio in *Measure for Measure.*) The chief motive that led Danvers to join the rebels, he said, was his "great obligation of love and duty" to Southampton.

But the king of honor had a temper, and patient of himself gave it scope. Playing at primero in the Presence Chamber, he struck the Queen's "squire of the body," Ambrose Willoughby. (Retaliating, this Willoughby pulled out some of his hair.) Fond of tilts and tourneys, he liked fighting best. Essex was the chimera, Parolles to his Bertram, who lured him to the wars. Any war would do, Normandy when he was still in his teens, Calais and Cadiz, the Azores' expedition. In 1599 he went with Essex to Ireland, and was with him two years later when Essex reached for the throne. Surviving his hero's wreck, he escaped with eighteen months in the Tower. Perhaps his lenient judges estimated their man. Essex, the fool of time, has his crazy panache, and "nothing in his life/Became him like the leaving it." Southampton lacks this glamor, except as Shakespeare supplies it.

ONLY THE DEDICATIONS say that Shakespeare knew him. But their orbits keep touching. In the next reign, Southampton's tutor supplies Shakespeare with a scene for *The Tempest,* and Southampton's stepfather suggests a new twist for *King Lear*. John Florio, an inmate of Southampton's household, is the tutor. Author of the first Italian dictionary, *A World of Words* (1598), he dedicated this to his patron and Shakespeare's. Later, he translated Montaigne. Shakespeare's Gonzalo, sketching his ideal commonwealth, belied by the world around him, has been reading this translation. Some think an ungrateful Shakespeare made fun of learned Florio in *Love's Labor's Lost*.

Sir Thomas Harvey, third husband of Southampton's mother, had a story for the household, worth Shakespeare's hearing. A version of the old tale Shakespeare tells in *King Lear,* it isn't indebted to Holinshed but real life. The dowager Countess dying in 1607, Harvey the widower took a new wife, Cordell or Cordelia, daughter of Brian Annesley. His wits had begun to turn and Cordelia's two sisters, pelican daughters who wanted the estate, petitioned to have their father declared insane. In 1603, before Shakespeare wrote his play, Cordelia sought the help of Secretary Cecil on behalf of this "poor aged and daily dying" man. Many versions of King Lear's story were available to Shakespeare but in none does the old king go mad.

Harvey was an overseer of Annesley's will on his death in 1604, and Thomas Russell of Shakespeare's. Russell had a half-brother, Sir Maurice Berkeley. In 1598 he traveled to France with Southampton. Later the two served together in Parliament, also in the Virginia Company, source of travel tips to Shakespeare, voyager in the "still-vexed Bermoothes." Berkeley, like Sir Henry Neville, shared Southampton's brief confinement when the three of them fell foul of the King (1604). This Neville, jailed with Southampton after the Essex fiasco, was father of Elizabeth, the wife of another of Thomas Russell's half-brothers.

Southampton, patron of poetry, enjoyed the theater too, spending his time "merrily in going to plays every day." Some of these plays were Shakespeare's. He knew *Henry IV,* Part One, and in 1599 a jocular letter from his wife tells the Earl of Sir John Falstaff and "his mistress Dame Pintpot." He knew *Richard II* too, the uncut version, and on the eve of the Essex rising helped persuade Shakespeare's company to revive this old play at the Globe. What Southampton and the others wanted from Shakespeare was the Deposition Scene, not played or printed in Elizabeth's reign. "Know you not I am Richard II," said the Queen. Released from the Tower after the Succession, Southampton set about entertaining Queen Anne. She liked her entertainment modish but he chose an out-of-date play to amuse her. The play, performed in 1604 "at my Lord of Southampton's," was *Love's Labor's Lost,* remarkable for in-jokes. Only those in the know took their point.

Taking the point preoccupied readers of *Willobie His Avisa,* a long poem of the 1590s, rhyming like Shakespeare's stanza in *Venus and Adonis.* Shakespeare figures in this poem, perhaps Southampton also. Sir Walter Ralegh, out of favor with the Queen in the early 1590s, lives on its periphery, dogged by the Earl of Essex and Southampton, this sworn enemy's friend. (Ralegh, like Shakespeare's patron, had a taste for imprudent amours.) Some think a poet-member of Ralegh's entourage intended the poem to make fun of Southampton; others, that it presents a penitent Earl, soliciting the (Virgin) Queen's favor. Tactless, if true.

A roman à clef with too many keys, *Willobie His Avisa* keeps its secret. But readers in the 1590s and later, teased by the cloying air of sexual anxiety, were in on the secret. The Court shared it too, and in 1599 the Queen's High Commission "called in" *Avisa* and burned this poem in Westminster Hall. It kept surfacing, though, even forty years afterwards, long life for so slight a vessel. Republished in 1609, it had impressive company, Shakespeare's sonnets and his *Troilus and Cressida,* each dating from an earlier time and first published this year without the author's permission. *Willobie His Avisa,* remembering things past, belongs in their context.

Entered in the Register on 3 September 1594, only a few months after *The Rape of Lucrece,* it tells the story of "a British Lucretia," vindicated where others succumb. In prefatory verses, Shakespeare— he paints "poor Lucrece' rape"—is noticed for the first time as a poet. But where Shakespeare's Roman heroine has only Tarquin to contend with, Avisa repels a troop of suitors, among them, many suppose, Shakespeare's Earl.

Five men court this "Britain bird" (Latin *avis* = bird). Outlandish cartoons like Portia's suitors in *The Merchant of Venice,* they ask to be deciphered, and scholars with a gift for detective work have obliged. All dudgeon and self-importance, First Nobleman gets nowhere. Cavelleiro, his successor, moves Avisa only "to fear the piles or else the pox." A Frenchman and an Anglo-German fare no better. "H.W." brings up the rear. Commentators note that his initials are Southampton's, Henry Wriothesley.

Lust tickles this concupiscent hero, refined to his "wanny face and sharpened nose." To make sure of Avisa, he brings along a companion, his "familiar friend W.S." The friend is his worser half, "one who goes with him" like tainted Parolles. This triangle resembles Shakespeare's in *Troilus and Cressida,* where the hero, a merchant or chapman in quest of a pearl, has his go-between to help him, "our convoy and our bark." Ideally cast for the go-between's role, W.S. "not long before

. . . [has] tried the courtesy of the like passion." Readers sit up at this, many glimpsing Shakespeare and his Dark Lady.

But W.S. differs from the anguished poet of the sonnets. Himself "newly recovered" from love's infection, this "miserable comforter" laughs in secret at H.W.'s folly as others, not long before, had laughed at his. "A dangerous and lascivious boy," he might be saying, like Parolles detecting young Bertram. Viewing from afar "the course of this loving comedy," the "old player" prompts the "new actor" from the wings. Theme for bitter expostulation in Shakespeare's sonnets, the player's discomfit is a theme for comedy now. He has been turning pages in Shakespeare, his source for cynical counsels poured in the open ulcer of H.W.'s love. A jingling couplet evokes lines in the early plays and sonnets:

> She is no saint, she is no nun,
> I think in time she may be won.

"Ply her still," says the player. But the raffish wisdom falls on deaf ears. In the end Avisa escapes them, her virtue still intact.

Affectively, though, this seems not true of her, and the poem's bleak moral (from Proverbs 12:4) points its readers in a different direction. "A virtuous woman is the crown of her husband, but she that maketh him all ashamed is as corruption in his bones." Corruption " 'mongst greatest sort" detains this poet with a chip on his shoulder, and partly his business is with "the nature, words, gestures, promises, and very quintessence . . . of such lewd chapmen as use to entice silly maids." Already in his first canto, England's soil has merged with Sodom's. Sodom, a code word, comes up again.

Willobie His Avisa, "poetically shadowed," is written in code, and under the "feigned name" of the heroine hides "something of truth." Perhaps the initials A.D. declare her. A mayor's daughter and an innkeeper's wife, she comes from the west of England. (Riddling details pinpoint the location, not so riddling that scholars can't sift them.) Ralegh lived in her neighborhood, licking his wounds. He kept a "school of atheism," enemies said, enrolling among his scholars Christopher Marlowe and George Chapman, favorite candidates for Shakespeare's Rival Poet in the sonnets.

But *Avisa* is "Willobie's," as the title proposes. He was Henry Willoughby of West Knoyle, Wiltshire, one of the Oxford men (a contemporary said) "able to sing sweetly." The avowed author of the poem, he isn't the "only begetter." Going abroad on Queen's business, he leaves the key to his study with his "chamber-fellow" Hadrian Dorrell, unknown to Oxford records. Dorrell, making free of Willoughby's papers, finds the poem and has it printed. This old stratagem, familiar in Shakespeare's time and before, says that Willoughby, a gentleman, feared the soilure of print. "The fault that I acknowledge in myself," said John Donne, "is to have descended to print anything in verse." Willoughby, like Donne, got his poem published but looked the other way.

Italian proverbs salt his narrative, telling of the dandified man. Seven of them turn up in a popular collection, published in 1591. John Florio was the collector. Also Willoughby had an in-law, the ubiquitous Thomas Russell, overseer of Shakespeare's will. Matter of fact, these peripheral details provoke speculation, and many have indulged it in print. They want to know, e.g., did Shakespeare, passing through Oxford en route to his "native country," meet Henry Willoughby through Thomas Russell? Did they cook up something spicy? share a wench between them, like Beaumont and Fletcher? Perhaps the woman who caught their eye was the A.D. of *Avisa,* not so chaste as her panegyrist pretended. Perhaps she was Shakespeare's Dark Lady. Hopeful commentators remember that Mistress Davenant, this poet's secret love (on the word of her son), kept a tavern in Oxford. Her given name, however, was Jane.

Ruttish young H.W., whoever he was in life, bears no resemblance to Southampton as he got older. Shakespeare's Earl, having sowed his wild oats, dwindled to a conformist, investor in the New World, and supporter of the Crown. (He hedged support, however, and the wind turning, veered round to the Parliament side.) As treasurer of the Virginia Company, "he carried his business closely and slyly," said a chronicler who knew him. A large island in Hudson's Bay and a town in Virginia remember Southampton. He died "of a lethargy" in 1624, eight years after Shakespeare.

HOW SHAKESPEARE, common player, involved himself with the noble Earl would make a scenario for a play of his, an unlikely one, *All's Well That Ends Well.* The connection once forged, though, Shakespeare exploited it. That is, he wrote sonnets, one hundred fifty-four of them. Not a mixed bag of lyrics but linked by theme and chains of imagery, they have a story line, dramatizing a connection like Shakespeare's with his patron.

But the story, resisting paraphrase, is hard to boil down. Individual sonnets redo or "confound" each other, the way that Time, giving, confounds what he gave. In no. 29, for instance ("When in disgrace with fortune and men's eyes"), Shakespeare's misery lifts when he remembers his friend. But pain gives pleasure in the companion poem (no. 30, "When to the sessions of sweet silent thought"), and the "dear friend," remembered, spoils his sentimental game. Point of view is a casualty of this back-and-forth, not credibility, however. Shakespeare at sonnets, immersed in his material, is essentially a dramatic poet. Egotism withers, and the dyer's hand acquires the color of the dye.

The sonnets as narrative fall into three parts. Linear in arrangement, they have the unity of what comes next, not the same as thesis-antithesis-synthesis. Only the publisher's authority backs up Shakespeare's sequence that doesn't come to conclusions, but it reads persuasively and most think the ordering hand is his. His narrative tells of two friends, a Fair Youth and a Poet, who pursue a married woman, the Dark Lady. The Youth, a man of quality "too dear" for the Poet's possessing, is Shakespeare's subject in Part One (nos. 1–126). He ought to marry and beget children (nos. 1–17), a way to be "new made" in age, and the Poet, solicitous, pushes this course. But the matter of Time eating seems to engage him more than his friend's renewal. Shakespeare, possibly spiteful, holds up a mirror, showing the Youth when Time has had its way with him, an old man with deep-sunken eyes. The summons to "breed" is anticipated by Sidney, also in a well-thumbed treatise on the art of rhetoric. Shakespeare, though bookish, wasn't insincere, and perhaps he found it in himself.

But his friend declines to marry. Playing the field, he takes up with a male rival, even fleshing his will on Shakespeare's mistress. Twenty-six poems (nos. 127–52) put the mistress before us, strikingly different from the blonde goddess preferred by most sonneteers. An anticonvention held that brunettes were better than blondes, and Shakespeare catered to this. Convention, followed slavishly, was death on sonnets. Meaning to be original, he described a mistress "not so bright/As those gold candles fixed in heaven's air."

Lust, mounting to hysteria, torments his Poet, and for multitudes of readers the sexual passion comes home as almost intolerably real: "had, having, and in quest to have, extreme." But at his most powerful, Shakespeare is most the technician. In no. 144, a rhetorical figure, antithesis or "the quarreler," presents his two loves, "of comfort and despair," he calls them. This artificial figure, not diluting his sincerity, assures it.

Two sonnets on Cupid (nos. 153–54), marked off from all the others and deliberately flattened, bring Shakespeare's cycle to an impersonal close. Dramatic poetry, anyway his, needs this quiet subsidence, "night walker's song after great cathedral gong." No thundering curtain comes down on Shakespeare's tragedies, and the sonnets, in this respect, are like the plays.

Shakespeare's loose plot, remembering Lyly's *Euphues*, has an analog in his own *Two Gentlemen of Verona*. Proteus, the antihero of this early comedy, is false to himself, his woman, and his friend, guilty of a "threefold perjury" is how Shakespeare puts it. But Shakespeare in the sonnets, adjusting this version of the Eternal Triangle, relegates "Proteus" to a supporting role. At the apex of the triangle stands the Poet, hero of his own *Bildungsroman*, below him the Fair Youth and Dark Lady. Irresolute Shakespeare wavers between the two, like Prince Hal assessing Falstaff and Hotspur. Finally, though, he grows up, rejecting both his tempters:

> Buy terms divine in selling hours of dross,
> Within be fed, without be rich no more.

A famous sonnet, no. 146, "Poor soul, the center of my sinful earth," supplies the quotation. Alone among the poems that make up Shakespeare's cycle, it appeals to the world over yonder. At the end, the soul, instructed, is headed for this better place. Along the way, though, it makes certain fiscal arrangements, and buying and selling portray a calculating soul. No doubt the bottom line, salvation, gets our approval. But approval is tempered and perhaps we feel uneasy at the shopkeeper-mix of calculation and virtue. Many of Shakespeare's sonnets and almost all the great ones beget this kind of equivocal response.

Reminiscent in feeling and sometimes in diction, the sonnets cast a wider net than early plays of Shakespeare's like the *Two Gentlemen*. Where Valentine loves Silvia and Proteus does too, Shakespeare's protean Poet has two loves, one male, the other female. Scholars, downplaying this, point out that males in Shakespeare's time addressed each other laconically in language later times devoted to sexual love. Antonio, not Portia, is the hero's "bosom lover" in *The Merchant of Venice*. Before Shakespeare wrote, love of a male subject inflamed some sonnet writers, Michelangelo, for one. Then there were the Greeks, in love with hyacinthine boys. They furnished a model, mostly literary, to English in the Renaissance. These facts put Shakespeare's sonnets in perspective. But every reader must feel an erotic attachment between the Poet and his masculine friend.

Shakespeare the homosexual, affronting some, unsettles most. Coleridge, reflecting his and his readers' discomfort, told them that in all Shakespeare there is "not even an allusion to that very worst of all possible vices." This disclaimer, first uttered or suggested not long after Shakespeare's death, still echoes today. E.g. a modern biographer: regarding the nature of Shakespeare's love for the Youth, "it was not homosexual—it was not sexual at all, but ideal." Shakespeare's early printer Benson, though not a Platonizer, isn't less protective of his subject's good name. Reissuing the sonnets in 1640, he altered Shakespeare's pronouns, turning "he" into "she." Not everyone was fooled, and in the nineteenth century one wideawake reader voiced his alarm: "Good Heavens! What do I notice? He instead of she? Can I be mistaken? Can these sonnets be addressed to a man? Shakespeare! Great Shakespeare! Did you feel yourself authorized by Virgil's example?"

Shakespeare in one sonnet parts company with Virgil, though. Loving his friend, he finds his love defeated, Nature having endowed the friend with "one thing to my purpose nothing." Being himself, Shakespeare makes the best of this:

> But since she pricked thee out for women's pleasure,
> Mine be thy love, and thy love's use their treasure.

"Pricked" means what it seems to mean and "use" is sexual use, available to women, not to heterosexual Shakespeare. He wasn't equable about this, however. An androgynous personality, he combined in himself both halves of Plato's sorb apple. Back in the beginning a jealous God cleft the apple. Wanting to diminish us, He reserved a plenary form to Himself. But Shakespeare gets round Him, and his sonnets, notably inclusive, throb with erotic longing, devoted impartially to a woman or a man.

Circulating in manuscript, the sonnets attracted the attention of shifty printers, hoping to find a windfall in the public domain. Thomas Thorpe, a "camp-follower of the regular publishing army," gave them to the world in June 1609. A cryptic dedication, not Shakespeare's but his, sowed the seeds of much discord in centuries to come:

> TO. THE. ONLY. BEGETTER. OF.
> THESE. ENSUING. SONNETS.
> MR. W.H. ALL. HAPPINESS.
> AND. THAT. ETERNITY.
> PROMISED.
> BY.
> OUR. EVER-LIVING. POET.
> WISHETH.
> THE. WELL-WISHING.
> ADVENTURER. IN.
> SETTING.
> FORTH.
> T.T.

Like individual sonnets, this dedication to all of them looks in different directions. It seems to say that "W.H." is the only begetter, the Fair Youth who inspired most of the poems. But in syntactical propriety, this begetter might as well be the poet. Some, not intending whimsy, think W.H. stands for William Himself, others, partisans of Southampton (Henry Wriothesley), that Thorpe reversed the letters to throw the vulgar off the scent. But "Mr.," no way to address a lord, raises eyebrows. Perhaps, more humbly, "begetter" means "procurer," the man who brought Shakespeare's manuscript to Thorpe. William Harvey, married to Southampton's mother, might have done this. (Tactful, he kept the yellowed bundle hidden until the Countess died in 1607.)

Thorpe's "Wisheth" gives trouble too, more than one antecedent being potential. Who is doing the wishing, publisher or poet? A surfeit of "points" or periods adds to the confusion. This clears, some believe, if you strike the period after W.H., allowing for the reading: "Mr. W. Hall." The William Hall thus engendered, a stationer and printer, is acknowledged gratefully by Thorpe. (He isn't rewarded, though, Thorpe hiring someone else to do the printing.) In *A Midsummer Night's Dream,* semiliterate characters don't "stand upon points," and their play-within-the-play, careless of punctuation, means different things to different readers. Thorpe's dedication is like this. Elizabethan prose has its glories, but readers who want to know where they are won't regret that the Age of Dryden, alert to hard-and-fast meanings, followed the Age of Shakespeare.

Piecing out his slender volume with *A Lover's Complaint,* Thorpe hired George Eld to print the sonnets at his shop in Fleet Lane. William Aspley and John Wright distributed Shakespeare's book to a public already bored with this innocent-seeming stuff. "Scorn" rhymed with "horn," apathetic readers said, and "school" with "fool," puerile endings that tickled Shakespeare. The month the book appeared, Edward Alleyn bought a copy for fivepence, cheap at the price. More than thirty years went by, however, before a second edition was called for. By 1609, the sonneteering vogue was passé.

With his world-famous book, Shakespeare most likely had nothing to do. Misprints disfigure it, much chaff in the wheat. One sonnet is too short, another too long, and the same couplet turns up twice. Deploring publication, Shakespeare otherwise ignored it. Perhaps he had forgotten all about his youthful effusions. Youthful most of them are, though not everyone thinks this. One way to be sure is to listen to young Shakespeare brooding on his old age. "Beated and chopped with tanned antiquity" (62), he knows his days are past the best (138). In one much-anthologized sonnet, "That time of year" (73), he appears in five different ways as a ruin. This is like young T. S. Eliot, the old eagle, or young Sir Philip Sidney, dead to "delight in the world." Sidney when he drew this self-portrait wasn't quite twenty-six.

Like many poets and poetasters in the 1590s, Shakespeare, starting out, found the artificial form appropriate to a beginner. (He chose the English variety, patented by the Earl of Surrey, it having fewer rhymes than the Italian.) Different from others, this beginner spoofed what he was doing: "none but minstrels like of sonnetting," etc. By 1598, his "sugared sonnets" (a contemporary's phrase) were making the rounds among "private friends." William Jaggard, a disingenuous printer, abstracted two of them for his poetical miscellany, *The Passionate Pilgrim* (1599). (Knowing how the famous name lured prospective buyers, he credited Shakespeare with all 21 poems in this collection.)

Often a mirror reflecting a mirror, sonnets of the time had a common ancestor, Sidney's *Astrophel and Stella* (1591). Shakespeare's cycle, imitative work with something to boot, tracks this Star Lover and Star. Shakespeare pays close attention to Sidney's epigones too, some of them poets of the first water like Drayton, Daniel, and Spenser, others not much remembered, most available to young Shakespeare before 1595. Schoolboy reading jogged his memory, and readers brought up on Ovid and Horace heard them in his ruminations on Time's fell hand. They heard the Bible also and the Book of Common Prayer: "Let me not to the marriage of true minds admit impediments."

Suggesting a time frame, Shakespeare quotes his own work, by and large the early plays and narrative poems. For example, no. 27, where the Fair Youth's shadow, an image coming up in sleep, is "a jewel hung in ghastly night." This remembers or looks forward to Romeo's first glimpse of Juliet:

> It seems she hangs upon the cheek of night
> Like a rich jewel in an Ethiop's ear.

Caveat lector, though. Shakespeare's beginning is in his ending, and the sonnets, looking backwards and forwards, intimate lines and phrases from most of the plays. This makes dating ticklish. Also it comments on the nature of Shakespeare's art, a coat of many colors but seamless.

No. 107 illustrates the dating problem and suggests how not to read Shakespeare's poems.

Not mine own fears, nor the prophetic soul
Of the wide world dreaming on things to come,
Can yet the lease of my true love control,
Supposed as forfeit to a confined doom.
The mortal moon hath her eclipse endured,
And the sad augurs mock their own presàge;
Incertainties now crown themselves assured,
And peace proclaims olives of endless age. . . .

Most commentators think Shakespeare's "eclipse" glances at a specific disaster, averted. Eclipses, giving notice of disaster, often frightened English people when he lived in London, 21 of them in the period 1592–1609. Maybe this eclipse is a metaphor, however, shrouding the "mortal moon," i.e. Queen Elizabeth, "Cynthia," as they knew her, chaste goddess of the night. In 1596 the Queen emerged whole from her 63rd or Grand Climacteric Year, an ominous conjunction arrived at by multiplying the mystic numbers 7 and 9. Many settle on this year as the date of Shakespeare's poem. Many, not all, and guesses range from 1571 when the Turks, invading Europe, were turned back at Lepanto, to 1603 when Queen Elizabeth died and Shakespeare's patron, free at last, quit the Tower of London. Once again men of letters vied for his favor, Shakespeare among them (says Southampton's biographer). In no. 107 he congratulates his "true love," no longer forfeit "to a confined doom."

But the poem, a nest of Chinese boxes, while it says that the moon, outlasting an eclipse, has survived it, says also that the moon, powerless to help itself, has endured an eclipse, submitting to its privation. Perhaps Southampton and the Queen (or the Turks or men of the Armada) play a part in Shakespeare's poem. But he doesn't salute them and they owe their promotion to his readers, not him.

His Poet, known for convenience' sake as Shakespeare, hearkens to doleful prophets who predict disaster. Their predictions aren't borne out, though, and Shakespeare finds them reproved by the happy event. Entertaining another possibility, he thinks the event, gloomy as may be, reproves the hopeful "presage" of these prophets, and this is why they are sad. The matter of fact he is dealing with is (1) triumphant (2) not so good. Historians hunting dates, if they read him with a poet's eye, won't find him helpful.

Despite his anxiety, optimistic Shakespeare tells himself that nothing can bring his love to an end. Or maybe the anxiety is justified by what happens, and the love, no fee-simple thing, isn't within his controlling. This Poet is a pessimist. And so on, here and elsewhere.

All poetry has its source—oozing like a gum "From whence 'tis nourished," says the poet in *Timon of Athens*—and likely this vexed sonnet begins with some historical event. But Shakespeare, hermetic or only artistic, assimilates fact to fiction. Spenser in his marriage hymn specifies his marriage day, and Sidney in one sonnet does really allude to the battle of Lepanto. In Shakespeare's sonnets, nothing, except the whole poem, precipitates out. This doesn't cancel the chance for autobiography but complicates the story he tells.

The Shakespeare Industry, rationalizing the sonnets, opposes its clarity to Shakespeare's complication. First chartered in the eighteenth century, it owes its real beginnings to John Benson, printer of the second quarto (1640). Fitting together individual poems, as many as five, he headed his scissors-and-paste work with descriptive titles. The sonnets when he got through with them were "serene, clear, and elegantly plain," he said, "no intricate or cloudy stuff to puzzle intellect." Benson's successors, like Freud reclaiming the Unconscious, mean to uncover Shakespeare's Zuyder Zee. Aware how an "alien pen," displacing his, has got the "use" of the friend, they want to know was he Samuel Daniel, tutor to a chief candidate for the role of the Fair Youth, highfalutin George Chapman, a panegyrist of the Earl of Essex, Christopher Marlowe, the poet as Ganymede.

The Dark Lady needs her identity too, more and less precise than Shakespeare's equivocal portrait. Majority opinion oscillates between Mary Fitton, mistress of the Earl of Pembroke, and Elizabeth Vernon, Southampton's mistress, later his wife. Some, wanting the best for Shakespeare, propose a liaison with Queen Elizabeth. The Age of Freud has its candidate, Shakespeare's mother. Victorians opted for Anne Hathaway, Shakespeare's wife.

Internal evidence, supplying clues to diligent readers, suggests to some an early female addict of tobacco. (Perfumes delight him more, candid Shakespeare confesses, than the breath that "reeks" or rises from his mistress.) The Dark Lady, being dark, suggests to others a quadroon or mulatto. Sponsors of Shakespeare's miscegenetic love affair, they link him with the prostitute, Lucy Negro. Prostitute, Court Lady, or middle-class housewife, her morals were loose, implying Latin blood. Commentators observe that French Jacqueline Field, wife of Shakespeare's first publisher, has this qualification. So does Emilia Bassano, daughter of an Italian musician at Court and paramour of old Lord Hunsdon, patron of the Chamberlain's Men. For each of these candidates, supporters, building their case, muster evidence, some of it ringing like truth. This truth shuttles, "guestwise," from one woman to another, though. Shakespeare's Dark Lady, like Shakespeare himself, is a bay in which all ships may ride.

The Fair Youth is like that, only more hospitable. Southampton, a sensualist reluctant to marry, heads the list of contenders, and the language of Shakespeare's dedications to his narrative poems, anticipating the sonnets, seems to merge the patron and friend: "Lord of my love, to whom in vassalage/Thy merit hath my duty strongly knit." A golden boy, capable of meanness, disloyalty too, looks out from Shakespeare's pages, his ambiguous praise still finding room in the eyes of posterity. But the Fair Youth isn't Southampton.

William Herbert, third earl of Pembroke, his chief rival for the part, looks too young to play it, being born in 1580. Other things tell in his favor, however. By age twenty, he had broken off four projected marriages. His father's company, Pembroke's Men, perhaps included Shakespeare, and he himself, when he served as Lord Chamberlain, was deep in theater business. "The greatest Maecenas . . . of any peer of his time," Aubrey called him. Shakespeare's editors dedicated the First Folio to this influential patron and his brother Philip, and Shakespeare's company played at Wilton, Pembroke's house, early in the reign of King James. Many, noting these facts, are sure that Pembroke is their man.

Other candidates are thick on the ground, though, among them Shakespeare's brother-in-law William Hathaway, his friend Henry Walker, and his nephew William Hart. Glamorous Essex makes the short list, also Henry Willoughby, supposed author of *Avisa,* and Hamnet Shakespeare, dying young but eluding mortality in eternal numbers. Some think Shakespeare names the friend in his ribald sonnet, no. 20, "A woman's face with Nature's own hand painted." Occupied with himself and a magnet to others, the friend is "A man in hue, all hues in his controlling." "Hues" is the key word, perhaps pronounced "use," so involving sexual license. Capitalized and printed in italic type (but that was the compositor's business, not the poet's), it introduces a boy actor, William or Willie Hughes. Oscar Wilde had fun with this.

Wilde knew better. "You *must* believe in Willie Hughes," he said. "I almost do myself." But the "master-mistress" of Shakespeare's passion, real as reality, isn't to be identified with this imaginary actor nor with any contemporary of Shakespeare's known to history by his given name and surname. The Dark Lady isn't any of the women put for her, and the Rival Poet whose "proud full sail" took the wind out of Shakespeare's has something in him of every poet of price. Life absorbed Shakespeare endlessly. Reliving the past, he works Stratford and its doings into his poems and plays, and some spear-carriers of his are named for people he knew. But he never draws from the life, and none of his protagonists has a real-life counterpart outside the theater or study.

In Shakespeare's boyhood, a Katherine Hamlet, lovelorn, drowned in the Avon near Stratford. Perhaps this woman's name and the way she died stuck in his memory. She isn't Ophelia, though. If he got hints from Cordelia Annesley's story, hints were all he wanted. His Cordelia is somebody else. Allegory, the binary kind, was beneath him. He couldn't have written *Willobie His Avisa*. Maybe a piece of Florio, Southampton's tutor, survives in the pedant of *Love's Labor's Lost*. But Holofernes is himself. Southampton, others too, participate in the sonnets. Cold-blooded and provident, Shakespeare made capital of his friends and acquaintance. He dispersed them, however, standard practice for this credentialed writer who understood how art and life aren't the same.

Sidney has a phrase for what Shakespeare is doing: "Ennobling new-found tropes with problems old." Exercising his craft, he isn't up front with readers, too cunning for that, and his truest poetry is "the most feigning." But the problems that beset him aren't make-believe. "The pangs of despised love," his or another's, afflict his wretched Poet. Hurt by life into poetry, he "whispers the o'erfraught heart," in his case to keep it from breaking. Self-abasing Valentine, entoiled "in a waste of shame," comes close to this Poet. "To be in love," what is it?

> If haply won, perhaps a hapless gain;
> If lost, why then a grievous labor won;
> However, but a folly bought with wit,
> Or else a wit by folly vanquishèd.

Harping on the same string, hero and Poet tell of the creator who endows both with life. In his sonnets and plays, Shakespeare, speaking through fictitious persons, "shadows of himself," is making a "recordation" to his soul.

Betrayal, often sexual, rouses his deepest feeling. He inhabits his two Antonios, the merchant and sea captain, each of them cast off by a handsome young man. "Oh, how vile an idol proves this god," appearance. Dido, abandoned, is among his obsessions, Philomela too. His Imogen, raped in all but deed, is reading her story when Iachimo, another Tarquin, comes stealing in the night, and tormented Shakespeare looks through the keyhole. It might be he, the "supervisor," who watches with Julia while her lover plays her false. (This scene, a more harrowing version, rivets Shakespeare's eye again in *Troilus and*

Cressida, "distasted with the salt of broken tears.") "The private wound is deepest," his Valentine says.

Shakespeare's biographer will want to notice his recurrences, perhaps involuntary. Odd tricks of phrase or feeling shooting out of the mind, they intimate the place he lived in, there where he garnered up his heart. But his sonnets and plays don't chronicle deprivation. Self-lacerating they may be in their beginnings, not in their endings, though, and the private and public life exist for him in a kind of symbiosis. Philomela's rape, like the story the sonnets tell, works out to song.

For catalytic Shakespeare, a cause of wit in other men, the role of looker-on seems appointed. It has its compensations, setting him apart from his dramatis personae, not above the battle but trapped by blood or *parti pris.* Neutral or rather absolutely engaged, he is like his long-lived crow in *The Phoenix and Turtle.* This outsider at the marriage feast engenders by breath alone.

The Poet of the sonnets has a disinterested rubric, "Look again!" Sorting through the same materials to different conclusions, he anticipates the playwright for whom "two truths are told." Sometimes his negative and positive truth, coexisting, make an emulsion. Or, like the knowledge of good and evil, they live in "the rind of one apple tasted." *Romeo and Juliet,* Shakespeare's tale of crossed loves, needs its comic recension, *A Midsummer Night's Dream,* not parody, however, only the other half of the apple.

The homoerotic content of the sonnets, a pitfall to many, discloses him on his comprehensive side. For univocal readers, making Shakespeare over in their own image, he is (1) a pederast, or (2) a man's man, confessing in every line "the normality of his sexual impulse." Either way, exclusive Shakespeare, like an eighteenth-century novel-character circumscribed by his "master passion," lets his readers know where to have him.

But his ardor is impartial, transcending either/or, immiscibles that shouldn't get together but do. Like double-faced Janus he looks both ways at once, or like the chameleon, his self-image from early days, he takes color from all his characters and participates in all his fictions. This doesn't argue the annihilating of personality (not the same thing as importunate ego) but its enlarging.

"Sweet," the epithet that most often describes him, as in "Sweet Will," looks like a misnomer. Not benevolent, only acquisitive, insatiably that, he annexes whatever territories butt on his own. This passes for caring. The old "termini," boundary gods venerated by the multitude, are nothing to him, and readers and auditors whose bias runs all one way think he has at heart their getting lost. Hating and loving, ever at ease and racked by uncertainty, superb in the consciousness of unrivaled powers but himself almost despising, he flattens our dichotomous world to a planisphere, merging north and south. This makes him a doubtful cicerone. Landing us up in an unchartered country where good penetrates evil and the other way round, he leaves us to shift for ourselves. This place of half-lights and shadows engaged his surveyor's interest more vitally than ever before in the sonnets. Over the next two decades, *anni mirabiles,* he went back many times, recording in his plays what he found there.

A Reading List

BOOKS AND PAPERS on Shakespeare's life, piled on one another, would overtop Mounts Pelion and Ossa. Surprisingly many are useful. So it seems ungrateful to boil them down to a short list. But that is what I have done, offering here only those relatively few works that seemed particularly valuable to me. Books on my short list are unequal in merit, some being repetitive and self-indulgent. But all have something important to offer, and anyone investigating young Shakespeare will want to consult them all.

Baker, Oliver. *In Shakespeare's Warwickshire and the Unknown Years.* London: Simkin Marshall, 1937.

Baldwin, T. W. *William Shakspere's Petty School.* Urbana: University of Illinois Press, 1943.

——*William Shakspere's Small Latine & Lesse Greeke.* 2 vols. Urbana: University of Illinois Press, 1944.

Chambers, E. K. *William Shakespeare: A Study of Facts and Problems.* 2 vols. Oxford: Clarendon Press, 1930.

——*The Elizabethan Stage.* 4 vols. Oxford: Clarendon Press (1928), 1961.

Eccles, Mark. *Shakespeare in Warwickshire.* Madison: University of Wisconsin Press, 1963.

Elton, Charles Isaac. *William Shakespeare: His Family and Friends.* London: J. Murray, 1904.

Fox, Levi. *The Borough Town of Stratford-upon-Avon.* Stratford: 1953.

Fripp, Edgar I. *Shakespeare Man and Artist.* 2 vols. London: H. Milford, Oxford University Press, 1938.

——*Shakespeare's Stratford.* London: Oxford University Press, 1928.

Gray, Joseph William. *Shakespeare's Marriage: His Departure from Stratford and Other Incidents in His Life.* London: Chapman and Hall, 1905. (Valuable for giving the documents.)

Halliwell-Phillipps, James O. *Outlines of the Life of Shakespeare.* 2 vols. London: Longmans, Green, 1889.

Lee, Sidney. *Stratford-on-Avon from the Earliest Times to the Death of Shakespeare.* London: Seeley, 1908 (revised edition).

Lewis, B. Roland, ed. *The Shakespeare Documents.* 2 vols. London: H. Milford, Oxford University Press, 1940.

Savage, Richard, ed. *The Registers of Stratford-on-Avon, County Warwick.* Parish Register Society. London: private printing, 1897.

Schoenbaum, S. *William Shakespeare: A Documentary Life.* New York: Oxford University Press, 1975.

Shakespeare's England. Walter Raleigh, Sidney Lee, and others, eds. 2 vols. Oxford: Clarendon Press (1916), 1950.

Stow, John. *Survey of London.* 1598. Everyman's Library. London: Dent; New York: Dutton, 1956.

Victoria History of the Counties of England: Warwickshire. 3 vols. London: Oxford University Press (1904), 1955.

Wheler, R. B. *History and Antiquities of Stratford-upon-Avon.* Stratford: J. Ward, 1806.

Notes

ABBREVIATIONS of Shakespeare's works, given here, are standard, as is the order in which the works appear, that of the Folio. Citations follow the Riverside edition (1974), to which the Harvard Concordance is keyed.

TMP	The Tempest
TGV	The Two Gentlemen of Verona
WIV	The Merry Wives of Windsor
MM	Measure for Measure
ERR	The Comedy of Errors
ADO	Much Ado About Nothing
LLL	Love's Labor's Lost
MND	A Midsummer Night's Dream
MV	The Merchant of Venice
AYL	As You Like It
SHR	The Taming of the Shrew
AWW	All's Well That Ends Well
TN	Twelfth Night
WT	The Winter's Tale
JN	King John
R2	Richard II
1H4	Henry IV, Part One

2H4	Henry IV, Part Two
H5	Henry V
1H6	Henry VI, Part One
2H6	Henry VI, Part Two
3H6	Henry VI, Part Three
R3	Richard III
H8	Henry VIII
TRO	Troilus and Cressida
COR	Coriolanus
TIT	Titus Andronicus
ROM	Romeo and Juliet
TIM	Timon of Athens
JC	Julius Caesar
MAC	Macbeth
HAM	Hamlet
LR	King Lear
OTH	Othello
ANT	Anthony and Cleopatra
CYM	Cymbeline
PER	Pericles
TNK	The Two Noble Kinsmen
STM	Sir Thomas More
VEN	Venus and Adonis
LUC	The Rape of Lucrece
PHT	The Phoenix and Turtle
SON	The Sonnets
LC	A Lover's Complaint

1. The Country

1.   Robert Greene said: *Groatsworth of Wit,* 1592.

1.   and well pronounced: MV, 1.2.10.

2.   of chaste lovers: Other poems and plays are sometimes attributed to him, most recently a nine-stanza lyric ("Shall I die"), copies of which exist in the Bodleian, Oxford, and the Beinecke, Yale.

3.   contemporary of Shakespeare's: William Vaughan, *The Golden Glove,* 1608.

3.   born on this day: He might have been born on Monday the 24th or Sunday the 23rd. Logic suggests—given the Prayer Book's injunction—that he couldn't have been born before St. George's Day. If his parents honored the injunction, and he was in fact born before, he would/should have been christened that Sunday.

3.   nothing but confusion: R2, 2.2.18–19.

3.   arrant knaves all: HAM, 3.1.128.

4.   Death is certain: 2H4, 3.2.40.

5.   their youthful sap: SON 15.7.

5.   "slaves of nature": R3, 1.3.229.

5.   to deadly use: 4.2.34–36.

5.   golden time convents: TN, 5.1.382.

6.   Salic law: H5, 1.2.11ff.

6.   dungy earth: ANT, 1.1.35; WT, 2.1.157.

6.   "of a peach": "Lichfield and Warwick" in *English Hours* (1905), 1981, p. 50.

6.   rank fumiter: LR, 4.4.3.

7.   of Burton Heath: Induction, 218.

7.   old John Naps: Ind., 293; and Sidney Lee, *A Life of William Shakespeare* (1898), 1916, pp. 238–39. 2H4, 5.1.41–45, 55–56.

7.   A knavish client: William Visor of Woncot (2H4, 5.1.39).

8.   the pebbled shore: SON 60.1.

8.   in the face: MAC, 1.4.12–13.

9.   a smug bridegroom: LR, 4.6.199.

9.   like a bride: MM, 3.1.83–84.

9.   at their doors: 2H6, 4.2.179–80.

9.   in my petticoat: G. R. Elton, *England under the Tudors,* 1955, p. 285.

10. "till they marry": Paul Hentzner, *Travels in England,* 1598.

10. in blood-sports: Bear-baiting in particular, maintained (said Privy Council in 1591) "for her Majesty's pleasure."

10. and the slaver: *Robert Laneham's Letter, 1575,* ed. F. J. Furnivall, 1907, p. 17.

10. fear and commiseration: *Annals,* 1625–29, III.16; Edgar I. Fripp, *Shakespeare Man and Artist,* 1938, I.161. The pamphleteer is John Stubbes.

10. Catholics . . . headed the procession: G. Elton, *England,* p. 308.

11. "breach of all": CYM, 4.2.10–11.

11. a "character" writer: Sir Thomas Overbury, *Characters,* 1614.

11. the "antique world": AYL, 2.3.56–65.

11. penalty of Adam: AYL, 2.1.5.

11.   of their fate: JC, 1.2.139.

11.   Hugh Latimer said: *Works,* ed. for Parker Society by G. E. Corric, 1968 reprint, I.101.

11.   of the world: JN, 2.1.574.

12.   "by indirections": HAM, 2.1.63.

12.   their warders' heads: MAC, 4.1.56–58.

12.   "Let order die!": 2H4, 1.1.154.

12.   and heaven together: 5.2.40–42.

12.   an "indigest": JN, 5.7.26.

12.   "unaccommodated" man: LR, 3.4.106–7.

12.   and violent sea: MAC, 4.2.21.

13.   the halcyon: LR, 2.2.78.

13.   *Measure for Measure:* 1.1.33–35 (remembering Matthew 5:15–16).

13.   "plough-torn leas": TIM, 4.3.193.

13.   a thousand furlongs: TMP, 1.1.65.

13.   "the merèd question": ANT, 3.13.10.

13.   of the rye: AYL, 5.3.22.

14.   potent in potting: OTH, 2.3.77.

14.   "high and disposedly": Peter Quennell, *Shakespeare The Poet and His Background,* 1963, p. 73.

14.   "of husbandry": John Fitzherbert's "Tract or Treatise," first pub. 1523, was reprinted frequently throughout the century.

14.   a greater power: ROM, 5.3.153.

15.   "as seasons fleet": 2H6, 2.4.1–4.

15.   frightened the ladies: ROM, 1.4.6.

15.   a crowkeeper: LR, 4.6.88.

15.   *Description of England:* In Raphael Holinshed, *The First and Second Volumes of Chronicles,* 1587; ed. F. J. Furnivall, 1877.

15.   Leicester hosted the Queen: *Laneham's Letter.*

16.   red with mirth: WT, 4.4.54.

16.   never merry days: 2H6, 4.2.8–9.

16.   "gilded puddle": ANT, 1.4.62.

16.   "bots" or worms: 1H4, 2.1.10.

16.   cuckoo-flowers: LR, 4.4.4.

16.   "murrion flock": MND, 2.1.97.

16.   "great oneyers": 1H4, 2.1.76.

16.   receipt of fern seed: 1H4, 2.1.86–87.

17.   no common: LLL, 2.1.224.

17.   young dace . . . old pike: 2H4, 3.2.330–31.

17.   "pelting" farms: R2, 2.1.60.

17.   this realm: R2, 2.1.50.

17.   his quillets shrilly: TIM, 4.3.155.

17.   light of enclosure: Sixteenth-century enclosures affected less than 3 percent of England's arable land: M. M. Reese, *Shakespeare*, 1980, p. 244.

18.   bells, and all: 2.1.28–34.

18.   to good pity: LR, 4.6.223.

18.   an imaginative playwright: Edward Bond, *Bingo*, 1974.

18.   Dugdale . . . describes the Ardens: *Antiquities of Warwickshire*, 1730.

19.   reminiscence of John Shakespeare: Thomas Plume, c.1657, quotes "Sir John Mennis."

20.   ragged as Lazarus: 1H4, 4.2.25–26.

21.   heavens . . . blazed forth: JC, 2.2.31.

22.   which you tickled: TN, 2.5.22.

22.   skimble-scamble stuff: 1H4, 3.1.152.

22.   in *Henry VIII*: 5.3.22.

22.   John Leland said: *The Itinerary*, ed. L. T. Smith, 1964, II.45.

23.   this wild wood: AYL, 5.4.154–59.

23.   die we must: 3H6, 5.2.27–28.

23.   seventeenth-century annalist: David Lloyd, 1665.

24.   Leland . . . said: *Itinerary*, II.27.

2. The Town

25.   "cupboarding the viand": COR, 1.1.100.

26.   excellent thing in woman: LR, 5.3.273–74.

27.   the rother's sides: TIM, 4.3.12, emending the Folio's "brothers."

27.   "cruel garters": LR, 2.4.7.

28.   like an apple: LR, 1.4.15–16.

28.   a local speculator: William Underhill.

28.   the meaner sort: John Davies of Hereford, "To Our English Terence, Mr. Will. Shakespeare," c.1610.

28.   Mislike me not: MV, 2.1.1.

28.   not an Englishman: Hentzner, *Travels*.

29.   Harrison said so: *Description of England*, pp. vi, xviin.

29.   saw, and overcame: CYM, 3.1.24.

29.   "hook-nosed fellow": 2H4, 4.3.41.

29.   "rough rugheaded kerns": R2, 2.1.156.

29.   "weasel Scot": H5, 1.2.170.

29.   the "French disease": E.g. AWW, 2.2.22.

29.   rest but true: JN, 5.7.117–18.

29.   two-headed Janus: MV, 1.1.50.

29.   like no brother: 3H6, 5.6.80.

30.   Sadler's son . . . William: Died at age two: Fripp, *Shakespeare*, II.312.

30.   Biographers imagine: E.g. A. L. Rowse, *William Shakespeare*, 1963, p. 62; Fripp, *Shakespeare*, I.338–39

30.   most noble father: MM, 2.1.7.

30.   Some . . . see in Tyler: Edgar I. Fripp, *Master Richard Quyny*, 1924, pp. 54–56.

31.   "penthouselike": LLL, 3.1.17–18.

31.   soul . . . is his clothes: AWW, 2.5.43–44.

31.   "old pantaloon": SHR, 3.1.37.

31.   and his thumb: 1H4, 1.3.37–38.

31.   about her ears: R3, 2.2.33 s.d.

31.   is a gentleman: LR, 3.4.143.

32.   "taking the wall": ROM, 1.1.12.

32.   this calamitous life: Elizabeth Burton, *The Pageant of Elizabethan England*, 1958, p. 166.

32.   it will come: JC, 2.2.36–37.

32.   of the tetter: 5.1.17–24.

32.   throws the meat: SHR, 4.1.165 s.d.

33.   a doleful "dump": ROM, 4.5.107.

33.   merrily set down: WT, 4.4.189.

33.   in one person: R2, 5.5.31.

33.   gives good words: JC, 5.1.30.

33.   bears sorrow better: JC, 4.3.147.

33.   mixed in him: 5.5.74.

33.   rite of May: MND, 4.1.133.

34.   carved in alabaster: MV, 1.1.83–84.

34.   "circummured": 4.1.28.

34.   John Parkinson . . . gardener: *Paradisi in Sole   Paradisus Terrestris* (1629), 1904.

34.   a grosser name: HAM, 4.7.169–70.

34.   faster it grows: 1H4, 2.4.440–42.

34.   but for some: ROM, 2.3.14 (and 9–10, 12).

35.   "in secret influence": SON 15.4.

35.   "bad revolting stars": 1H6, 1.1.4.

35.   Horatio said this: HAM, 1.1.125.

35.   Jonathus the Jew: My identification.

36.   a star danced: 2.1.335.

36.   The Harvard House: Rebuilt after the fire of 1594.

36.   needed no bush: AYL, Epil.3–4.

36.   mine hostess' door: JN, 2.1.289.

37.   the passing bell: VEN, 11.674–702.

37.   of your house: MND, 3.1.192–93.

37.   corn and grass: *Itinerary,* II.49.

37.   discredit their "mystery": MM, 4.2.29.

37.   prince of Hell: Philip Stubbes, *Anatomy of Abuses,* 1583 (2d ed.).

37.   "good counsel": MM, 2.1.252–54.

37.   on Cotsall hills: WIV, 1.1.88–89.

37.   bears like . . . Sackerson: WIV, 1.1.294–96.

37.   Dun-in-the-Mire: ROM, 1.4.41.

38.   they capered: TN, 1.3.121.

38.   in a cinquepace: TN, 1.3.130–31.

38.   knew the pavan: TN, 5.1.200–1.

38.   our "mingled yarn": AWW, 4.3.71–74.

38.   day of season: AWW, 5.3.32–34.

38.   a "baby figure": TRO, 1.3.344–45.

38.   lord of his reason: ANT, 3.13.3–4.

38.   control his fate: OTH, 5.2.265.

38.   inch of raw mutton: Marlowe's Lust in *Dr. Faustus*, 2.2.169–70.

38.   on Lethe wharf: HAM, 1.5.32–33.

39.   Herod of Jewry: WIV, 2.1.20.

39.   bloody-hunting slaughtermen: H5, 3.3.38–41.

39.   Consent to swear: HAM, 1.5.151–52.

39.   delight were played: TGV, 4.4.159.

40.   kind of Puritan: 2.3.140.

40.   "cakes and ale": TN, 2.3.114–16.

40.   famous party [at Kenilworth]: *Robert Laneham's Letter*, pp. 8, 34, 44–46, 71. M. C. Bradbrook identifies the author of the letter with John Laneham, one of the leading actors of Leicester's Men, and thinks the letter describes a comic work from the company's repertory. *The Rise of the Common Player: A Study of Actor and Society in Shakespeare's England*, 1962, ch. 6.

40.   watched the goings-on: This is inference, building on the plays.

41.   boy on the dolphin: TN, 1.2.15.

41.   sea maid's music: MND, 2.1.149–54.

41.   honest Harry Goldingham: Burton, *Pageant*, p. 135.

41.   a Wild Man: *Laneham's Letter*, pp. 14–15.

41.   near to beast: LR, 2.3.9.

41.   "termini" at Theobalds: Burton, *Pageant*, p. 59.

41.   print . . . of goodness: TMP, 1.2.352.

42.   "Stripes" . . . might move: TMP, 1.2.345.

42.   fury of his heart: LR, 3.4.131–33.

42.   I/Acknowledge mine: 5.1.275–76.

43.   that "scarfèd bark": MV, 2.6.14–15.

43.   "sheer" or pure: Ind. 2.21–24.

43.   pitchers having . . . ears: R3, 2.4.37.

43.   "most senseless": 3.3.23.

44.   is in Messina: 4.2.82.

44.   his bones aching: 5.1.93.

44. his "everlasting rest": ROM, 5.3.109–10.

44. Prince be willing: ADO, 3.3.80.

44. game of ticktack: MM, 1.2.190–91.

44. title is affeered: MAC, 4.3.34.

45. plain-dealing man: 2H6, 4.2.102–04.

45. on his forefinger: ROM, 1.4.55–56.

46. "too slightly timbered": HAM, 4.7.21–24.

46. shot his arrow: 5.2.243–44.

46. the other forth: MV, 1.1.140–43.

46. Moralists: Like Cassius, JC, 1.2.139–41.

46. unthought-on accident: WT, 4.4.538–41.

46. Rebels in Durham: Wallace MacCaffrey, *The Shaping of the Elizabethan Regime*, 1968, ch. 13.

47. shears between them: MM, 1.2.27–28.

47. "glimpse of newness" . . . feel the spur: MM, 1.2.158–62.

48. like old Hamlet: HAM, 1.5.76.

48. on antique time: COR, 2.3.119.

48. his soul's consent: R2, 4.1.249.

49. stand on quillets: 2H6, 3.1.261.

49. but do't: PER, 4.1.82–83.

3. "I, Daedalus"

51. from others' books: LLL, 1.1.86–87.

51. drunk ink: LLL, 4.2.25–26.

51. exchequer of words: TGV, 2.4.43–44.

51. old vice still: TGV, 3.1.284.

51. "Figures pedantical . . . three-piled": LLL, 5.2.408.

51. *timor occupat artus:* 2H6, 4.1.117.

51. lakes, and groves: TMP, 5.1.33.

51. Shakespeare made acquaintance: George A. Plimpton, *The Education of Shakespeare*, 1933, offers a brief and lucid survey of the texts he probably used and the method in which he was instructed. A fuller account is Virgil K. Whitaker, *Shakespeare's Use of Learning*, 1953.

51. "good old Mantuan": LLL, 4.2.94–95.

52. her "dim light": Francis Beaumont (to Ben Jonson), 1615.

52.   learning was . . . little: Bishop Thomas Fuller, *Worthies of England,* 1662.

52.   among the Goths: AYL, 3.3.8–9.

52.   an English translation: 90 percent of Shakespeare's references to the *Metamorphoses* come from Arthur Golding's trans., 1569.

52.   a Latin couplet: Lifted, it must be said, from the "florilegia," collections of elegant extracts.

52.   in heavenly minds: 2H6, 2.1.24.

52.   grammar long ago: TIT, 4.2.23.

52.   I slew him: JC, 3.2.24–27.

52.   good "latin" spoons: Sir Nicholas L'Estrange (1629–55), in E. K. Chambers, *William Shakespeare: A Study of Facts and Problems,* II.243.

52.   Horace . . . told him: In his *Ars Poetica.*

52.   wondrous strange snow: MND, 5.1.59.

53.   tide of times: JC, 3.1.256–57.

53.   mother and foundation: Bishop Waynflete, founder of Magdalen College, Oxford.

53.   in the children: Statutes of St. Paul's School, London, 1518.

53.   and Christian religion: Royal Commission of 1547, prescribing for Winchester College.

53.   tropes and taffeta phrases: LLL, 5.2.406.

54.   end of reckoning: MM, 5.1.45–46.

54.   John Shakespeare . . . brooded: Fripp, *Shakespeare,* I.52.

54.   in Newgate prison: Fripp, I.194.

54.   thing on thing: MM, 5.1.62.

54.   the "endless jar": TRO, 1.3.116–17.

54.   "mining all within": HAM, 3.4.148.

54.   a "breeching scholar": SHR, 3.1.18.

54.   bred in a book: LLL, 4.2.24.

54.   on his head: LLL, 5.1.47–48.

54.   i' the church: TN, 3.2.75–76.

55.   it to them: LLL, 4.2.74–80.

55.   butt of malmsey: R3, 1.4.155.

55.   Leland came through: *Itinerary,* II.27, 49.

56.   "Dunghill for *unguem*": LLL, 5.1.79–80.

56.   sermons and "homilies": Alfred Hart, *Shakespeare and the Homilies*, 1934.

56.   by the Lord: R2, 3.2.57.

56.   an abated flood: JN, 5.4.53–57.

57.   you and me: JN, 1.1.39–41.

57.   "foolish mild man": LLL, 5.2.581–84.

57.   an Absey book: JN, 1.1.196–99.

57.   the letter "G": R3, 1.1.54–59.

57.   with heavy looks: ROM, 2.2.156–57.

58.   lost his ABC: TGV, 2.1.22–23.

58.   in the speech: Byrd, *Psalms, Sonnets, and Songs of Sadness and Piety*, 1588.

58.   said one pedagogue: Roger Ascham, *The Schoolmaster*, 1570.

58.   Holofernes . . . teaches . . . hornbook: LLL, 5.1.46.

58.   "jerks of invention": LLL, 4.2.123–25.

58.   swept their living: Apropos John Owen, author of Latin *Epigrams*, tr. 1624.

58.   course of praying: *Primer* of 1545.

58.   ventricle of memory: LLL, 4.2.68.

58.   the "choughs' language": AWW, 4.1.19.

58.   o'er the boy: LLL, 3.1.177.

59.   they called "abbominable": LLL, 5.1.17–25.

59.   to write fair: HAM, 5.2.34–36.

59.   a teacher meet: Francis Clement, *The Petty School*, 1587.

59.   ear could endure: 2H6, 4.7.38–41, 43–46.

60.   to all men: 1H4, 2.1.95.

60.   quotes the Latin: TN, 2.3.2–3.

60.   study leaves . . . "bias": LLL, 4.2.109.

60.   in the Hesperides: LLL, 4.3.338–41.

60.   voice "for barbarism": LLL, 1.1.112.

60.   end of study: LLL, 1.1.55.

60.   fritters of English: WIV, 5.5.143.

61.   be a whore: WIV, 4.1.17–63.

61.   honor and virtue: George Sandys, introducing his commentary on the *Metamorphoses,* tr. 1626.

61.   wanton Cupid's hose: LLL, 4.3.56.

61.   "honey-tongued" Shakespeare: Francis Meres, *Palladis Tamia,* 1598.

61.   the crystal tide: VEN, 11.956–57.

61.   renew old Aeson: MV, 5.1.1–14.

62.   Greek to me: JC, 1.2.282–84.

62.   "the Greek thing": *Res Graeca,* a phrase of Pliny's.

62.   a bosom "franchised": MAC, 2.1.28.

62.   of mighty opposites: HAM, 5.2.60–62.

62.   cause, not we: TN, 2.2.31.

62.   "two truths": MAC, 1.3.127–29.

63.   to the world: AWW, 1.3.18.

63.   giddy and unfirm: TN, 2.4.29–33.

63.   the neighbor bottom: AYL, 4.3.78.

63.   let it drink: TN, 1.3.70.

64.   to the place: AYL, 4.3.76–80.

64.   all the lawyers: 2H6, 4.2.76–77.

64.   in corners thrown: AYL, 2.3.38–42.

65.   A faded drawing: Dated 1708; F3 copy (1664) in Colgate University library, Hamilton, N.Y.

65.   time didn't amble: AYL, 3.2.324–25.

65.   Thomas Russell: Peter Alexander, *Shakespeare,* 1964, p. 33 (after Leslie Hotson, *I, William Shakespeare,* 1937).

66.   'fore these witnesses: WT, 4.4.389.

66.   One biographer, imagining: Sidney Lee, *A Life of William Shakespeare,* pp. 30–31.

67.   "cautels" or tricks: LC, 11.302–33.

67.   well-balanced form: MM, 4.3.100.

67.   of your rings: TN, 5.1.156–59.

67.   it is solemnized: AYL, 3.2.331–33.

67.   that day's celebration: TMP, 4.1.28–29.

67.   "sour-eyed disdain": TMP, 4.1.20.

67.   what marriage is: AYL, 3.3.84–86.

68.   to her maidenhead: SHR, 3.2.225.

68.   Local people insist: S. W. Fullom, *History of William Shakespeare*, 1862, p. 202.

68.   timber warp, warp: AYL, 3.3.86–89.

68.   love is . . . "untrussing": MM, 3.2.179.

68.   elegance of fancy: George Steevens, 1773.

69.   best in his plays: John Leyland, *The Shakespeare Country*, n.d., p. 30.

69.   our author's career: James D. Halliwell-Phillipps, *Outlines of the Life of Shakespeare*, 1889, I.66–67.

69.   "too much liberty": MM, 1.2.125.

69.   drink we die: MM, 1.2.128–30.

69.   of "outward order": MM, 1.2.144–49.

69.   "woodman" Shakespeare: MM, 4.3.162.

69.   overlusty at legs: LR, 2.4.10.

69.   begot between codfish: MW, 3.2.109.

69.   i' the blood: TMP, 4.1.53.

69.   and burns on: AWW, 5.3.6–8.

69.   "Natural rebellion": AWW, 5.3.6.

70.   rite be ministered: TMP, 4.1.15–17.

70.   upon better acquaintance: WIV, 1.1.246–50. ("Contempt" is Theobald's emendation for Folio's "content.")

70.   grave with him: Letter of 1693 by "Mr. Dowdall"; Chambers, *WS*, II.259.

70.   Shakespeare, closet Puritan: Some biographers suggest that Anne Hathaway was the Puritan, a reason for their estrangement, e.g. Marchette Chute, *Shakespeare of London*, 1949, pp. 53–55; F. E. Halliday, *The Life of Shakespeare*, 1961, p. 45.

71.   little kingdom, man: 2H4, 4.3.107–09.

71.   the "trampling courser": VEN, 11.295–98.

71.   and shoulder-shotten: SHR, 3.2.50–56.

71.   glover's paring knife: WIV, 1.4.20–21.

71.   schoolmaster in the country: Perhaps, says one tradition, at a noble house in Gloucestershire (Ivor Brown, *Shakespeare*, 1949, pp. 70–71).

72.   a calf there: HAM, 3.2.100–06.

72.   a parish clerk: Whose reminiscence is recorded by "Mr. Dowdall"; Chambers, *WS*, II.259.

72.   "wooing of wenches": Halliwell-Phillipps, *Outlines*, I.73.

72.   Diana's foresters: 1H4, 1.2.25–26.

73.   old coat well: WIV, 1.1.19–20.

73.   the nether lip: 1H4, 2.4.404–05.

73.   nail, one nail: COR, 4.7.54.

73.   to the cushion: COR, 4.7.43.

73.   Like the chameleon: 3H6, 3.2.191.

73.   water, swooning paleness: LC, 11.303–5.

74.   Shakespeare in Lancashire: The most recent account is E. A. J. Honigmann, *Shakespeare: The 'lost years,'* 1985.

74.   "William Shakeshafte": "In Snitterfield records Richard [Shakespeare's grandfather] is also sometimes called Shakstaff and Shakeschafte": E. K. Chambers, *Sources for a Biography of Shakespeare,* 1946, p. 10.

74.   His will: Chambers, *Sources*, p. 18, gives the details.

74.   Fulk Gyllome: A guildsman, he played in the Chester miracles. Halliday, *Shakespeare*, p. 51.

74.   the Stanley seats: Seventeenth-century epitaphs, engraved on Sir Edward Stanley's tomb in Shropshire and copied by Dugdale the antiquarian, were ascribed by him to "William Shakespeare, the late famous tragedian": *Visitation to Shropshire, 1664*. Chambers, *WS*, II.33–34, notes that the Queen's Men were at the Earl of Derby's house, New Park in Lancs., Oct. 16, 1588, and at Lathom in Lancs., another of his houses, July 12–13. They visited him a third time at Knowsley in Lancs., Sept. 11–13.

75.   "hardhearted adamant": MND, 2.1.195.

75.   his own nature: LR, 5.3.244–45.

76.   deity in his bosom: TMP, 2.1.277–78.

76.   "words, words, words": HAM, 2.2.192.

76.   a black heart: AWW, 1.3.93–95.

76.   deer i' the herd: AWW, 1.3.50–55.

76.   A "shallow plash": SHR, 1.1.21–24.

76.   he would tread: 3H6, 3.2.135–36.

77.   the open air: 3H6, 3.2.174–77.

77.   the world abroad: TGV, 1.1.6.

77.   small experience grows: SHR, 1.2.50–52.

77.   ever homely wits: TGV, 1.1.2.

77.   Shakespeare . . . "sluggardized": TGV, 1.1.7.

77.   in the world: TGV, 1.3.20–21.

77.   "prodigious son": TGV, 2.3.3–4.

77.   why he's sad: MV, 1.1.1.

77.   "a hasty spark": JC, 4.3.111–13.

77.   in his pride: 1H6, 4.7.14–16.

77.   "I, Daedalus": 3H6, 5.6.21.

77.   fool was drowned: 3H6, 5.6.20.

77.   drunken Christopher Sly: SHR, Induction, sc. 1.

78.   out-Herods Herod: HAM, 3.2.8–14.

78.   at his pleasure: Fuller, *Worthies*.

78.   Muly Mahomet: A character in Peele's *Battle of Alcazar*, about 1589.

78.   "tickle o' the sere": HAM, 2.2.324,

4. Shadows of Himself

79.   said John Aubrey: *Brief Lives,* 1st pub. 1813.

79.   wife and children: Some biographers (like J. Q. Adams) imagine a domestic Shakespeare settled in London with his family. Evidence suggests that in later years, at least, when he gave testimony in a London law suit, he was living alone.

79.   stood like "forfeits": MM, 5.1.321.

80.   "by the same": *Description.*

80.   carried ginger roots: 1H4, 2.1.26–30.

80.   of the Thames: John Earle, *Micro-cosmographie,* 1628.

80.   let out horses: Fynes Moryson, *Itinerary,* 1617.

80.   needed "brawn" buttocks: AWW, 2.2.18–19.

80.   "the voyage miscarries": Earle, the same.

80.   these "masterless men": Pp. 3–5, 27 in Frank Aydelotte, *Elizabethan Rogues and Vagabonds* (1913), 1967, the standard work on this subject.

80.   men must live: 1H4, 2.2.90–91.

80.   "St. Nicholas' clerks": 1H4, 2.1.61–62.

80.   *Hamlet* included: Cited by "Ratsey" in a book retelling his exploits, *Ratsey's Ghost*, 1605.

81.   old cast cloak: Thomas Dekker, *Satiromastix*, 1601, 4.1.130.

81.   lash drew blood: E. K. Chambers, *The Elizabethan Stage*, 1923, IV.324.

81.   "fruitful and pleasant": *Antiquities*, I.544.

81.   got its name: B. C. A. Windle, *Shakespeare's Country*, 1899, pp. 200–1.

81.   governed by spleen: 1H4, 5.2.19.

81.   of our enemies: Windle, the same.

81.   of this cheese: WIV, 1.1.128.

81.   In country inns: Moryson, *Itinerary*.

82.   of the water: Harrison, *Description*.

82.   road for fleas: 1H4, 2.1.14–21.

82.   prone to "misplacing"; MM, 2.1.88.

82.   saucy and audacious: MND, 5.1.99–103.

82.   Leland . . . said: *Itinerary*, II.112.

83.   "bare ruined choirs": SON 73.4.

83.   Camden . . . rehearsed: In *Britannia*, 1586, revised and trans. by various hands under the editorship of Edmund Gibson, 1695; facsimile 1971, p. 280.

83.   at their rut: *Laneham's Letter*, p. 31.

83.   chimes at midnight: 2H4, 3.2.214.

83.   loved a glass: Chambers, *Sources*, p. 64.

84.   "a pretty thoroughfare": Leland, II.114.

84.   *Love's Labor's Lost:* 4.3.51–52.

84.   the fat knight: Nathaniel Field, *Amends for Ladies*, 1618, 4.3.

84.   two and two: 1H4, 3.3.90.

85.   in this life: John Stow, *Survey of London*, 1598 (Everyman ed., 1945), p. 393.

85.   his own tobacco: *A Catalogue of Plants Cultivated in the Garden of John Gerard . . . 1596–1599*, ed. B. D. Jackson, 1876.

85.   at Staple Inn: Burton, *Pageant*, p. 56.

86.   than he promised: 1H4, 1.2.209.

86.   be most delicate: H5, 2.4.38–40.

86. like "summer grass": H5, 1.1.65–66.

86. a sullen ground: 1H4, 1.2.212.

86. "our terrene state": TNK, 1.3.14.

86. the second city: Fuller, *Worthies*, "London."

86. twice this number: A. H. Dodd, *Life in Elizabethan England*, 1961, p. 34.

87. a famous scene: 1H6, 2.4.

87. Whitefriars: R3, 1.2.226.

87. and take it: R3, 3.7.51.

87. his dull life: "Letter to Ben Jonson."

87. "immoderate quaffing": Stow, p. 76.

87. almost 900 taverns: Says a record of 1574 in Henry Thew Stephenson, *Shakespeare's London*, 1905, p. 334.

87. the Pegasus: SHR, 4.4.4–5.

87. tapster's arithmetic: TRO, 1.2.113.

87. tapster's oath: AYL, 3.4.30–31.

87. this small beer: 2H4, 2.2.5–6.

88. grown upon trees: William Bullein, *A Dialogue against the Pestilence*, 1573 (1st ed. 1564).

88. pipes . . . brought water: Stephenson, pp. 75–76.

88. fetched by hand: Stephenson, pp. 185–86.

88. of our reign: 2H6, 4.6.1–4.

88. "Such a thundering": After Thomas Dekker, *The Seven Deadly Sins of London*, 1606.

88. almost stopped up: Moryson, *Itinerary*.

88. the Lord's sake: MM, 4.3.19.

88. bowl or clackdish: MM, 3.2.126–27.

88. born in Kent: 24 October 1568, in Henry Huth, *Ancient Ballads & Broadsides*, 1867, pp. 288–92.

88. journey by night: *La Cena delle Ceneri*, 1584.

89. mold of form: HAM, 3.1.153.

89. "general gender": HAM, 4.7.18.

89. with many heads: COR, 4.1.1–2.

89. forms, windows, anything: JC, 3.2.257–59.

89. overpeering their "list": HAM, 4.5.100.

89.   poet to pieces: JC, 3.3.

89.   "A needy adventurer": Dr. Johnson in 1765, getting the story from his amanuensis Robert Shiels, who got it ultimately from Davenant.

89.   for Richard Field: Joseph Quincy Adams, *A Life of William Shakespeare*, 1923, p. 126. (Adams is doubtful.)

89.   countryman, John Sadler: Mark Eccles, *Shakespeare in Warwickshire*, 1963, summarizes his career, pp. 60, 99.

89.   "in simple time": WIV, 3.3.72–73; Stow, p. 74.

89.   possession of dirt: HAM, 5.2.87–88.

89.   deceased in beggary: MND, 5.1.53.

90.   "prove an usurer": *Groatsworth of Wit.*

90.   of his friend: MV, 1.3.134.

90.   Some suggest: E.g. E. A. J. Honigmann, *Shakespeare's Impact on His Contemporaries*, 1982, esp. ch. 1.

90.   this unedifying story: Recorded by Halliwell-Phillipps, *Outlines*, 1.185; and summarized in Chambers, *WS*, II.52.

90.   the Subsidy Rolls: J. Q. Adams, *Shakespeare*, p. 197.

90.   a strolling player: In *Ratsey's Ghost, 1605.*

90.   his own despite: "The First Epistle of the Second Book of Horace."

90.   his mistress' eyebrow: AYL, 2.7.149.

90.   a "serviture": William Castle, parish clerk of Stratford, b.1614.

91.   Malone . . . says: In 1780.

91.   and tapestry hangings: John Downes, 1708.

91.   at Whitehall Palace: Chambers, *Sources*, p. 25.

91.   a contemporary said: John Davies of Hereford, "To Our English Terence, Mr. Will. Shakespeare."

92.   sung a song: William Oldys, about 1750–60, reporting a story told him by the actor John Bowman.

92.   a "looker-on": MM, 5.1.317.

92.   said reminiscent Aubrey: Following William Beeston. Aubrey doesn't stand on "points" or punctuation, and the punctuation here is mine.

92.   and rebellious liquors: AYL, 2.3.49.

92.   not his wife: JC, 2.1.285–87.

92.   one of the theaters: The Curtain, in "The View of the City of London from the North towards the South," now in the University of Utrecht. J. C. Adams gives the view, plate 7 in *The Globe Playhouse* (1942), 1961.

92. and a brook: Leland, II.114.

92. the ax's edge: 3H6, 5.2.11.

93. by their manners: Bullein, *A Dialogue*.

93. few Jews . . . left: Cecil Roth, *A History of the Jews in England*, 1964.

93. of the lions: TGV, 2.1.28.

93. Shakespeare's characters supposed: R3, 3.1.69–74; R2, 5.1.1–2.

94. blood of Lancaster: 3H6, 5.6.61–62.

94. Richard of Gloucester: Fabyan's *Chronicles*, 1st printed 1516; ed. of 1553, sig.CCXX.

94. little pretty ones: R3, 4.1.100.

94. words almost verbatim: H8, 2.1.102–3.

94. to his son: H5, 4.3.49–59.

95. "toused" or tore: MM, 5.1.311–12.

95. a name, "Polypus": Donald Lupton, *London and the Country Carbonadoed*, 1632.

95. *The Tamer Tamed*: 1606, 1.3.

95. the drawbridge: Raised for the last time in 1500: Adrian Prockter and Robert Taylor, *The A to Z of Elizabethan London*, 1979, p. xi.

95. of them died: Gordon Home, *Old London Bridge*, 1931, pp. 190–91.

95. it is obstructed: Fuller, *Worthies*, "London."

95. hides of dogs: Jonson, "On the Famous Voyage," ll. 145–46.

95. Hucksters exhibited "prodigies": TMP, 2.2.27–33.

96. a great tool: H8, 5.3.34.

96. mad Shallow yet: 2H4, 3.2.14–15.

96. down the Savoy: 2H6, 4.7.1–2.

96. "great oneyers": 1H4, 2.1.76.

96. One chronicler: Thomas Fairman Ordish, *Shakespeare's London*, 1904, pp. 263–77.

97. shoals of honor: H8, 3.2.435–36.

97. fell like Lucifer: H8, 3.2.361–62, 371.

97. "That's past": H8, 4.1.95.

97. died for sin: Francis Beaumont, "On the Tombs in Westminster."

98. "the fishful river": William Fitzstephen, 12th century, in Stow, p. 10.

98. rivers in Europe: Fuller, *Worthies,* "London."

98.   "Then westward ho!": TN, 3.1.134.

98.   Shakespeare, leaving Blackfriars: After Ordish, *Shakespeare's London*, pp. 298–99, 305.

98.   he nearly drowned: "The Voyage . . . in a Boat of browne-Paper, from London to Quinborough in Kent," in *The Works of John Taylor the Water Poet* (1630), facs. repr. 1973.

98.   a respectful Londoner: Lupton, *London*.

99.   strength is bootless: 3H6, 1.4.19–21.

99.   and slanderous matter: Acts of the Privy Council, New Series, XXVI (1597), p. 338.

99.   limbs of Limehouse: H8, 5.3.62–63.

99.   tree at Wapping: *Description of Tyburn*.

99.   this "dead shepherd": AYL, 3.5.81–82.

100.   Shakespeare . . . first appears: J. Q. Adams, *Shakespeare*, p. 197.

100.   new-come soul: Gaveston speaks for him in *Edward II*, 1.1.10–11.

100.   Parolles reported this: AWW, 4.3.269–70.

100.   Is this Moorfields: H8, 5.3.33.

100.   melancholy of Moorditch: 1H4, 1.2.77–78.

100.   enacted Poor Laws: E. M. Leonard tells the story in *The Early History of English Poor Relief*, 1900.

101.   fast-growing "sprays": R2, 3.4.34–35.

101.   "pain forty dure": *peine forte et dure*.

101.   prostitute or "punk": MM, 5.1.522–23.

101.   "The land's epitome": Earle, *Micro-cosmographie*.

101.   the horse fair: Bishop James Pilkington of Durham, d.1576.

101.   on dancing horses: LLL, 1.2.56–57; "The Dancing Horse of 'LLL' " R. A. Fraser, *Shakespeare Quarterly*, 5 (Jan. 1954), 98–99.

101.   not few pockets: Earle, *Micro-cosmographie*.

101.   "The ears' brothel": Earle, the same.

102.   him in Paul's: 2H4, 1.2.52.

102.   said a proverb: Fuller, *Worthies*, "London: Proverbs."

102.   had a vision: Quotations from Donne's "Second Anniversary."

102.   recorded the event: *Henslowe's Diary*, ed. R. A. Foakes and R. T. Rickert, 1961, pp. 17–20.

102.   phrase is . . . Jonson's: Prologue to *Every Man in His Humor*, 1598, 1616.

102.   Coventry ... tapestry: Described (and illustrated) by A. F. Kendrick, *Burlington Magazine*, 44 (1924), 83–88; and George Scharf, *Archaeologia*, 36 (1855), 438–53.

103.   rain, and cold: 1H6, 2.1.5–7.

103.   hive of ... bees: 2H6, 3.2.125–27.

103.   or summer flies: 3H6, 2.6.8.

103.   "the greater gust": 3H6, 3.1.88.

103.   The great wheel: LR, 2.4.72–74.

103.   vultures of sedition: 1H6, 4.3.47.

103.   one theater-goer: Thomas Nashe, *Pierce Penniless*, 1592, ed. R. B. McKerrow, 1904–5 (1966), I.212.

103.   "imaginary puissance": H5, Prologue, l. 25.

103.   "shadow of himself": 1H6, 2.3.62.

103.   tells the time: SON 12.1.

103.   "multitudinous seas incarnadine": MAC, 2.2.59.

103.   I sport myself: 3H6, 2.5.31–34.

103.   of tedious days: R3, 4.4.28.

104.   of forced breath: HAM, 1.2.79.

104.   out of France: 1H6, 1.1.58.

104.   copious in exclaims: R3, 4.4.135.

104.   "silly stately style": 1H6, 4.7.72.

104.   clamor in a vault: 3H6, 5.2.44. "Clamor" is the reading of the "bad" Quarto, "cannon" of the Folio.

104.   against the wind: 3H6, 2.5.5–13.

104.   expect a dearth: R3, 2.3.31–35.

105.   smiles and says: 3H6, 3.1.43–46.

105.   "Pucelle or puzzel": 1H6, 1.4.107.

105.   change of mood: TIM, 1.1.84.

105.   mouth of death: R3, 4.4.1–2.

105.   thorns ... weeds ... "stock": 2H6, 3.1.67 and 31–33; 2.2.58.

105.   caterpillars eat ... leaves: 2H6, 3.1.90.

105.   knife is set: 3H6, 6.47–50.

105.   the withered vine: 1H6, 2.5.11–12.

105.   "growing time ... ripened": 1H6, 2.4.99.

105.   the tree die: CYM, 5.5.264–65.

105. pluck on sin: R3, 4.2.64.

105. Lancaster's long jars: Jonson's Prologue to *Every Man in His Humor*.

106. successive stage directions: 1H6, 5.3.29 s.d. and 5.3.44 s.d.

106. their mockeries be: H5, 4. Prol. 53.

106. Parliament of England: 2H6, 4.7.14–15.

106. stand for law: 3H6, 4.1.49–50.

5. Wild-Goose Chase

107. characters of his: E.g., Viola in TN, 1.2.43; Isabella, MM, 5.1.116.

107. wondrous strange show: MND, 5.1.59.

107. cities and boroughs: Lee, *WS*, p. 164; Lee, *Stratford-on-Avon from the Earliest Times to the Death of Shakespeare*, 1908, p. 270; Eccles, *Shakespeare*, pp. 132–33, 164; Fripp, *Shakespeare*, II.670, 725, 762–63; Chambers, *WS*, II.96, 151–53.

107. found an audience: Discussion draws on Alfred Harbage, *Shakespeare's Audience*, 1941.

107. seeing a play: Thomas Nashe, *Pierce Penniless*, 1592; McKerrow edn. (1958 reprint), I.212.

108. "six-penny damnation": Nashe, *Christ's Tears*, 1593; *Pierce Penniless;* McKerrow, II.148, I.217.

108. "Two-hours' traffic": ROM, Prologue, l. 12.

108. "Winchester geese": TRO, 5.10.54; 1H6, 1.3.35, 53.

108. Bridges . . . warned: In 1909; *Collected Essays*, 1927, I.29.

108. Some . . . say: E.g. Anne Jennalie Cook, *The Privileged Playgoers of Shakespeare's London 1576–1642*, 1981.

108. of their joy: H8, 4.1.58–59.

108. kept the wind: 1H4, 1.3.45.

109. for bitten apples: H8, 5.3.60–61.

109. fill the ear: Hentzner, *Travels*.

109. "near a thousand": Fripp, *Shakespeare*, I.163; William Fleetwood, London's City Recorder, to Lord Burghley, 6/18/1584.

109. to help him: Moryson, *Itinerary*.

109. wanted the throne: HAM, 5.2.65.

109. in a nutshell: 2.2.254–55.

109. short of breath: 5.2.287.

109. scourge to them: 3.4.175.

109.   to the general: 2.2.437.

109.   tale of bawdy: 2.2.506.

109.   a Puritan writer: William Crashaw, *Parable of Poison*, 1618, p. 24.

109.   a traveler observed: Friedrich Gerschow, in A. M. Nagler, *Shakespeare's Stage*, 1958, p. 94.

109.   A modern historian: Chambers, *Eliz. Stage*, II.387.

109.   "swarms of wives": Robert Anton, *Vice's Anatomy Scourged and Corrected*, 1617.

110.   some other things: JC, 1.2.52–53.

110.   A stubborn fellow: Charles William Wallace, "The First London Theatre," *Nebraska University Studies*, 1913, XIII.141–42; Chambers, *Eliz. Stage*, IV.298.

110.   be at rest: Minshieu, *Ductor in Linguas*, 1617, quoted C. I. Elton, *William Shakespeare: His Family and Friends*, 1904, p. 194.

110.   beneath the fire: Dugdale, *Origines Juridiciales*, 1666, quoted Elton, *Shakespeare*, p. 194.

110.   The Boar's Head: J. Q. Adams, *Shakespeare*, p. 105; C. J. Sisson (with Stanley Wells), *The Boar's Head Theatre*, 1972; Herbert Berry, *The Boar's Head Playhouse*, 1986.

111.   a secret key: Chambers, *Eliz. Stage*, II.388; Wallace, XIII.142–43.

111.   "scaffold" and "stage": "Scaffold" means "stage" in H5, pro. 10; and executioner's block in R3, 4.4.243.

111.   and comedies upon: Thomas Whythorne, *Autobiography* (1560s), ed. James M. Osborne, 1961.

111.   divorce of steel: H8, 2.1.76.

111.   This theatrical figure: From Marvell's "Horatian Ode."

111.   eyes dropped millstones: R3, 1.3.352.

111.   said an expert: Reginald Scot, *Discovery of Witchcraft*, 1584, Bk. 13, ch. 34.

111.   Sackerson the bear: WIV, 1.1.294–96.

111.   "head-lugged" bear: LR, 4.2.42.

111.   stag or hart: JC, 3.1.204.

111.   fight the course: MAC, 5.7.1–2 (and LR, 3.7.54).

112.   heart can think: TN, 3.1.118–20.

112.   to the Mayor: H8, 5.4.69–70.

112.   whoredom and adultery: I. F., *Covenant between God and Man*, 1616, pp. 381–83 (Bb7–8).

112.   claimed two victims: Chambers, *Eliz. Stage*, IV.208; R. A. Fraser, *The War Against Poetry*, 1970, p. 26.

112.   plagues are plays: T. W., *A Sermon Preached at Paul's Cross*, 1578, C8v.

112.   They pointed to: Ordinance of 12/6/1574; J. Q. Adams, *Shakespeare*, pp. 108–10.

112.   ought to say: LR, 5.3.325.

113.   colony of Jews: Roth, pp. 139–44.

113.   Shakespeare [at] . . . Cross Keys: Between 1594 and spring 1597.

113.   a Puritan writer: William Prynne, *Histrio-mastix*, 1633. John Aubrey amplifies in his *Natural History and Antiquities of Surrey*, quoted Chambers, *Eliz. Stage*, III.424.

113.   to pull down: J. Q. Adams, *Shakespeare*, pp. 108–9.

113.   wouldn't be bound: Fleetwood to Burghley, 6/18/1584; *Eliz. Stage*, IV.298.

113.   John Brayne: J. Q. Adams, *Shakespeare*, p. 114; Chambers, *Eliz. Stage*, II.387.

113.   The Red Lion: William Ingram, "The Early Career of James Burbage," forthcoming in *The Elizabethan Theatre X*; Chambers, *Eliz. Stage*, II.379–80.

114.   first public theater: Glynne Wickham, *Early English Stages 1300 to 1660*, 1963, II, Part 1, 166–68, describes a "game-house" in Great Yarmouth, built 1538/9. But Burbage remains the pioneer "in devoting his playhouse predominantly to stage-plays."

114.   *Castle of Perseverance:* Hardin Craig, *English Religious Drama of the Middle Ages* (1955), 1960, esp. pp. 119–20 and 348–49.

114.   "rogues and beggars": Wallace, XIII.4.

114.   The Theater: Elton, p. 50; Lee, *WS*, pp. 58–60.

115.   young men "breathed": Stow, p. 87.

115.   concourse of people: *Tarlton's News Out of Purgatory, c.*1589.

115.   "the great house": J. Q. Adams, *Shakespeare*, pp. 113–16.

115.   chapel of Satan: Anon, *A Second and Third Blast of Retreat from Plays and Theaters*, 1580.

115.   the Bankside "gardens": John Foxe in 1539 has the king attend bear-baiting at Paris Garden. In Braun and Hogenberg's map of London, 1554–58, two amphitheaters on Bankside are labeled "The Bear-Baiting and the Bull-Baiting." Bear gardens and playhouses differed in design, so weren't used interchangeably: Oscar Brownstein, "Why

Didn't Burbage Lease the Beargarden?" in *The First Public Playhouse,* ed. Herbert Berry, 1979, pp. 81–96.

115.   all men's eyes: *Second and Third Blast,* p. 139.

116.   Forest of Arden: AYL, 2.4.15.

116.   Evidently a novelty: Discussion draws on Glynne Wickham, " 'Heavens,' Machinery, and Pillars in the Theatre and Other Early Playhouses," *The First Public Playhouse,* ed. Berry, pp. 1–15.

116.   prologue of 1598: To *Everyman in His Humor.*

116.   in the heavens: Peter Thomson, *Shakespeare's Theatre,* 1983, p. 42.

116.   Robert Greene requires: *Alphonsus, King of Aragon* (pub. 1599).

116.   "on the top": TMP, 3.3.19. Many believe TMP to be a text related to a Court performance or to a Blackfriars' one. Since the same s.d. occurs in 1H6, this suggests the kinship of public and private theater.

116.   a torch burning: 1H6, 3.2.23, 25 s.d.

116.   "arts inhibited": OTH, 1.2.79.

117.   of the bell: John Stockwood, *A Sermon Preached at Paul's Cross,* 1578, p. 23.

117.   Shakespeare, exploiting this: LLL, 5.2.185; MND, 3.1.3: ANT, 3.5.16–17.

117.   A minor poet: Edmund Gayton, *Festivous Notes on Don Quixote,* 1654, p. 3.

117.   stood "on tiptoe": Anthony Scoloker, *The Shakspere Allusion-Book,* C. M. Ingleby, L. T. Smith, F. J. Furnivall, J. Munro (1909), 1932, pp. 133–35.

117.   Pretentious Dame Eleanor: 2H6, 1.3.83.

117.   this "masquing stuff": SHR, 4.3.87–91, 142–44.

118.   Older Shakespeareans: Beginning with Malone and Capell in 18th-century England and followed by 19th-century Germans.

118.   a skeptical view: E.g. P. Thomson, p. 50; Richard Hosley, *The Revels History of Drama in England,* 1975, III.119–36. No inner stage or alcove, say Hosley et al.: rather, an opened door in the tiring-house facade. Better if there were a middle or third door instead of De Witt's two; and best if a curtain hung in front of the doorway. (So far, this looks like the old "inner stage.") Mostly, though, these revisionists think, properties like Desdemona's bed, hung with curtains, were carried on stage, obviating the need for an alcove. Hosley, III.183, 233ff.

118.   "A historical curiosity": Herbert Berry (characterizing J. C. Adams,

The Globe Playhouse, 1942), "Americans in the Playhouses," *Shake-speare Studies IX,* ed. J. Leeds Barroll, 1976, p. 43.

118.   displayed her caskets: MV, 3.2.

119.   object poisoning sight: OTH, 5.2.363–65.

119.   Falstaff slept: 1H4, 2.4.528–29, 543.

119.   found Polonius: HAM, 3.4.24.

119.   redeeming all sorrows: LR, 5.3.267.

119.   past is prologue: TMP, 2.1.253.

119.   allowed of "penetration": Andrew Marvell.

119.   cribbed, and confined: MAC, 3.4.23.

119.   the "base court": R2, 3.3.180.

120.   mead or garden: TNK, 3.1.5–7.

120.   "unworthy scaffold": H5, Prologue, l. 10.

120.   wooden palings: Not in De Witt's sketch but the Fortune employed them (Andrew Gurr, *The Shakespearean Stage 1574–1642,* 1970, p. 91).

120.   our "dungy earth": ANT, 1.1.35.

120.   in *Pericles:* 2.1.

120.   props: P. Thomson, pp. 166–67, gives an inventory of properties belonging to the Admiral's Men, 1599.

120.   dug a pit: TIT, 2.3.

120.   glimpses of the moon: HAM, 1.4.53.

120.   repassed the seas: 3H6, 4.7.5.

121.   the dying Bedford: 1H6, 3.2.40 s.d.

121.   a coffin: R3, 1.2.1 s.d.

121.   hear the sea: LR, 4.6.4.

121.   earth . . . . air: ANT, 4.3.13–17.

121.   "like a harpy": TMP, 3.3.52 s.d.

121.   his crystalline palace: CYM, 5.4.113.

121.   pursued by a bear: WT, 3.3.58 s.d.

122.   play is done: Ralegh, "What is our life?"

122.   never ran smooth: MND, 1.1.134.

122.   these "abridgements": MND, 5.1.39–59.

122.   a torturing hour: MND, 5.1.37, 39.

122.   non-load-bearing wall: Lee, WS, p. 59.

122. Burbage got control: In 1585. William Ingram, "Henry Lanman's Curtain Playhouse . . . 1585–1592," *The First Public Playhouse*, ed. Berry, pp. 24–25.

122. of stage plays: W. Ingram, "The Playhouse at Newington Butts," *Shakespeare Quarterly*, 21 (1970), 393.

122. best to lodge: TN, 3.3.39–40.

122. of the way: Chambers, *Eliz. Stage*, II.405, IV.313.

122. bank called Stews: Chambers, *Eliz. Stage*, II.405.

123. played the Swan: 1596–97.

123. Francis Langley's theater: W. Ingram, *A London Life in the Brazen Age F.L., 1548–1608*, 1978.

123. of the Bank: Jonson, "Execration upon Vulcan."

123. said Henry Chettle: *Kind Heart's Dream*, 1592.

123. down the "houses": MM, 1.2.95–96.

123. not their terror: MM, 2.1.4.

123. are all frail: MM, 2.4.121.

123. stew of corruption: MM, 5.1.318–19.

123. is very laughable: Henslowe Papers; Chambers, *Eliz. Stage*, II.454, 458.

123. additions in *Jeronimo: Henslowe's Diary*, p. 182.

123. Rose was Henslowe's: And John Cholmley's, grocer of London.

123. Queen Victoria Street: Lee, *WS*, pp. 65n, 66n.

124. boy-players: Enrolled in two dominant troupes: Children of St. Paul's (until 1606) and, under various names, Children of the Chapel Royal (until 1616).

124. leased the . . . friary: In 1577. The fullest account of the boy companies is Harold N. Hillebrand, *The Child Actors*, 1926. Later accounts supplement this: Irwin Smith, *Shakespeare's Blackfriars Playhouse: Its History and Its Design*, 1966; Gurr, pp. 33–37 (*re* the boys' companies); Michael Shapiro, *Children of the Revels*, 1977.

124. "eyrie of children": HAM, 2.2.339.

124. shut them down: As in 1590, likely for meddling in the Marprelate controversy, matter of Divinity and State. Hillebrand, p. 143.

124. *Othello . . . Macbeth*: Chambers, *Eliz. Stage*, II.337, 348.

124. Some annalists of theater: Alfred Harbage insists at book length on the duality of Elizabethan drama in *Shakespeare and the Rival Traditions*, 1952. The classic statement of this position is G. E. Bentley's, "Shakespeare and the Blackfriars Theatre," *Shakespeare Survey*, I

(1948); followed and amplified by Bernard Beckerman, *Shakespeare at the Globe 1599–1609*, 1962.

124.   Public came to mean: Louis B. Wright, *Middle Class Culture in Elizabethan England*, 1935, p. 609.

124.   a beer-brewer: John Marston, *Jack Drum's Entertainment*, 1600.

124.   jig to boot: Prologue to Thomas Goffe, *The Careless Shepherdess*, acted after 1629; C. R. Baskervill, *The Elizabethan Jig*, 1929, p. 115.

125.   waiters upon vanity: *Bartholomew Fair*, 5.3.

125.   a common playhouse: Hillebrand, p. 155; P. Thomson, Appendix C, p. 170.

125.   charge and trouble: Cuthbert Burbage in 1635, quoted Hosley (*Revels History*, III.204), who describes the second coming of the boys, after Burbage's death, and the renovated theater they played in (III.197–226).

125.   and yet live: Quoted G. K. Hunter, *John Lyly*, 1962, p. 86.

125.   napkin for children: *Euphues and His England*, 1580.

126.   not charmed her: TN, 2.3.18.

126.   first taught them: Edward Blount, *Six Court Comedies*, 1632.

126.   smoke of rhetoric: LLL, 3.1.63.

126.   own too much: HAM, 4.7.118.

126.   sooner it wears: 1H4, 2.4.399–402.

126.   "govern the ventages": HAM, 3.2.357.

126.   the late 1580s: Dating is inferential. ERR, probably the first play, is followed by TGV, both before 1589; SHR was written by 1592; LLL not later than a year or two after this. Alexander, *Shakespeare*, 1964, pp. 68, 70–71; Hazelton Spencer, *Art and Life of WS*, 1940, pp. 130, 135.

126.   throat of death: LLL, 5.2.855.

127.   "the liver vein": LLL, 4.3.72.

127.   Educated contemporaries: John Davies of Hereford; Francis Meres, 1598; the anon. author of the preface to TRO, 1609; Thos. Freeman, 1614; Ben Jonson, 1623; *Gesta Grayorum*, an account of the Christmas revels at Gray's Inn, 1594–95, pub. 1688.

127.   "by a figure": TGV, 2.1.148.

127.   banquet the mind: LLL, 1.1.25.

127.   known to others: ERR, 2.2.189.

127.   pantaloon . . . son: SHR, 3.1.36–37, 5.1.68–70.

127. child who "repairs": CYM, 1.1.132.

127. "Florentius' love": SHR, 1.2.69.

127. mine own eyes: Bertram in AWW, 2.3.107–8.

127. "by a parable": TGV, 2.5.39–40.

127. "folded" or covert: ERR, 3.2.36.

128. well with her: TGV, 2.5.20–23.

128. by the yard: LLL, 5.2.667–69.

128. talk until Doomsday: LLL, 4.3.270.

128. "set of wit": LLL, 5.2.29.

128. "Wit's peddlar": LLL, 5.2.315–18.

128. solid things, "dislimning": ANT, 4.14.10–11.

128. good to none: TGV, 3.2.51–53.

128. part the word: LLL, 5.2.249.

128. sense of sense: LLL, 5.2.256–59.

129. "bolting hutch": 1H4, 2.4.450.

129. in his *Survey:* P. 72.

129. "a cheveril glove": TN, 3.1.11–12.

129. they kiss, consume: ROM, 2.6.10–11; 3.2.76.

129. for all things: ERR, 2.2.65–109.

130. full of books: Stow, *Survey,* p. 69.

130. whereof comes this: LR, 1.4.290.

130. an ell broad: ROM, 2.4.83–84.

130. wild-goose chase: ROM, 2.4.71.

131. best stick her: TGV, 1.1.70–102.

131. In thy tail: TGV, 2.3.37–49.

131. the same joke: SHR, 2.1.218.

131. to other folks: Juan Vives, *The Instruction of a Christian Woman,*
      1557.

131. ass, my anything: SHR, 3.2.230–32.

132. and their lords: ERR, 2.1.18–24.

132. "in ladies' eyes": LLL, 4.3.312.

132. all the world: LLL, 4.3.348–50.

132. good without "respect": MV, 5.1.99.

132. foul contending rebel: SHR, 5.2.159.

132.   Giddy, she thinks: SHR, 5.2.20.

132.   by "counterfeit supposes": SHR, 5.1.117.

132.   what thou wilt: WIV, 4.4.6.

133.   a "haggard": SHR, 4.2.39.

133.   calls them "informal": MM, 5.1.236 (and ERR, 5.1.105).

133.   reeking and smoking: VEN, ll. 55–64, 547–55.

133.   head, thy sovereign: SHR, 5.2.146–47.

133.   "quiet life": SHR, 5.2.108.

133.   I give thee: TGV, 5.4.83.

133.   my seat forbear: SON 41.9.

133.   badge of Hell: LLL, 4.3.250.

133.   sun-expelling mask: TGV, 4.4.153.

134.   goose a goddess: LLL, 4.3.72–73.

134.   on the ground: SON 130.12.

134.   do the deed: LLL, 3.1.196–98.

134.   cuckold and a whore: TRO, 2.3.72–73.

134.   "will and will not": MM, 2.2.33.

134.   Jack doesn't get Jill: LLL, 5.2.875.

134.   "Sweet and happy": SHR, 5.2.110.

134.   dreamed till now: SHR, Induction II, 68–69.

134.   "feeble, shallow, weak": ERR, 3.2.35.

134.   Wandering in illusions: ERR, 4.3.43.

134.   "mated" [heroes]: ERR, 3.2.54 and 5.1.282.

134.   of human reason: ERR, 5.1.189.

134.   "privy marks": ERR, 3.2.141–44.

134.   "remedy" presents itself: MM, 3.1.198–99.

134.   by special grace: LLL, 1.1.151–52.

134.   the "old Adam": ERR, 4.3.13–14.

135.   comes "by miracle": ERR, 5.1.265.

135.   chalks forth the way: TMP, 5.1.203.

135.   are not steered: CYM, 4.3.46.

135.   grief, such nativity: ERR, 5.1.407.

135.   feels the future: MAC, 1.5.57–58.

6. A Motley to the View

136. Scholar playwrights: Kyd, an apparent exception, graduated from the Merchant Tailors' School, London.

136. the "basest trade": 2 *Return from Parnassus, c.*1600.

136. in our colors: Greene, *Francisco's Fortunes,* 1590 (second part of his *Never Too Late*).

136. a "daily counterfeit": John Cocke of Lincoln's Inn, "A Common Player," 1615; quoted Gurr, p. 62.

136. condescended to "Roscius": 3H6, 5.6.10; HAM, 2.2.390–91.

136. bred public manners: SON 111.4.

136. be wiped away: LUC, ll. 607–8.

137. in Finsbury Fields: *Piers Penniless,* 1592, McKerrow ed., I.240.

137. anti-Stratford cult: Chronicled in Frank W. Wadsworth, *The Poacher from Stratford: A Partial Account of the Controversy over the Authorship of Shakespeare's Plays,* 1958; G. E. Bentley, *Shakespeare A Biographical Handbook,* 1961, ch. 1; S. Schoenbaum, *Shakespeare's Lives,* 1970.

137. "siege" or seat: OTH, 1.2.21–22.

138. livery of learning: Thomas Dekker, *A Knight's Conjuring,* 1607.

138. the infinitive mood: *The Plays and Poems of Robert Greene,* ed. J. Churton Collins (2 vols.), 1905, I.16 (the source of most detail about Greene in what follows).

139. "the English Ovid": Thomas Warton's phrase.

139. of the pox: Meres, *Palladis Tamia.* Material on Peele's life comes from David H. Horne, *The Life and Minor Works of George Peele,* 1952.

139. most noted poet: Anthony Wood, *Athenae Oxoniensis.* 1691.

139. "Privy" ... moths: Gosson, Sigs. G8v, A3, D4. (And I. G., *Refutation of the Apology for Actors,* 1615, A3, H4v.) Attacks on the stage are mustered in R. Fraser, *The War Against Poetry,* 1970.

139. Lodge: The career is given by N. Burton Paradise, *Thomas Lodge The History of an Elizabethan,* 1931; and Charles J. Sisson, "Thomas Lodge and His Family," pp. 1–164, in *TL and Other Elizabethans* (1933), 1966.

140. Thomas Nashe: R. B. McKerrow tells his story, *The Works of TN* (1904–10), 1966, V.1–156.

140. to the world: *The Spanish Tragedy,* 5.1.69–72.

140.   "Young Juvenal": *Groatsworth.*

140.   "English Aretine": *Wit's Misery and the World's Madness,* 1596.

140.   half-penny purse: LLL, 5.1.74.

141.   His best song: From *Summer's Last Will and Testament,* 1600.

141.   sack and sugar: Dekker, *Knight's Conjuring.*

141.   "Niobe, all tears": HAM, 1.2.149.

142.   wit and invention: Fuller, *Worthies.*

142.   compared him to the . . . ant: E. A. J. Honigmann, *Shakespeare's Impact on His Contemporaries,* 1982, pp. 2–6.

142.   "fortune's fool": ROM, 3.1.136.

143.   Greene called himself: Preface to *Groatsworth.*

143.   says the editor: Henry Chettle, *Kind-Heart's Dream.*

144.   a vile phrase: HAM, 2.2.111–12.

144.   perhaps a plagiarist: R. B. Gent., eulogizing Greene in *Greene's Funerals,* 1594: "the men that so eclipsed his fame" were the same who "Purloined his plumes" (often taken as referring to Shakespeare but perhaps referring to Greene's enemy, Gabriel Harvey).

144.   a woman's hide: 1.4.137.

144.   show of virtue: R3, 3.5.29.

144.   published an apology: *Kind-Heart's Dream.*

145.   an unknown bottom: AYL, 4.1.207–08.

146.   or thirty years: Herford and Simpson ed. (1938), 1954, VI.16.

146.   nuptial of Lucentio: 1.5.31–40.

146.   now eleven years: 1.3.23.

146.   the collied night: MND, 1.1.145.

146.   pale as lead: ROM, 2.5.17.

146.   Meres, listed: In *Palladis Tamia* (TGV, ERR, LLL, "Love Labours Wonne" [existing only in a bookseller's notice], MND, MV, R2, R3, H4 [no distinction between parts 1 and 2], JN, TIT, ROM).

146.   Shakespeare gets credit: Fifteen of the quartos, good and bad, bear his name, though it doesn't appear before 1598 (LLL) and sometimes represents a false ascription. Chambers, *WS,* I.206.

147.   E. K. Chambers: He gives his chronology in *WS,* I.270–71. And see pp. 244–69. Malone, *A Dissertation on the Three Parts of Henry VI,* 1790, credited Greene with the originals of 2 and 3H6: "The First

Part of the Contention between . . . York and Lancaster" and "The True Tragedy of Richard Duke of York," qtos. of 1594 and 1595.

147.   His biographer takes the view: Following "revisionists" like Honigmann, *Shakespeare's Impact*, pp. 70, 78, 88–90; and most notably Peter Alexander, *Shakespeare's Life and Art*, 1939, pp. 42–49; and *Shakespeare*, 1964, pp. 97–98.

147.   bones wanting "paste and cover": AWW, 1.1.103; R2, 3.2.154.

148.   like a sponge: HAM, 4.2.15–21.

148.   progeny of his: E.g. *Taming of a Shrew* is a "bad qto" of Shakespeare's SHR. Ann Thompson's New Cambridge ed., 1984, dates Shakespeare's play before 1592, perhaps as early as 1590 (pp. 1–9). See also Irving Ribner, *William Shakespeare*, 1969, p. 173.

148.   "high-viced" city: TIM, 4.3.109–11.

148.   a combined company: Gurr, pp. 25–26; Chambers, *Eliz. Stage*, II.120–21.

148.   he cared not: Chambers, *WS*, I.42.

148.   gracer of tragedians: Greene, *Groatsworth*.

149.   Chamberlain this year: From 1585. Two successive Lords Hunsdon, Henry and George Carey, father and son, held the office with a short interval (July 23, 1596–March 17, 1597) between their tenures.

149.   "cry" or pack: HAM, 3.2.275–78.

149.   Burbage . . . called himself: Wallace, XIII.11–12.

150.   sleek-headed men: JC, 1.2.192–93.

150.   mind is seized: E.g. in LLL, 1.2.109–10, 4.1.65–66; R2, 5.3.80; 2H4, 5.3.102; ROM, 2.1.14.

150.   motley to the view: SON 110.2.

150.   a fellow-poet: John Davies of Hereford, *Microcosmus*, 1603; Alexander B. Grosart ed. (1878), 1968, I.82. The initials W.S. and R.B. (for Burbage) follow l. 3 in the penultimate stz.: "And some I love for painting, poesy."

150.   and men's eyes: SON 29.1.

150.   strong as plague: SON 111.10.

150.   An anecdotist remembered: Fuller, *Worthies*.

150.   Marlowe died: Leslie Hotson tells the story, *The Death of CM*, 1925.

151.   "brave translunary things": Michael Drayton's phrase.

152.   my declining fall: *Edward II*, 5.6.59–63.

152.   his special "luster": ANT, 2.3.28.

153.   water-wallèd bulwark: 2.1.23–27.

153.   some recent scholarship: Honigmann's Arden ed. of JN, 1954; Wm. H. Matchett's Signet ed., 1966; Alexander, *Shakespeare*, 1964, pp. 166–72.

153.   "traded" . . . pilots: TRO, 2.2.64.

153.   ends of John: 3.3.164–68.

153.   together in calamity: 3.3.64–67. (Sc. divisions in this play differ depending on the ed.)

154.   acts of death: 2.1.375–76.

154.   order orderless: 3.1.253.

154.   Herald . . . "Two kings . . . .": 2.1.

154.   "hard with kneeling": 3.1.309–10.

154.   fall from thee: 3.1.320.

155.   sweet child's death: 4.2.80–81.

155.   "himself alone": After 3H6, 5.6.83.

155.   powers above . . . Mother England: 5.6.37, 5.2.153.

156.   of the 1580s: *The Spanish Tragedy* is recorded by Henslowe as being played at the Rose 3/14/1591–92 by Strange's Men. Generally dated after 1582 and before 1590—probably before the Spanish Armada (1588), it not being mentioned. Philip Edwards, the Revels editor of the play, puts it closer to 1590.

156.   Lodge recalled: In *Wit's Misery*, 1596.

157.   In *Titus Andronicus*: 2.4.1 s.d.

157.   please my soul: 4.5.12.

157.   murder and misdeeds: 3.2.1–4.

158.   avouch of eyes: HAM, 1.1.57–58.

158.   thy luster now: KL, 3.7.83–84.

158.   one playwright: Edward Ravenscroft.

159.   bright-burning Troy: 3.1.68–69.

159.   on the ground: 2.3.12–15.

159.   ne'er it ruinate: 5.3.203–4. This passage, not in the 1st Qto, is from the 2nd Qto (followed by Q3 and F), and is perhaps a compositor's addition.

159.   "the valued file": MAC, 3.1.92–95.

159.   "reach of hell" R3, 4.1.42 (another instance of the Shakespearean watershed).

160.   *Henry IV*, Part One: 5.4.65. TIT (5.3.17): "What, hath the firmament moe suns than one?" But the speaker is Saturninus, a villain.

160.   end of *Cymbeline:* 5.5.476–78; and TIT, 1.1.144–45.

160.   of Coriolanus: TIT, 4.4.68.

160.   their mockeries be: H5, 4.pr.53.

160.   References to negritude: 2.3.72, 78, 83; 3.2.78; 4.2.175; 5.1.44.

160.   base a hue: 4.2.71.

160.   shows of dross: MV, 2.7.20.

160.   "sooty bosom": OTH, 1.2.70.

160.   in his mind: 1.3.252.

161.   wilderness of tigers: 3.1.54.

161.   a cruel heart: Kyd's life and documents bearing on it are given in Frederick S. Boas, *The Works of TK,* 1901: Introduction (Life); Kyd's letter to the Lord Keeper, Sir John Puckering, an apologia; "atheistical" fragments found in Kyd's papers; Baines' note accusing Marlowe (pp. xiii–cxvi).

162.   could take him: Marlowe, brought before Privy Council May 20, was released, then sought for again.

162.   a little room: AYL, 3.3.15.

162.   on Whitsun Eve: June 2, 1593. The scribe errs, and Marlowe died three days before, not after.

162.   . . . God's wrath: Title of a tract by Edmund Rudierde, 1618.

162.   plain rogues: *The Just Censure and Reproof* (a Martinist pamphlet), 1598.

7. The Dyer's Hand

163.   victim to plague: The long-standard account is F. P. Wilson, *The Plague in Shakespeare's London* (1927), 1963; much amplified by J. F. D. Shrewsbury, *A History of Bubonic Plague in the British Isles,* 1970. Matter of fact, unless otherwise indicated, comes from these two books.

163.   where they died: Donne in a letter of 1625.

163.   four major visitations: 1592–93, 1603–4, 1608–9, 1609–10. Gurr, p. 56, dates the plague years.

163.   "harbinger and prologue": HAM, 1.1.122–23.

164.   resolved to dust: Donne, XXVI Sermons, no. 18 (January 15, 1625), in *The Sermons of JD,* ed. Evelyn M. Simpson and George R. Potter (1962), VI. 362.

164.   Dekker . . . saw them: *The Seven Deadly Sins,* 1606.

164.   grinned at his pomp: R2, 3.2.162–63.

164.   plague . . . petered out: A useful locus for discussion of this issue is Andrew B. Appleby, "The Disappearance of Plague: A Continuing Puzzle," *The Economic History Review,* 2nd series, vol. 28, no. 2 (May 1980), pp. 161–73.

165.   to disorder wander: TRO, 1.3.92–96.

165.   at the pesthouse: John Webster, *The White Devil,* 5.3.176–77.

165.   runs presently mad: ADO, 1.1.87–88.

166.   full of O's: LLL, 5.2.45.

166.   handsome and clean: Hentzner, *Travels.*

166.   of butcher's offal: WIV, 3.5.5.

166.   throng and press: London Common Council ordinance, 12/5/1574, in J. Q. Adams, *Shakespeare,* p. 109.

167.   into the country: Lee, *WS,* p. 85, lists the cities.

167.   temple-haunting martlet: MAC, 1.6.3–4.

167.   the common ferry: MV, 3.4.53–54.

167.   itinerary . . . in the sonnets: Following Fripp, *Quyny,* pp. 69–73.

167.   of each soil: 1H4, 1.1.63–64.

168.   The Stationers' Register: *A Transcript of the Registers . . . 1554–1640,* ed. Edward Arber, 5 vols. (1875), 1950.

168.   licensed this poem: April 18, 1593.

168.   A year later: S.R., May 9, 1594.

168.   Entries . . . were minatory: On the licensing of books, see Chambers, *WS,* I.138; and *Eliz. Stage,* III, ch. 22.

168.   are no deeds: H8, 3.2.154.

168.   excess begs all: Ll. 39–42.

168.   souls should have company: After LUC, l. 1110.

168.   in one person: R2, 5.5.31.

168.   at the flats: HAM, 4.5.100–01.

169.   own too much: HAM, 4.7.118.

169.   his grand sea: ANT, 3.12.9–10.

169.   "forest of feathers": HAM, 3.2.275.

169.   man might play: HAM, 1.2.84.

169.   *Henry VI,* Part Three: 3.2.190.

169.   kept coming back: E.g. in CYM, 3.4.59.

169.   chameleon . . . serpent: 3H6, 3.2.191; MAC, 1.5.66.

169.   veil of wildness: H5, 1.1.63–64.

169.   single copy survives: See the entries in the *Short-Title Catalogue* . . . *1475–1640,* ed. A. W. Pollard and G. R. Redgrave, 2d ed., 1976, II(I–Z).327.

170.   an indifferent eye: G. E. Bentley, *The Profession of Dramatist in Shakespeare's Time 1590–1642* (1971), 1986, pp. 279–80. Honigmann, *Shakespeare's Impact,* p. 49, disputing the standard view of indifferent Shakespeare, points to the replacing of "bad" quartos with good. He cared, this writer thinks, for his injured reputation, or had enough pull with his fellows to insist on corrected publication.

170.   of such treasures: Richard Tottel, epistle "To the Reader" in his famous "Miscellany," 1557.

170.   willing or no: George Wither, *The Scholar's Purgatory,* c.1625.

170.   Two errors surface: Following G. E. Bentley, *Shakespeare and His Theatre,* 1964, ch. 1: "Shakespeare and the Readers of His Plays."

170.   "fire-hot" heroine: John Weever in an epigram of c.1597, *Ad Gulielmum Shakespeare.*

170.   Ovid . . . gave him his lead: He had other models in Lodge's *Scillaes Metamorphosis,* 1589 (reissued in 1610 as *Glaucus and Scilla*), Daniel's *Complaint of Rosamond,* 1592, and Nashe's *The Choice of Valentines,* written before July 1593 and too erotic to be printed but circulating in MS.

171.   motto from Ovid: *Amores,* Bk. 15.

172.   his dyer's hand: SON 111.7.

172.   "incorpsed and demi-natured": HAM, 4.7.85–87.

172.   with "wit's regard": R2, 2.1.28.

173.   *Hero and Leander:* Posthumously licensed September 28, 1593, but not printed until 1598.

174.   to a pleurisy: HAM, 4.7.117.

174.   *Measure for Measure:* 2.1.89–94, 131.

175.   with less art: HAM, 2.2.95.

175.   copy . . . brought £15,000: J. Q. Adams, *Shakespeare,* p. 154.

176.   earl of Southampton: Details, unless otherwise indicated, are from A. L. Rowse, *Shakespeare's Southampton Patron of Virginia,* 1965; and G. P. U. Akrigg, *Shakespeare and the Earl of Southampton,* 1968.

177. one from Oxford: August 19, 1592 (*Register of the University,* II.i.353; cited Fripp, *Shakespeare,* I.322).

177. cherisher . . . of poets; Quennell, p. 114. For dedications to him, see Lee, *WS,* p. 200, and App. IV, pp. 662–68.

177. at Maecenas' grave: Francis Beale, "Tears of the Isle of Wight," 1624.

177. Nashe, adulating: In his dedication of *The Unfortunate Traveler,* 1593.

177. Southampton . . . is Narcissus: The title of a Latin poem dedicated to him in 1591.

177. portraits: Listed Lee, *WS,* p. 224 and n.

178. An informer's letter: Of 1601; Salisbury MSS; Quennell, pp. 117–18.

178. "brooch" or pendant: TRO, 2.1.114–15.

178. "his masculine whore": TRO, 5.1.15–17.

178. with tender down: John Sanford, *Apollinis et Musarum Euktika Eidyllia,* 1592.

179. Stow's characterization: Akrigg, p. 258n., cites Howes's 1631 augmenting of Stow's *Annals,* sig. XxxIr.

179. *Measure for Measure:* 3.1.82–84.

179. fool of time: After SON 124.13.

179. the leaving it: MAC, 1.4.7–8.

180. "still-vexed Bermoothes": TMP, 1.2.229.

180. plays every day: Halliwell-Phillipps, *Outlines,* I.176.

180. mistress Dame Pintpot: Chambers, *WS,* II.198.

180. Lord of Southampton's: Sir Walter Cope to Cecil, 1604; Salisbury MSS, XVI.415.

181. a long poem: Ed. G. B. Harrison, 1926.

181. goes with him: AWW, 1.1.99.

181. and our bark: TRO, 1.1.104.

182. and lascivious boy: AWW, 4.3.219–21.

182. the open ulcer: TRO, 1.1.53.

182. plays and sonnets: E.g. R3, 1.2.227–28, SON 41.5, 1H6, 5.3.79, TIT, 2.1.83 (the nearest echo).

182. "Ply her still": Fripp, *Quyny,* p. 91, thinks this passage (from canto 47, stz. 3) redacts verses from poem XIX, ll. 25–30, in *The Passionate Pilgrim,* a miscellany of the 1590s passed off as Shakespeare's. The redacting, if that is what it is, is more generic than particular.

182. to sing sweetly: *Polimanteia*, 1595; quoted J. Q. Adams, *Shakespeare*, p. 195n. Willoughby, matriculating at St. John's College, Oxford, in 1591, transferred to Exeter College, taking his degree there four years later.

182. unknown to . . . records: A Thomas Darell studied at Brasenose College, Oxford, during these years.

183. said John Donne: In the *Anniversaries*.

183. an in-law: In 1590 his elder brother married Eleanor, one of the Bampfield sisters, and Eleanor's sister Katherine married Thomas Russell. See Hotson, *I, William Shakespeare*; and Eccles, *Shakespeare in Warwickshire*, pp. 116–18.

183. closely and slyly: Arthur Wilson, II (sect. vi).736, in *A Complete History of England: with the Lives of All the Kings and Queens*, 1706.

183. "of a lethargy": Wilson, II.789.

183. what he gave: SON 60.8.

184. "too dear": SON 87.1.

184. "new-made": SON 2.13.

184. deep-sunken eyes: SON 2.7.

184. well-thumbed treatise: Thomas Wilson, *The Art of Rhetoric*, 1553 (including the trans. of "An epistle to persuade a young gentleman to marriage, devised by Erasmus in behalf of his friend").

184. in heaven's air: SON 21.11–12.

184. to have, extreme: SON 129.10.

185. a "threefold perjury": 2.6.5.

185. "bosom lover": 3.4.17.

185. Coleridge, reflecting: Anecdotage here and later draws on the New Variorum Sonnets, ed. H. E. Rollins, 2 vols., 1944.

185. all, but ideal: Rowse, *WS*, p. 144.

186. use their treasure: SON 20.10–14.

186. regular publishing army: Lee, *WS*, p. 160.

187. "Mr. W. Hall": Some other candidates: Wm. Hammond, a patron; Wm. Haughton, a dramatist; Wm. Hatcliffe of Lincolnshire, Prince of Purpoole (Lord of Misrule) in the Gray's Inn Revels of 1587–98. This is Hotson's proposal, *Mr. W.H.*, 1964.

187. "stand upon points": 5.1.118.

187. "Scorn" . . . "fool": ADO, 5.2.38–39.

187. nothing to do: Some time after 1604, the poet Wm. Drummond of

Hawthornden writes of "Sir William Alexander and Shakespeare, who have lately published their works." Chambers, *WS*, I.559 and II.220–21, citing *Works of WD of H*, 1711, p. 226 (an ed. I have not been able to see), dates this reference *c.*1614, allowing for the possibility that Shakespeare did actually enable Thorpe's publication. Thomas Heywood in his *Apology for Actors*, 1612, complaining of W. Jaggard's publication of his poems and Shakespeare's in *The Passionate Pilgrim* (1st ed. 1599, augmented with Heywood's poems in the 3d ed. of 1612, following an undated 2d qto.), says that Shakespeare, "to do himself right, hath since published them in his own name." Jaggard drops Shakespeare's name from the title-page of his miscellany in a subsequent issue.

187.   too short . . . too long: SON 99 has 15 ll., 126 has 12 ll., 145 is in tetrameter, 36 and 96 employ the same couplet.

188.   in the world: Sidney to his brother Robert, 10/18/1580.

188.   like of sonnetting: LLL, 4.3.156.

188.   has "sugared sonnets": Meres in *Palladis Tamia*.

188.   Jaggard . . . abstracted two: Nos. 138, 144.

188.   he credited Shakespeare: Chambers, *WS*, I.547–48, assigns the non-Shakespearean poems.

188.   others not much remembered: E.g. Henry Constable, Thomas Watson, Bartholomew Griffin, Barnabe Barnes, Richard Barnfield, Giles Fletcher.

188.   Let me not: SON 116.

188.   an Ethiop's ear: ROM, 1.5.45–46.

189.   says Southampton's biographer: Akrigg, p. 254.

190.   *Timon of Athens:* 1.1.21–22.

190.   got the "use": SON 78.3.

190.   breath that "reeks": SON 130.8.

191.   duty strongly knit: SON 26.1–2.

191.   eyes of posterity: SON 55.10–11.

191.   played at Wilton: Allegedly, in 1603: Chambers, *WS*, II, App. D.

191.   Wilde had fun: In *The Portrait of Mr. W.H.*, 1889.

191.   the "master-mistress": SON 20.2.

191.   "proud full sail": SON 86.1.

192.   new-found tropes: *Astrophel and Stella*, no. 3, l. 6.

192.   "the most feigning": AYL, 3.3.19–20.

192.   pangs of despisèd love: HAM, 3.1.71.

192.   the o'erfraught heart: MAC, 4.3.210.

192.   waste of shame: SON 129.1.

192.   by folly vanquishèd: TGV, 1.1.32–35.

192.   "shadows of himself": After 1H6, 2.3.62.

192.   making a "recordation": TRO, 5.2.116.

192.   proves this god: TN, 3.4.365.

192.   he, the "supervisor": OTH, 3.3.395–96.

192.   plays her false: TGV, 4.2.

192.   *Troilus and Cressida:* 5.2.

193.   of broken tears: TRO, 4.4.48.

193.   wound is deepest: TGV, 5.4.71.

193.   of the mind: ANT, 4.2.14–15.

193.   up his heart: OTH, 4.2.57.

193.   cause of wit: 2H4, 1.2.10.

193.   truths are told: MAC, 1.3.127.

193.   one apple tasted: Milton in *Areopagitica.*

193.   his sexual impulse: Rowse, *WS,* p. 193.

Index